James Madison, the South, and the Trans-Appalachian West, 1783–1803

James Madison, the South, and the Trans-Appalachian West, 1783–1803

Jeffrey Allen Zemler

LEXINGTON BOOKS
Lanham • Boulder • New York • Toronto • Plymouth, UK

Published by Lexington Books
A wholly owned subsidiary of Rowman & Littlefield
4501 Forbes Boulevard, Suite 200, Lanham, Maryland 20706
www.rowman.com

10 Thornbury Road, Plymouth PL6 7PP, United Kingdom

British Library Cataloguing in Publication Information Available

Library of Congress Cataloging-in-Publication Data

Zemler, Jeffery Allen, 1958– .
James Madison, the South, and the trans-Appalachian West, 1783–1803 / Jeffery Allen Zemler.
p. cm.
Includes bibliographical references and index.
ISBN 978-0-7391-8217-8 (cloth) — ISBN 978-0-7391-8218-5 (electronic)
1. Southern States—Politics and government—1775–1865. 2. Madison, James, 1751–1836—Politi-
cal and social views. 3. United States—Politics and government—1783–1809. 4. Northwest, Old—
History—1775–1865. 5. Sectionalism (United States)—History—18th century. 6. Sectionalism
(United States)—History—19th century. I. Title.
F213.Z46 2014
973.5'1092—dc23
2013039342

Printed in the United States of America

For Cathy

Contents

Acknowledgments

A project of this magnitude cannot be accomplished alone. It requires the concerted efforts of a myriad of individuals helping the author along the path to completion. Fortunately, I had the combined wisdom of a truly supportive cast, for which I am very grateful. I would like to express my appreciation and thanks to the following libraries and archives whose helpful staffs aided my efforts: The Filson Historical Society; Kentucky Historical Society; Library of Congress; Southern Historical Collection, University of North Carolina Library; Tennessee Historical Society; Underwood Law Library, Southern Methodist University; University of Chicago Library; University of Virginia; Virginia Historical Society; William R. Perkins Library, Duke University; Willis Library, University of North Texas; and Wisconsin Historical Society. I would also like to thank Drs. Guy Chet, Micheal F. Sayler, F. Todd Smith, Laura I. Stern, and Elizabeth Hayes Turner for their critiques of the manuscript. I would especially like to thank Dr. Harland Hagler, my friend and mentor, for his critical comments and his patience and willingness to serve as my sounding board. Most importantly, I would like to thank my wife, Cathy, and my children, Mary Hope, Keene, Emma, Sarah, and Madeleine, for allowing me the time to fulfill a dream.

Editorial Note

In the 1780s, the term "eastern" referred to the New England states and, quite often, to the middle states, and the term "easterner" referred to the people who inhabited this region. By the late 1790s, both terms had developed a more distinctive New England connotation, whereas "North" and "northern-er" had become the more accepted terms for people living in this expansive region. Outside of quotations, the terms "northerner" and "New Englander" will be used to prevent any confusion on the part of the reader. Similarly, the term "southerner" generally referred to a person living in Virginia, North Carolina, South Carolina, and Georgia and the term "South" reflected this geographic reality. Maryland inhabited a twilight area, but usually found itself grouped with the southern states and, therefore, is a southern state for the purpose of this study. During this period, a "westerner" was someone who lived west of the Allegheny Mountains, primarily in Kentucky and Tennessee, and was distinct from a "southerner" and a "northerner." This distinction is maintained. For the purpose of this study, the "West" reflects the area upon which southerners concentrated their efforts—the region south of the Ohio River, west of the Appalachian Mountains, and east of the Mississippi River.

Finally, it should come as no surprise to anyone who has spent time working with documents from this period that the spelling ability of men and women in the late-eighteenth century reflected little standardization. Granted, this little problem can be annoying for the modern reader, but for the sake of authenticity, I have chosen to retain the original spelling, grammar, and abbreviations contained in the documents, except when clarification was absolutely needed.

Chapter One

Introduction

In December 1801, Natchez resident Seth Lewis wrote Tennessee resident Andrew Jackson about a shared western and southern interest. "[T]he time is not very distant," he told Jackson, "when we become a State & thus add two Senators & proportionate Share of representatives in Congress to the Western & Southern Interest."[1] This "Western and Southern interest," spoken so fondly of by Lewis, had its beginnings in the 1780s, as farsighted southerners looked westward.

Twelve years earlier, Virginian Adam Stephen had begun to grasp this relationship when he alerted James Madison to the fact that the "Western Country is daily moving into greater importance.... Proper Attention to that Country is Absolutely Necessary, in time it will give Law to America."[2] Likewise, at the Virginia ratifying convention in 1788, William Grayson, an Anti-Federalist, remarked that he looked upon "this as a contest for empire . . . whether one part of the continent shall govern the other."[3]

This western and southern interest, gradual in its evolution but important in its outcome, lacked form in the 1780s and 1790s. No single issue during this period had the power to unite all southerners into a unified block defending the West against political and economic attacks, often from northerners but sometimes from people within their own region. Instead, southerners more often responded to what they perceived as insensitivities on the part of northerners and others to the needs of the West and westerners. Within their defense of the West lay the foundation for the strong relationship that the two sections would have in the nineteenth century as they merged to form what scholars have termed the Old South.

For decades, historians have debated when a conscious South first appeared. Some, such as Charles S. Sydnor, placed it around the time of the Missouri crisis. Others, such as Avery O. Craven, argued that it occurred much later, during the 1850s. A few historians, such as John R. Alden, even concluded that a southern consciousness was evident at the time of the American Revolution. Seldom did historians see any activity in this regard between the establishment of the republic under the federal Constitution and the debate over Missouri statehood. One historian who did was Jesse T. Carpenter, who argued that from the beginning of the federal republic, the South envisioned itself a minority member, and, as a result, southern political thinkers thought it necessary to adopt various strategies to protect their region within the republic.[4]

Within this debate over the emergence of a southern consciousness, historians have overlooked one important factor in its development—the West. Whereas I do not hold the position that a southern consciousness began in the 1780s or 1790s, I do argue that southerners began to look at the West during this period as something more than just virgin territory. Some southerners, especially James Madison, saw the South's political future entwined with the West's advancement and worked to ensure that a strong political relationship between the two regions developed. For people like Madison, this political merger of the two sections is what they meant when they talked about the southern and western interest.

I further believe historians should not take the close relationship between the South and the trans-Appalachian West for granted. Indeed, the two regions shared many interests, family and slavery being just two, but the close political relationship that developed did so, I believe, because of the hard work and dedication of a handful of forward-looking southerners. William J. Cooper Jr. has detected a southern commitment to westward expansion. He believes that western land claims and a desire for "future prosperity" caused southerners to champion "southern or southern-dominated western states [so that they] could act as a sectional equalizer for a South facing a commercially superior North."[5] James E. Lewis Jr. who also has taken a cursory look at the interaction between the seaboard states and the trans-Appalachian West during this period, argues that "multiple sovereign nations, whether individual states or partial confederacies, in a single neighborhood could not coexist peacefully."[6] To avoid problems that might develop between neighborhoods—"collisions over laws, trade, and borders"—the Founders sought stability under a federal Constitution that linked all three sections—North, South, and West—but when the Spanish empire started to collapse, their old fears about neighborhoods, including their effect on a tenuously attached trans-Appalachian West, reemerged.[7] As some historians can attest, the trans-Appalachian West's role in the new union is far more complicated than once imagined and described. Still, I see the region's role foremost in terms of its political alignment with the South.

In this book, I place James Madison at the center of this evolving southern and western relationship. His political growth, from an ardent nationalist in the 1780s to a vocal opponent of the Washington and Adams administrations in the 1790s, highlights the evolutionary nature of this southern and western relationship. Although not the first to see the potential of this relationship, Madison would become its champion, arguing on behalf of the West when few others felt so inclined. His tenacity would eventually pay off, for, by the late 1790s, he and other champions of the West would feel confident enough in this budding relationship to redirect their attention eastward and address, with the help of westerners, other pressing matters, such as the Sedition Act.

NOTES

1. Seth Lewis to Andrew Jackson, 9 December 1801, in *The Papers of Andrew Jackson*, eds. Sam B. Smith et al. (Knoxville: University of Tennessee Press, 1980), 1:262.

2. Adam Stephen to James Madison, 12 September 1789, in *The Papers of James Madison*, eds. Charles F. Hobson et al. (Charlottesville: University Press of Virginia, 1979), 12:398.

3. *The Documentary History of the Ratification of the Constitution*, eds. John P. Kaminski and Gaspare J. Saladino (Madison: State Historical Society of Wisconsin, 1993), 10:1259.

4. Charles S. Sydnor, *The Development of Southern Sectionalism, 1819–1848* (Baton Rouge: Louisiana State University Press and the Littlefield Fund for Southern History of the University of Texas, 1948); Avery O. Craven, *The Growth of Southern Nationalism, 1848–1861* (Baton Rouge: Louisiana State University Press and the Littlefield Fund for Southern History of the University of Texas, 1953); John R. Alden, *The First South* (Baton Rouge: Louisiana State University Press, 1961); John R. Alden, *The South in the American Revolution, 1763–1789* (Baton Rouge: Louisiana State University Press and the Littlefield Fund for Southern History of the University of Texas, 1957); Jesse T. Carpenter, *The South as a Conscious Minority, 1789–1861: A Study in Political Thought* (New York: The New York University Press, 1930).

5. William J. Cooper Jr., *Liberty and Slavery: Southern Politics to 1860* (New York: Alfred A. Knopf, 1983), 54.

6. James E. Lewis Jr., *The American Union and the Problem of Neighborhood: The United States and the Collapse of the Spanish Empire, 1783–1829* (Chapel Hill: The University of North Carolina Press, 1998), 9.

7. Ibid.

Chapter Two

What to Do with the West?

"I have got all my back-Lands judiciously located, in one Body," wrote George Mason, author of the Virginia Declaration of Rights, to his son, George Mason Jr., in January 1783. "These lands will cost me, by the time the Title is completed, not less than 1,000 [pounds] Specie; but if I can secure & settle them, they will, in twenty years, be worth forty or fifty thousand Pounds to my family."[1] Mason was not the only person residing in the southern United States who had set his eyes on the West and had envisioned this immense wilderness teeming with productive Americans. Many southerners had dreamed at the close of the American Revolution of amassing small fortunes from the American acquisition of the trans-Appalachian West, although few had taken the time to consider the important question of the West and its place within the Union. This situation is particularly surprising when one remembers that the southern states claimed most of the lands west of the Appalachian Mountains and that a number of their residents had braved many dangers, chiefly Indian attacks, to move into the area in the early 1770s.[2]

Between 1775 and 1782, the American Revolution had caused most southerners to focus their attention on the events occurring east of the Appalachians. Yet, the Revolution did not cause a halt to the westward migration of southerners. Settlers continued to pass through the Cumberland Gap, a mountain pass on the border of Virginia, Kentucky, and Tennessee, and claim lands lying south of the Ohio River. The rapid expansion of the West began before the end of hostilities with Great Britain. In the decade dominated by the American Revolution, the population of Kentucky increased from approximately 15,700 in 1770 to 45,000 in 1780. During this time period, the population of Tennessee grew tenfold, from 1,000 to 10,000.[3]

When the United States took possession of the vast, untamed region stretching from the Appalachian Mountains to the Mississippi River in 1783, Americans for the first time had to sit down and decide what the role of the West would be in the new republic. Would it be economic, political, or a combination of the two? No one was sure, although the debate initially centered on the economic relationship between the West and the Atlantic seaboard states. For years many Americans had gazed west and dreamed of obtaining financial security for themselves and their families. For some men, this security took the form of huge profits, which they acquired from speculating in western lands. For others, it meant moving west with their families and starting a new life. Regardless of their different approaches, these men had one thing in common—all viewed the West as a possession capable of bestowing untold wealth on its owner.

The first few years of debate following the 1783 Treaty of Paris illustrated how little southerners comprehended what they had achieved through the treaty with Great Britain. Besides granting its former colonies their independence, Great Britain awarded the United States its territory east of the Mississippi River and the right to navigate the river from its source to the ocean. The British decision, however, to limit the United States on the south by the Spanish colonies of East and West Florida and the thirty-first parallel would complicate American efforts to access the Mississippi River. During the war, southerners, while cognizant of activities in the West, did not take the time to develop a consensus regarding the western role in a new country. When they allowed the West to distract them temporarily, many southerners viewed it principally as a source of income for themselves and for their states. In the 1770s and 1780s, few southerners worried about the political orientation of the West. When southerners did think about western politics, they generally thought about the local administration of government, which centered on two primary economic considerations. First, how heavy an economic burden would it be for the individual state to preserve law and order in the West? Secondly, how great an economic restraint would the lack of an organized West be on the owners of western land or on the nation in general? Indeed, economic considerations caused politicians in Virginia to allow the Illinois County charter of 1780 to lapse in 1782.

In December 1778, George Rogers Clark, a colonel in the Virginia militia, victoriously led a small force of backwoodsmen against British outposts in the Illinois country. As a result of the success of Clark's military campaign, Virginia became responsible for preserving law and order in the Illinois country. Virginia politicians acted quickly. On 9 December 1778, the Virginia General Assembly created the county of Illinois. Governor Patrick Henry appointed John Todd county lieutenant and instructed him to organize this newest Virginia county. On Todd's arrival in the Illinois country, he held an election to allow residents to select local judges and other county officials.

Unfortunately, Virginia managed to do little else. During the remaining years of the American Revolution, Illinois County fended for itself because Virginia lacked the necessary funds to administer the county properly. Although they did not anticipate any problems when they created the county, legislators in Virginia wrote into the bill creating the county a requirement that the legislature re-establish the county every two years. After citing the immense distance from the capital and the exorbitant cost of running such a distant government, the Virginia General Assembly in January 1782 exercised its option and allowed the Illinois County charter to expire. Afterwards, the Illinois country became part of the territory lying north of the Ohio River that Virginia would offer to the United States. [4]

Virginians' three year struggle to cede their Ohio lands to the United States stirred southerners to begin thinking about the West. Because of the Treaty of Paris of 1783, southern politicians no longer possessed the luxury of blaming Parliament for all the ills plaguing the West. The burden now fell on them to make important decisions about it. Unfortunately, southern congressional delegations did not know what those decisions should be. The Virginia Cession marked the beginning of a long process among southerners of building a common opinion regarding the political role of the West within the Union.

Maryland occupied a unique position among southern states because it claimed no land west of the Appalachian Mountains. Yet, that condition did not lessen the interest of Marylanders in the West. They refused to ratify the Articles of Confederation and thus join the Union as long as the landed states retained their western lands. From their first rejection of the compact in March 1778, Marylanders adamantly predicated their admittance into the Union on the principle of common interest in, if not common ownership of, the West. [5] They championed the position that the West belonged to all Americans. Although speculative ventures in western lands caused some Marylanders to support their state in its defiant stand, a majority of Marylanders put aside their personal interests and supported their political leaders as they fought for this principle of American ownership of the West. Even after their state signed the Articles of Confederation on 1 March 1781, Maryland residents still retained their commitment to this principle. At one point during a debate on the cession, the Maryland delegates asked Congress to delay its deliberations while they communicated with the Maryland General Assembly. "The Western territory," they wrote, "is so important in itself, and in its consequences that we have thought it advisable to transmit a full detail of the late proceedings of Congress on this Subject." [6]

For Virginians, the defiant position of the people in Maryland, in conjunction with the pressing need to create a national government, forced them to set aside their personal interests in the West and to act like nationalists. Although they were careful to offer only enough western land to satisfy the demands of Maryland and thus ensure their possession of Kentucky, Virginians in 1783 still believed that they had made the correct decision. The cession, the Virginia delegates wrote, was "a matter so important to the welfare of our state . . . and to the U. States in General" that Virginians had no other choice but to set aside their personal interests in the West to guarantee passage of the Articles of Confederation. [7]

Despite these nationalistic pronouncements, some southerners worried more about who would have access to the western lands and how settlers would use the land than about the welfare of the nation. Virginians addressed petitions to their representatives in the General Assembly expressing their disapproval of the request by the Confederation Congress in 1780 that all landed states cede their western lands to the government for the common good. "We are also at a loss," one group of petitioners wrote, "to know whence Congress derives the powers of demanding cessions of lands and of erecting new States before such powers have been granted them by their constituents."[8] Beside these nagging legal questions, most petitioners believed that Congress would not use the land to benefit all Americans but would convert the land "to private, instead of public purpose."[9] "The intrigues of the great land companies," they cried, "and the methods by which they have strengthened their interest are no secret to the public."[10] Virginia's delegation to the Confederation Congress shared their concern. Fearing that the history of repeated congressional delays in dealing with land cessions would ensure that the land came under the control of "adventurers," the Virginia delegates affirmed the right of their state to sell the land "if Congress will not."[11] Partially in response to the lobbying campaign of their fellow citizens, the Virginia delegation informed Congress that it would not "execute the deed" if Congress placed it on the table and allowed it to languish for eighteen months while speculators divided the cession among themselves.[12] This determined response to congressional foot-dragging worked. Congress ratified the Virginia act of cession on 1 March 1784.[13]

Of the southern states represented in Congress at the time of the vote, only South Carolina expressed any opposition to the bill. Its two-man delegation divided at the time of the final vote.[14] Jacob Read, who voted for the cession, did so because he believed that, like his former congressional colleagues John Rutledge and Ralph Izard, it would "produce a Valuable fund for satisfying the Army and Public Creditors."[15] Like Read, those southerners who approved of the Virginia cession viewed it as an economic necessity, not a national policy of westward expansion. The American Revolution had left the states and national government deeply in debt to domestic and international creditors, and southerners sought ways to rid themselves of this economic burden. In their eyes, southerners viewed a large national debt as tantamount to "a chain of slavery," with the borrower transformed into a servant and the lender into the master.[16] "These debts," they argued "which on [are] the necessary cause of taxation must prove the necessary source of grief."[17] The American Revolution provided a vivid reminder of such "grief." To these men, the West offered financial insurance against such a disaster.[18]

The cession also provided the national government with the means of honoring its pledges of military bounties in the West to Revolutionary War veterans.[19] Even though the New York act of cession in 1781 awarded title to the area between the Ohio River and the Great Lakes to the United States, the United States still lacked a clear title to the land because Virginia also claimed the same territory. This situation prevented the national government from fulfilling its promises of western military bounties to Revolutionary War veterans. It also stopped the national government from selling the land to pay its debts, which included a sizeable amount of back pay to Continental Army officers.[20] In March 1783, some army officers impatient with the inability of the national government to honor its promises conspired to demand, perhaps with arms, that Congress end its delay. Fortunately, General George Washington, who adamantly refused to take part in the conspiracy, managed to persuade his officers to drop their threatening plans against Congress by appealing to their love of country and to their feelings for him. Despite its peaceful conclusion, the Newburgh Conspiracy, as the affair became known, awakened thoughtful men throughout the South to the dangers that the national government faced because of inadequate sources of revenue. With the Virginia cession, the national government was finally able to begin honoring its promises of military bounties, which made the prospects of a military uprising highly unlikely.[21]

Although many southerners supported Virginia in its decision to cede its Ohio lands, the excessive delays of Congress in accepting the cession caused many thoughtful men in the South to become apprehensive about further cessions of western lands to the United States.[22] In 1783, the North Carolina delegation was "not a little embarrassed" that they had "accepted the cessions of two States from which it is expected North Carolina will receive advantages equally with the other States, and altho[ugh] we have an extensive Western territory we have not ceded any."[23] However, by 1784, the political leadership in North Carolina was split in its opinion over the cession of their western territory. The congressional delegation even refused to act on the issue until state officials had clarified their position. After watching what had happened with the Virginia cession, its delay in Congress, and the actions of the "land-jobbers," some North Carolinians, such as Richard Dobbs Spaight, reached the conclusion that they would "be sorry to see any part of our State at the disposal of Congress."[24] Other residents of North Carolina, however, argued that the state did not immediately have to cede its western lands because more favorable terms might be forthcoming. Despite some misgivings, North Carolina ceded its lands in June 1784.[25]

The haunting doubts, nevertheless, continued, and in November, a new North Carolina legislature withdrew the offer.[26] In explaining the actions of the legislature, Governor Alexander Martin noted "that the situation of our Public accounts was somewhat changed since the last Assembly, and that the Interest of the State should immediately be consulted and attended to, [and] that every citizen should reap the advantages of the vacant territory."[27] With these points in mind, the North Carolina governor declared that legislators "[judged] it ill timed generosity at this crisis to be too liberal of the means that would so greatly contribute to her honesty and justice."[28] The apparent inconsistencies in the actions of the North Carolina legislature revealed just how difficult the western question had become for many southerners. By 1785, southerners had started to wonder whether their local interests and needs outweighed the needs and interests of the national government.

The only group of southerners that appeared happy over the Virginia cession consisted of large land speculators who rejoiced at the thought of increased land prices. Looking on the West with hungry eyes, William Blount was one such speculator. As a former governor of North Carolina, he knew the economic pressures that the landed states were under to administer their western claims, and he thought he could turn these pressures to his advantage. Interested in establishing a settlement near Natchez or in Tennessee, Blount wrote to his business partners admonishing them "not [to] fail to impress on the minds of your Brother Commissioners the Value of western land to individuals and the little Advantage it will be to the State of Georgia."[29] Thus, as Blount viewed the situation, the West was an economic liability for state governments and offered "a Reason for both the Cessions that have taken place in this State [North Carolina] and Virginia and that will certainly and unavoidably take Place in Georgia in a short Time!"[30]

Like Blount, other speculators longed for the day when the states of Georgia and North Carolina would emulate Virginia and cede their western territories to the United States. Yet, before these states could cede their lands, speculators had started to acquire title to their western holdings from them rather than from the national government in the belief that the states granted more favorable terms than Congress. By the time North Carolina ceded its land to Congress in 1784, speculators had already acquired three million of the four million acres in Tennessee. Most of this land the North Carolina legislature had sold for as little as £10 (the equivalent of $5) per 100 acres. Similarly, land speculators benefited from the generosities of another legislature eleven years later when Georgia sold its thirty-five million-acre Yazoo tract to four land companies for $500,000.[31]

Within less than two years, many southerners, except for the land speculators, had lost most of their enthusiasm for their states making any additional western land cessions. Although congressional delays helped create some of this growing uncertainty about western lands, a growing provincial attitude among planters and political leaders caused many southerners to reevaluate their opinions concerning the West. In 1784 and 1785, the orderly development of the West particularly concerned southerners. Many southerners took for granted western growth and noted "that a wise government should look forward to the numerous States that are fast rising out of the Western Territory."[32] This optimistic pronouncement, however, concealed a fundamental concern over the direction that this expansion might take. Congress could enact a series of laws for the governance of the West and the orderly settlement of immigrants on the land, but Congress had no real control over the western immigrant. Notwithstanding the monetary benefits that might accrue to southerners from the sale of western land to immigrants, some southerners became increasingly convinced that they should end westward expansion, or, at least slow its pace. As they viewed the situation, the West posed a real threat to the political and economic survival of the South Atlantic states.

In the southernmost state, residents at first did not fear western expansion; they welcomed it.[33] Georgia emerged from the war with nearly 100 million acres of public land, 62 million acres comprising its western territory—most of the present-day states of Alabama and Mississippi. Even though title to the land was at best dubious, Georgians viewed the unsettled lands as their economic salvation. On 25 February 1784, the Georgia House of Assembly established a bounty land grant system designed to attract out-of-state settlers. For each head of family who produced a sworn statement attesting to his honesty and integrity, Georgia awarded 200 acres free of charge, provided the person paid a small filing fee.[34] A year later, the state eliminated the small filing fee.[35] As speculators learned how to acquire large tracts of land using the laws, and sometimes in spite of those laws, Georgians suddenly lost their enthusiasm for the haphazard settlement of their back country.[36] They were not alone.

"Alarming" was the word that some southerners used to describe the western exodus. "I have ever viewed," wrote one man from Maryland, "selling or settling it [the West] speedily, is the most ruinous policy, as opening a door for our citizens to run off and leave us, as a means of depreciating all our landed property already settled, and disabling us from paying taxes and funding the debts already contracted."[37] Those who shared such views could appreciate that it was natural for a man to flee from economic oppression, but they did not believe it honorable to burden another man with one's responsibilities.[38] These southerners were not simply decrying the loss of a few taxpayers. They were lamenting the potential collapse of their economies. Still, economically dependent on tobacco cultivation, Virginian James Madison foresaw a time when the price would fall due, in large part, to its cultivation in the West. "It will be politic," he noted, "for the people here [Virginia] to push the culture of this article whilst the price keeps up."[39]

Within these growing economic fears an underlying general assumption about westward expansion existed: "the [economic] interests of that Country and the Atlantick States Will certainly interfere."[40] Many southerners believed that as emigrants moved west, their political, commercial and economic ties with the Atlantic seaboard states would lessen, especially if westerners had access to the Mississippi River and the port of New Orleans. Some southerners tried to reduce this potential drain on their economies by establishing a strong transportation network with the West.[41]

As part of the process of creating this commercial link with the West, supporters of the James and Potomac rivers transportation projects in Maryland and Virginia hoped their efforts to open the two waterways to western trade through a series of locks and canals would prevent, or at least reduce, the westward drain of people from their states. Like most supporters of the projects, Maryland assembly member David McMechen believed that the Potomac River project "would be an immense source of wealth" to his state.[42] He noted, however, that if "local prejudices" managed to prevent the completion of the project and if Spain opened the Mississippi River to American commerce, Maryland (and the Atlantic states) would lose the western market forever.[43] Likewise, George Washington realized that the Atlantic states had to have a strong system of navigable rivers in place before Spain opened the Mississippi River to American commerce.[44] "There is nothing," he wrote Henry Lee, "which binds one country or one state to another but [commercial] interests," and the long-term commercial needs of the Atlantic states had to take precedence over the everyday needs of the western settlers.[45]

Besides the commercial advantages of opening new markets, supporters of the projects for these "great and important"[46] James and Potomac rivers believed that they would not only form an important communication link with the West but would also "double the value of half the lands within the Commonwealth [Virginia], . . . extend its commerce, [and] link with its interests those of the Western States."[47] More astute southerners saw internal improvements performing an even more important role. Richard Henry Lee noted that improving the navigation of the western waters would prevent a war with Spain over the exclusive rights to the Mississippi.[48] The Marylander McMechen predicted that if a strong commercial relationship were not established with the West through a system of navigable rivers, "the vast continent of America . . . [might be] a divided empire," a fear that Washington also expressed.[49]

Washington was acutely aware of the political danger that the West presented to the Union. Westerners, he argued, were the type of people who naturally had a low regard for constituted authority. If the Atlantic states could not maintain westerners' allegiance to the nation through economic ties, Washington believed westerners, in pursuit of commercial intercourse, would turn to either Spain or Great Britain, form a commercial and political alliance, and, in the process, become a distinct people and a "formidable and dangerous neighbour."[50] Thus, Washington's advocacy of the improvement of the James and Potomac rivers took on a tone of urgency, as he feared for the political stability of the young nation.

Still, some southerners remained unconvinced that the best solution to their problem was simply a program of internal improvements. Residents of Baltimore severely chastised David McMechen for voting for the Potomac bill in the Maryland General Assembly.[51] For these and like-minded southerners, the logical solution to this problem was simple—support the Spanish policy of prohibiting American commerce on the Mississippi River. "Should the Navigation of the Mississippi continue open," Hugh Williamson argued, "Vast Bodies of People would migrate thither whose mercantile Connections could be of no Use to the old States. In Taxation their assistance would be very inefficient."[52] Conversely, they reasoned "let the Navigation of the Mississippi be shut and the Country joining our present Settlements will be first improved and durable commercial and civil intercourse established."[53] James Monroe, who placed the interest of his native Virginia above all else, chastised his own state specifically and the United States generally for acting in ways that "instead of weakening . . . [westerners' interest] and making it subservient to our purpose[,] we [Virginians] have given it all the possible strength we . . . [could]."[54] Nevertheless, Monroe, who wanted the Mississippi River to remain closed, reluctantly agreed that concerted southern efforts to open it to American commerce were a necessary goal, provided southerners retained their western territories and did not divide them into new states. Then, together, southerners and westerners could work toward unified goals and objectives. Monroe concurred with Washington, however, that if they severed their political ties through "dismemberment" [statehood], westerners would eventually withdraw from their common economic "pursuit" with the Atlantic states and eventually the Union itself.[55]

Some southerners, however, failed to see any benefit in closing the Mississippi River. Besides the likelihood that residents in the West would not idly stand by and watch Spain close the great waterway to American commerce, some southerners argued that the nations of Europe relied too heavily on American agricultural staples to permit Spain to close the river.[56] In fact, they envisioned New Orleans as the premier mercantile port in the world.[57] Still others, such as James Madison, asserted that the opening of the Mississippi was not only "beneficial to all the nations who either directly or indirectly trade with the U.S." but also vital for the continuation of the republican dream of a nation of small farmers.[58] "Shut up the Mississippi and discourage the settlements on its waters," wrote Madison, "and what will be the consequences?"[59] First, with an ever-increasing population, he reasoned, southern farmers would have to turn to the production of food crops, abandoning, or at least drastically reducing, their production of cash crops. With a decrease in supply, prices for cash crops would increase, forcing European consumers to pay higher prices.[60] Secondly, and undoubtedly the most alarming aspect of the scenario in Madison's eyes, the "hands without land at home[,] being discouraged from seeking it where alone it could be found, must be turned in a great degree to manufacturing."[61] With the settlement of the back country and free access to the Mississippi River, Madison, however, felt confident that "by a free expansion of our people[,] the establishment of internal manufacturers will . . . be long delayed" and the agricultural trade with Europe would continue.[62]

Initially, most Americans assumed that the major contribution of the West to the nation would be the elimination of the national debt through the sale of western lands. On this point, James Madison told Congress in early 1783 that it had to settle the question of land valuation before it could entertain any "other essays for the public relief."[63] However, as southerners began evaluating the financial aspects of western expansion, they noted with growing alarm the precarious state in which they found the West. Western migrants' tendency to settle on land still under Indian ownership, land to which the United States did not have legal title, was a source of irritation for many southerners. Besides the potential Indian conflicts, "the first of many evil consequences that must result from such lawless measures,"[64] the situation also raised the specter of Congress having to establish a standing army to protect the frontier.[65] Of course, Congress could choose to leave the frontier unguarded, but for many southerners neither option was acceptable. Succinctly evaluating the situation, James Monroe noted that no matter what method Congress adopted it would not be possible to "[prevent] the adventurers from setling where they please."[66] Monroe did mention, however, that the former option, the establishment of a standing army, carried with it a graver risk—the "loss of our liberty."[67]

Monroe was not the only southerner to believe that lawlessness on the frontier was a threat to the tenets of the American Revolution. John F. Mercer and Arthur Lee, fellow Virginians and delegates to Congress, wrote Governor Benjamin Harrison a lengthy discourse on the inherent evil of western expansion. Underscoring the inordinate cost of protecting the frontier inhabitants from Indian attacks and the actions of "lawless banditti," the two men spoke of a threat to the very fabric of American society. Westerners, in their opinion, were likely to form governments "not only on dissimilar principles to those which form the basis of our Republican Constitutions, but such as might eventually prove destructive to them."[68]

Thus, for southerners, the establishment of orderly government in the West took on a tone of urgency in 1784 and 1785. Still, not all southerners agreed with Lee, Mercer, and Monroe that the frontier tended to erode the settlers' democratic underpinnings and reduce them to a state of barbarity.

John Marshall, the future chief justice, who at one time contemplated moving to Kentucky, believed that westerners were destined to create a form of government superior to that created on the Atlantic coast.[69] Many southerners, however, were unsure as to whose interest should take precedence in the development of the West—those of the governments and residents of Virginia, North Carolina, and Georgia; those of the national government; or those of western residents.[70]

Still, southerners agreed that the westerners' proclivity for settling on Indian lands and the apparent lawless condition of the region were definite threats to the ability of the national government to sell land to prospective settlers, particularly in the region north of the Ohio River, one of the few areas where the national government had a clear title to the land. As a result, Congress enacted two laws intended to eliminate these anticipated problems in that region. The Ordinance of 1784 established a system of temporary governments in the West under the direct supervision of Congress, whereas the Ordinance of 1785 disposed of western lands in an orderly manner through a grid-like system of townships. Southerners appeared resigned to accept the acts without much debate. They knew that if a prolonged debate ensued, the land would soon come into the possession of squatters and "put the United States to more expence to dispossess them, than the soil will afterwards sell for."[71] A number of southerners saw the retiring of the national debt with the proceeds from land sales as the crucial issue for a young nation just establishing itself.[72] They believed these two acts accomplished that essential task.

Of even greater importance in the eyes of many southerners was the territory south of the Ohio River, where the vast majority of Americans, particularly southerners, were migrating. Like the Illinois country, Kentucky periodically stretched the ability of officials in Virginia to govern its rapidly developing area. This situation started Virginians wondering about the future political relationship of these two regions in the mid-1780s. In late September 1783, General William Irvine reported that Virginians were crossing the Ohio River from Kentucky and settling on treaty lands in Ohio. Virginia officials feared an Indian war and the possible depopulation of their western territory.[73] Virginia governor Benjamin Harrison remarked candidly that even if he were to do everything within his power to prevent the illegal emigration, he would not be able to stem the tide of westward migration. Citing the governor's lack of power to punish lawbreakers, Harrison predicted that even if he called out the militia to remove the settlers from the region north of the Ohio River, the settlers would "refuse obedience to the orders and escape all kinds of punishment."[74] He further predicted that Virginia, not Kentucky, would "soon be the Seat of anarchy and confusion unless our law makers find out that Government cannot be supported without lodging powers somewhere to enforce obedience to the law."[75]

Not all Virginians, however, shared the governor's pessimistic attitude. Thomas Jefferson possessed faith in the ability of Virginia to enforce its laws in the West, provided Virginia reduced the size of its western territory. He believed that the mouth of the Kanawha River provided an excellent location for Virginia to draw its western boundary. The Kanawha River, which flowed through western Virginia (present-day West Virginia) into the Ohio River, provided a natural boundary with future western states. More importantly, in Jefferson's view it promised Virginia a virtual monopoly "of the Western & Indian trade."[76] Besides these economic and defensive reasons, Jefferson believed that the Kanawha River was the farthest point west where Virginia could establish its border and still provide an efficient and convenient system of government for its residents.[77]

As residents of Kentucky began petitioning the Virginia legislature for the right to separate from their political mother and enter the Union as a state, their agitations forced Virginians to consider the question of who had the ultimate right to govern the western lands.[78] Given the precedent of the ordinances of 1784 and 1785, a number of southerners had accepted the position that new states would develop in the West. Still, not everyone supported state-making. James Monroe disliked the idea of new states forming in the West. Instead of Virginia permitting Kentucky to become a state, he proposed that "we model our regulations as to accommodate our government to their convenience."[79] As Monroe viewed the situation, "the more we diminish the state the less consequence she will have in the union."[80] The only hope, he further explained, was for Virginia and the rest of the Atlantic states to "fix their numbers as much as possible" to avoid them "outnumber[ing] us in Congress."[81] Still, he was resigned to the inevitability of western statehood, and like Jefferson, believed that the Atlantic states should not arbitrarily ignore the interests of westerners, which might imperil the Union.[82]

If western statehood were inevitable, most southerners believed that the new state should enter the Union after receiving permission from its parent state and not through the process of armed revolt, as the proponents of the "State of Franklin" and its supporters in Washington County, North Carolina, were trying to do.[83] When the North Carolina legislature withdrew its western land offer, residents in the eastern part of what would become Tennessee refused to accept the decision. Despite objections from North Carolina officials, they proceeded to elect a legislature and governor and asked for admission into the Union as the fourteenth state.[84] The situation in which North Carolina found itself regarding the disturbance in Franklin caused some southerners to champion strict plans for the creation of new states. A few men, such as William Grayson and Richard Henry Lee, worried that northern states already jealous of the size of Virginia might take advantage of a similar disturbance in Kentucky and dismember Virginia "with't [without] admitting the new state into the Confederation."[85] To protect his state from such an eventuality, Lee proposed the establishment of a convention, at which time the three affected parties—the parent state, the future state and the United States government—would sit down and draft a compact explicitly stating the procedure for admittance and what the parent state would receive, if anything, for allowing the division to take place. [86] Jefferson feared that if a plan were not in place, "our several states will crumble to atoms" in the face of every "little canton" demanding statehood. [87]

Members of the Virginia legislature voiced a similar fear. In January 1786, they wrote certain guarantees into "An Act concerning the Erection of the District of Kentucky into an Independent State" to ensure that Kentucky became a state once Virginia granted it independence. [88] With the realization, however, that they did not have a good argument to prevent Kentuckians from achieving statehood, most Virginians seemed to echo the sentiments of George Washington, who believed that Virginia could only "meet them upon their own ground, draw the best line, and best terms we can of separation, and part good friends." [89]

Although southerners worried about the economic and political implications of future westward expansion, they acted as if the situation did not demand their immediate attention. However, in the summer of 1786, the issue of the closure of the Mississippi River became a major political issue. John Jay, whom Congress had authorized to negotiate a commercial treaty with Spain, and Diego de Gardoqui, the Spanish *chargé d'affaires* to the United States, had reached a tentative agreement whereby the United States would agree to the temporary closure for twenty-five or thirty years of the Mississippi River in return for a treaty guaranteeing American possessions in North America and the opening of Spanish ports to American trade. The United States would also accept Spanish territorial claims in the trans-Appalachian West and open American ports to Spanish commerce. [90] Jay's instructions from Congress, however, did not give him the power to negotiate away the use of the Mississippi River by residents of the United States. [91] When Jay informed Congress of his progress, many southern members, including some who now abandoned earlier, contrary positions, objected to the closing of the all-important western waterway. Undaunted, northern members, through sheer number, tried to incorporate permission into Jay's instructions for the temporary occlusion of the Mississippi River to American commerce but lacked the required nine votes. The southern states united to condemn the change and, through their combined ability to defeat any modification to the original instructions, managed to frustrate Jay and retain American rights to the Mississippi River. [92]

Even though a few southerners failed to unite in opposition to the revised instructions, most southerners steadfastly opposed what the northern states had attempted to do in Congress. [93] Explaining his actions as a member of that body to the North Carolina legislature, Timothy Bloodworth believed that the federal compact did not invest Congress "with power to Dispose of any of the priveledges, whether natural, or acquired, of the Individual States, without their consent first obtain'd."[94] "Admit the position," he noted, "and our Dearest priveledges are rendered precarious, and insecure."[95] Bloodworth also asserted that it was not right for the southern states "to pay the purchase, by giving up the Missecippey" while the northern states received all the economic benefits from the treaty.[96] Finally, Bloodworth emphasized the "pernicious Consequences" that would befall southerners, specifically the reduction in the value of western lands and the political alienation of western settlers.[97] This last possibility, which Bloodworth interpreted to mean the desire of the northern states to foster the political alienation of the West from the South, explained why the northern states willingly agreed to the closure of the Mississippi River. Bloodworth was not alone in his suspicions. William Grayson, on the floor of Congress, maintained that occlusion "would separate the interest of the western Inhabitants, from that of the rest of the Union and render them hostile to it."[98] It would, he noted, "weaken if not destroy the union by disaffecting the S[outhern] States when they saw their dearest interest sacrificed and given up to obtain a trivial commercial advantage for their brethren in the East."[99]

James Monroe, who favored the opening of the Mississippi River only if the South and the West remained unified in purpose, reacted strongly to the perceived attack on the South. "The object in the occlusion," Monroe wrote, "is to break up so far as this will do it, the settlements on the western waters, prevent any in future, and thereby keep the States southward as they now are—or if settlements will take place, that they shall be on such principles as to make it the interest of the people to separate from the Confederacy, so as effectually to exclude any new State from it."[100] For Monroe, the purpose of "Jay and his party in congress" was clear—"either as the means of throwing the western people and territory without the govt. of the U.S. and keeping the weight of population of govt. here, or of dismembering the govt. itself, for the purpose of a separate confederacy."[101] Thus, he argued southerners, for their own self-preservation and that of their ultra-montane brethren, should work for the defeat of Jay's instructions.

On 16 August, Charles Pinckney of South Carolina delivered a lengthy speech on the proposed treaty with Spain. Like those southerners who had spoken in opposition to the treaty, Pinckney blasted the Atlantic states for forsaking those residents who depended on the Mississippi River for their economic survival. The treaty, he argued, was nothing more than Spain taking advantage of a weak and financially strapped United States to protect its colonial possessions from "intimacy" with Americans.[102] Spain's commercial concessions, he told members, were fanciful, since "she proposes nothing more than she will always be willing to grant you without a treaty."[103] What was at stake with this treaty, the South Carolinian explained, was the relationship between the Atlantic states and the West. "Nature has so placed this country," he noted, "that they must either be the future friends or enemies of the Atlantic states, and this will altogether depend upon the policy they shall observe towards them."[104] Render them dependent on Spain, he warned all members, and they will "immediately . . . [throw] themselves into her arms for that protection and support which you have denied them."[105]

The few southerners who supported the occlusion measure did so purely for pragmatic reasons, for they believed that "a cession for a limited time" might prove beneficial to the United States.[106] First, they claimed a commercial treaty with Spain would provide immediate rewards to the mercantile states by "relieving the distresses which oppress their citizens, most of which they [the New England states] say flow from the decay of their commerce."[107] Secondly, they saw the issue disrupting the relationship of the states to each other. They believed the southern states should acquiesce in the dispute and end "the fatal effects of discord."[108] Finally, and most tellingly, they argued "that in agreeing to the occlusion of the navigation of the Mississippi, we [the United States] give in fact nothing, for the moment our western country becomes populous and capable, they will seize by force what may have been yielded by treaty."[109] Thus, in effect, the United States was not relinquishing any material right to the Mississippi River, only agreeing to the continuation of the present situation. On the other hand, Henry Lee believed that the agreement did not abandon the right of the United States to the Mississippi River at all. Instead, it tacitly strengthened the American claims, for the willingness of Spain to negotiate a treaty for a twenty-five or thirty year closure of the river to American commerce implicitly stated an American right to the river.[110]

Despite southern pleas, Congress, on 29 August, rescinded Jay's previous instructions on the Mississippi River by a vote of seven to five.[111] The following day, by the same vote, Congress issued revised instructions to Jay.[112] These series of votes upset southern members, for they had previously stated as part of their argument against revision that since nine states were needed to approve a treaty, nine states were needed to craft instructions. Northern states, however, failed to heed this argument and considered their efforts successful. To ensure that Jay fully understood the precarious nature of his situation, Charles Pinckney drafted a letter to Jay reminding him that since the ratification of any treaty required the approval of nine states, "common sense" dictated that he should not continue "upon any other principles than those stipulating, the free navigation of the Mississipi and the fixing the territorial limits agreeable to the treaty with Great Britain."[113] Pinckney, however, never sent his letter to Jay. Monroe explained to Madison that cooler heads had prevailed, worried that Pinckney's tone "might have an intemperate & factious appearance."[114] Furthermore, he noted that the southern states had faithfully adhered to the Articles of Confederation and to the rules of Congress and intended to continue along that same path. [115]

After wrestling with the basic issues of westward expansion for nearly three years, southerners were just beginning to understand the complexities of the subject. In 1783, economic considerations dominated southern opinions on the West. The sale of land in the West was an easy and painless way to eliminate the national debt and enrich the commercial interests of the Atlantic states. However, in 1785 and 1786, the issue became more complicated with Kentucky's demands for statehood and the Mississippi occlusion controversy. These events forced southerners to begin the slow process of developing a coherent western policy—a policy that would benefit not only those people living on the Atlantic coast but also those people living in the trans-Appalachian West. By 1786, southerners had come to realize the importance of the southern-western economic relationship. Only a few southerners, however, had started thinking about the political relationship of the two regions. [116]

NOTES

1. George Mason to George Mason Jr., 18 January 1783, in *The Papers of George Mason, 1725–1792*, ed. Robert A. Rutland (Chapel Hill: The University of North Carolina Press, 1970), 2:761.

2. James Harrod founded Kentucky's first permanent settlement, Harrodsburg, in 1775. Its settlers were by no means the first British colonists to visit the region, for exploration of the region had begun a decade or so earlier. Lowell Hayes Harrison and James C. Klotter, *A New History of Kentucky* (Lexington: The University Press of Kentucky, 1997), 24–25.

3. United States Department of Commerce, Bureau of the Census, *Historical Statistics of the United States, Colonial Times to 1970, Part One* (Washington, DC: United States Government Printing Office, 1975), 1168.

4. Clarence Walworth Alvord, *The Illinois Country, 1673–1818* (Chicago: A. C. McClurg & Company, 1922), 358; Arthur Clinton Boggess, *The Settlement of Illinois, 1778–1830* (Chicago: Chicago Historical Society, 1908), 31.

5. John Henry to Thomas Johnson, 10 March 1778, in *Letters of Delegates to Congress*, eds. Paul H. Smith et al. (Washington, DC: Library of Congress, 1982), 9:259. For an overview of the Maryland position, see Merrill Jensen, *The Articles of Confederation: An Interpretation of the Social-Constitutional History of the American Revolution, 1774–1781* (Madison: The University of Wisconsin Press, 1940), 190–93.

6. Maryland Delegates to the Maryland General Assembly, 3 November 1783, in *Letters of Members of the Continental Congress*, ed. Edmund C. Burnett (Washington, DC: Carnegie Institution of Washington, 1934), 7:368.

7. Virginia Delegates to Governor Benjamin Harrison, 29 April 1783, in Ibid., 7:153.

8. "Fairfax County Freeholder's Address and Instructions to Their General Assembly Delegates," 20 May 1783, in Rutland, *Papers of George Mason*, 2:782.

9. Ibid.

10. Ibid.

11. Thomas Jefferson to Governor Benjamin Harrison, 3 March 1784, in Burnett, *Letters of Members*, 7:459.

12. Ibid.

13. Jacob Read to Governor Benjamin Guerard, 1 March 1784, in Ibid., 7:457.

14. Only Virginia, North Carolina and South Carolina voted on the issue. Maryland and Georgia were not present. Virginia cast four yes votes, North Carolina two, and South Carolina one. Richard Beresford voted against the Virginia cession. *Journals of the Continental Congress, 1774–1789,* ed. Worthington C. Ford et al. (Washington, DC: Government Printing Office, 1928), 26:117

15. Jacob Read to Governor Benjamin Guerard, 1 March 1784, in Burnett, *Letters of Members,* 7:457.

16. Hugh Williamson to Governor Martin, 19 March 1784, in Ibid., 7:476.

17. Ibid.

18. Arthur Lee to Joseph Reed, 5 April 1784, in Ibid., 7:485.

19. . Ibid.

20. North Carolina Delegates to Governor Alexander Martin, 26 September 1783, in Ibid., 7:313.

21. Richard H. Kohn, "The Inside Story of the Newburgh Conspiracy: America and the Coup d'etat," *William and Mary Quarterly,* 3rd Series, 27:2 (April 1970), 209–10; Richard B. Morris, *The Forging of the Union, 1781–1789* (New York: Harper & Row, Publishers, 1987), 42–50.

22. Richard Dobbs Spaight to Governor Alexander Martin, 30 April 1784, and Hugh Williamson to Alexander Martin, 30 September 1784, both in Burnett, *Letters of Members,* 7:510 and 597.

23. North Carolina Delegates to Governor Alexander Martin, 26 September 1783, in Ibid. 7:313.

24. Richard Dobbs Spaight to Governor Alexander Martin, 30 April 1784, in Ibid., 7:509.

25. Governor Alexander Martin to Hugh Williamson and Richard D. Spaight, 4 June 1784, in *State Records of North Carolina,* ed. Walter Clark (Goldsboro, NC: Nash Brothers, Book and Job Printers, 1899), 17:78–79.

26. Governor Alexander Martin to His Excellency the President of Congress, 4 December 1784, in Ibid., 17:110. See "An Act to Repeal an Act of the Congress of the United States Certain Western Lands Therein Described, and Authorising the Delegates from this State in Congress to Execute a Deed or Deeds for the Same," in *State Records of North Carolina,* ed. Walter Clark (Goldsboro, NC: Nash Brothers, Book and Job Printers, 1905), 24:678–79.

27. Alexander Martin to "The Inhabitants of the Counties of Washington, Sullivan and Greene," 25 April 1785, in Clark, *State Records of North Carolina,* 17:442.

28. Ibid.

29. William Blount to Joseph Martin, 26 October 1783, in Draper Mss 4XX17 of the Tennessee Papers of the Lyman C. Draper Collection, Wisconsin Historical Society, Madison, WI.

30. Blount to John Donelson, Joseph Martin and John Sevier, 31 May 1784, in *John Gray Blount Papers,* ed. Alice Barnwell Keith (Raleigh: State Department of Archives and History, 1952), 1:168.

31. Abner Nash to Samuel Purviance, 19 August 1784, in Purviance Family Papers, 1757 (1776–1920) 1932, Manuscript Department, William R. Perkins Library, Duke University, Durham, NC; Richard A. Bartlett, *The New Country: A Social History of the American Frontier, 1776–1890* (New York: Oxford University Press, 1974), 60–66.

32. Benjamin Hawkins and Hugh Williamson to Alexander Martin, 24 October 1783, in *State Records of North Carolina,* ed. Walter Clark (Goldsboro, NC: Nash Brothers, Book and Job Printers, 1899), 16:909.

33. George Walton to the Walker County Grand Jury, in *Savannah Gazette of the State of Georgia,* 14 April 1785.

34. Oliver H. Prince, *Digest of the Laws of the State of Georgia, Obtaining All Statutes and the Substance of all Resolutions of a General and Public Nature, and Now in Force, which have been Passed in this State, Previous to the Session of the General Assembly of Dec. 1837, with Occasional Explanatory Notes, and Connecting References, to which is added an Appendix, containing the Constitution of the United States, the Constitution of the State of Georgia as Amended; the Statute of Frauds and Perjuries, the Habeas Corpus Act, [e]tc. Also a Synopsis*

of the Local Acts, Arranged to Each County, and Classed under Appropriate Heads, with a Copious Index, 2nd ed. (Athens: Published by the author, 1837), 527–31.

35. Thomas R. B. Cobb, *Statute Laws of the State of Georgia, in Force prior to the Session of the General Assembly of 1851, with Explanatory Notes and References; Together with an Appendix, Containing the Constitution of the United States; the Constitution of the State of Georgia; the Statute of Frauds and Perjuries; the Habeas Corpus Act; The Judiciary Act of 1799, and the Local Laws of Applicable to Each County, Compiled and Published under the Authority of the General Assembly* (Athens: Published by Christy, Kelsea & Burke, 1851), 671.

36. Farris W. Cadle, *Georgia Land Surveying History and Law* (Athens: University of Georgia Press, 1991), 86–88.

37. *Annapolis Maryland Gazette*, 8 September 1785.

38. Richard Henry Lee to Madison, 20 November and 26 November 1784, both in *The Papers of James Madison*, eds. William T. Hutchinson, William M.E. Rachal et al. (Chicago: The University of Chicago Press; Charlottesville: University of Virginia Press, 1973), 8:145, 150.

39. Madison to Jefferson, 20 August 1784, in *The Papers of Thomas Jefferson*, ed. Julian P. Boyd (Princeton: Princeton University Press, 1953), 7:403.

40. Archibald Stuart to Jefferson, 17 October 1785, in *The Papers of Thomas Jefferson*, ed. Julian P. Boyd (Princeton: Princeton University Press, 1953), 8:646.

41. Henry Lee to Richard Bland Lee, 28 October 1786, in *Letters of Delegates to Congress, 1774-1789*, ed. Paul H. Smith et al. (Washington, DC: Library of Congress, 1996), 23:618.

42. *Virginia Journal and Alexander Advertiser*, 27 October 1785.

43. Ibid.

44. Washington to Richard Henry Lee, 22 August 1785, in *The Writings of Washington from the Original Manuscript Sources, 1745–1799*, ed. John C. Fitzpatrick (Washington, DC: United States Government Printing Office, 1938), 28:231.

45. Ibid. Washington expressed similar sentiments to Henry Lee the following year. See Washington to Henry Lee, 18 June 1786, in Ibid., 28:460. For an examination of Washington's western attitudes see: Thomas P. Slaughter, *The Whiskey Rebellion: Frontier Epilogue to the American Revolution* (New York: Oxford University Press, 1986): 75–89, and Charles H. Ambler, *George Washington and the West* (Chapel Hill: The University of North Carolina Press, 1936).

46. *Virginia Journal and Alexandria Advertiser*, 19 May 1785.

47. Madison to Jefferson, 9 January 1785, in Hutchinson et al., *Madison Papers*, 8:226.

48. Richard Henry Lee to Madison, 27 December 1784, in Burnett, *Letters of Members*, 7:638.

49. *The Virginia Journal and Alexandria Advertiser*, 27 October 1785.

50. Washington to Henry Knox, 5 December 1784, in Fitzpatrick, *Writings of Washington*, 28:4. Washington expressed similar sentiments to multiple people. See Washington to James Warren, 7 October 1785, to Barbé-Marbois, 21 June 1785, to Benjamin Lincoln, 5 February 1785, and to the Marquis de Lafayette, 25 July 1785, all in Ibid., 28:291, 169, 64, 207, respectively.

51. *Virginia Journal and Alexandria Advertiser*, 27 October 1785.

52. Hugh Williamson to Jefferson, 11 December 1784, in Burnett, *Letters of Members*, 7:623.

53. Ibid.

54. James Monroe to Jefferson, 19 January 1786, in *The Papers of James Monroe: Selected Correspondence and Papers, 1776–1794*, ed. Daniel Preston (Westport, CT: Greenwood Press, 2006), 2:265.

55. Ibid.

56. Edmund Pendleton to Richard Henry Lee, 7 March 1785, in *The Letters and Papers of Edmund Pendleton, 1734-1803*, ed. David John Mays (Charlottesville: Published for the Virginia Historical Society by the University Press of Virginia, 1967), 2:475.

57. Pendleton to Richard Henry Lee, 8 August 1785, in Ibid., 2:482.

58. Madison to Jefferson, 20 August 1784, in Boyd et al., *Jefferson Papers*, 7:403.

59. Madison to the Marquis de Lafayette, 20 March 1785, in Hutchinson et al., *Madison Papers*, 8:252.

60. Ibid.

61. Ibid.

62. Madison to Jefferson, 20 August 1784, in Boyd et al., *Jefferson Papers*, 7:405.

63. Madison to Edmund Randolph, 11 February 1783, in Smith et al., *Letters of Delegates*, 19:676.

64. Virginia Delegates to Governor Benjamin Harrison, 8 September 1783, in *The Papers of James Madison*, eds. William T. Hutchinson and William M. E. Rachal (Chicago: The University of Chicago Press, 1971), 7:300.

65. Richard Henry Lee to Monroe, 5 January 1784, in *The Letters of Richard Henry Lee*, ed. James Curtis Ballagh (New York: The Macmillan Company, 1914), 2:287.

66. Monroe to Richard Henry Lee, 16 December 1783, in Preston, *Monroe Papers*, 2:71.

67. Ibid.

68. Virginia Delegates to Governor Benjamin Harrison, 1 November 1783, in Smith et al., *Letters of Delegates*, 21:139.

69. John Marshall to Arthur Lee, 17 April 1784, in *The Papers of John Marshall*, eds. Herbert A. Johnson et al. (Chapel Hill: University of North Carolina Press, 1974), 1:119.

70. Marshall to George Muter, 9 January 1785, in Ibid., 1:133.

71. Richard Dobbs Spaight to Governor Richard Caswell, 5 June 1785, in Burnett, *Letters of Members*, 7:135.

72. Richard Henry Lee to Washington, 18 April 1785, in Ballagh, *R. H. Lee Letters*, 2:349.

73. Virginia Delegates to Governor Benjamin Harrison, 8 September 1783, in Hutchinson, *Madison Papers*, 7:300; Harrison to Virginia Delegates, 19 September 1783, in Ibid., 7:349.

74. Harrison to Virginia Delegates, 26 September 1783, in Ibid., 7:358.

75. Ibid.

76. Jefferson to Madison, 20 February 1784, in Smith et al., *Letters of Delegates*, 21:368.

77. Jefferson to Washington, 15 March 1784, in Burnett, *Letters of Members*, 7:450.

78. John Harvie to Arthur Campbell, 30 November 1785, in Arthur Campbell Papers, The Filson Historical Society, Lexington, KY.

79. Monroe to Jefferson, 25 August 1785, in Boyd et al., *Jefferson Papers*, 8:442.

80. Ibid.

81. Ibid.

82. Monroe to Jefferson, 16 July 1786, in Burnett, *Letters of Members*, 8:403; Jefferson to Madison, 16 December 1786, in *The Papers of Thomas Jefferson*, ed. Julian P. Boyd (Princeton: Princeton University Press, 1954), 10:603.

83. For a general overview, see Kevin T. Barksdale, *The Lost State of Franklin: America's First Secession* (Lexington: University Press of Kentucky, 2008).

84. Patrick Henry to Jefferson, 10 September 1785, in Boyd et al., *Jefferson Papers*, 8:508; *Savannah Georgia Gazette*, 17 November 1785.

85. William Grayson to Madison, 21 August 1785, in Burnett, *Letters of Members*, 8:194.

86. Richard Henry Lee to Madison, 11 August 1785, in Ibid., 8:180.

87. Jefferson to Richard Henry Lee, 12 July 1785, in Boyd et al., *Jefferson Papers*, 8:287.

88. *The Statutes at Large; Being a Collection of all the Laws of Virginia from the First Session of the Legislature, in the Year 1619*, ed. William Waller Hening (Richmond: George Cochran Printers, 1823; repr., Charlottesville: Published for the Jamestown Foundation of the Commonwealth of Virginia by the University Press of Virginia, 1969), 12:37-40.

89. Washington to Jefferson, 26 September 1785, in Boyd et al., *Jefferson Papers*, 8:556. Also see Richard Henry Lee to Madison, 30 May 1785, in Burnett, *Letters of Members*, 8:131.

90. *Journals of the Continental Congress*, 31:467-84.

91. Ibid., 29:658.

92. Calvin Jillson and Rick K. Wilson, *Congressional Dynamics: Structure, Coordination & Choice in the First American Congress, 1774-1789* (Stanford: Stanford University Press, 1994), 273; *Journals of the Continental Congress*, 31:621; Monroe to Madison, 3 September 1786, in *The Papers of James Madison*, ed. William M. E. Rachal (Chicago and London: The University of Chicago Press, 1975), 9:112-14 .

93. Edward Rutledge of Virginia was one person who retained his previous position. Writing Jay, he noted: "If from our relinquishment at present, she can retain for a number of years, the exclusive navigation of the river, it is well—it will stop migration, it will concenter force, because the settlers can have no vent for their productions of that country but down the Mississippi, and, therefore, think they will not be fond of immediately of inhabiting her banks." Rutledge to Jay, 12 November 1786, in *The Correspondence and Public Papers of John Jay*, ed. Henry P. Johnston (New York: G. P. Putnam's Sons, 1890), 3:218.

94. Timothy Bloodworth to the North Carolina Assembly, [n.d.], in Burnett, *Letters of Members*, 8:521.

95. Ibid.

96. Ibid., 8:522. Bloodworth continues his attack on the proposal in several letters to Governor Richard Caswell. He concluded that if the northern states could impose such a treaty on the country, then "there remains no security for any possession," a possible reference to the institution of slavery. Bloodworth to Governor Richard Caswell, 29 September 1786, in Burnett, *Letters of Members*, 8:474; For the slavery interpretation of this passage, see David Waldstreicher, *Slavery's Constitution: From Revolution to Ratification* (New York: Hill and Wang, 2009), 56.

97. Charles Thomson, "Minutes of Proceedings," 16 August 1786, in Burnett, *Letters of Members*, 8:427.

98. Ibid.

99. Ibid.

100. Monroe to Patrick Henry, 12 August 1786, in Smith et al., *Letters of Delegates*, 23:465.

101. Monroe to Madison, 14 August 1786, in Burnett, *Letters of Members*, 8:427. Monroe continued this dismemberment theme in a second letter to Madison, arguing that the break would occur at the Potomac River. Monroe to Madison, 3 September 1786, in Ibid., 8:461.

102. "Mr. Charles Pinckney's Speech, in Answer to Mr. Jay, Secretary for Foreign Affairs, on the Question of a Treaty with Spain, Delivered in Congress, August 16, 1786," in *Journals of the Continental Congress*, 31:938.

103. Ibid., 31:942.

104. Ibid., 31:944.

105. Ibid., 31:945.

106. Rutledge to Jay, 12 November 1786, in Johnston, *Papers of Jay*, 3:217.

107. Henry Lee to Washington, 11 October 1786, in Burnett, *Letters of Members*, 8:482.

108. Ibid.

109. Henry Lee to Washington, 7 August 1786, in Ibid., 8:417.

110. Henry Lee to Washington, 11 October 1786, in Ibid., 482-83. This point did not go unchallenged. Charles Pinckney noted that "to me appears most extraordinary that a doctrine should be attempted to prove, that because we have not at present a government sufficiently energetic to assert a national right, it would be more honorable to relinquish it." See "Mr. Charles Pinckney's Speech, in Answer to Mr. Jay, Secretary for Foreign Affairs, on the Question of a Treaty with Spain, Delivered in Congress, August 16, 1786," in *Journals of the Continental Congress*, 31:943.

111. Connecticut, Massachusetts, New Hampshire, New Jersey, New York, Pennsylvania, and Rhode Island voted in favor of the motion, and Georgia, Maryland, North Carolina, South Carolina, and Virginia voted against it. See *Journals of the Continental Congress*, 31:595.

112. Ibid., 31:601.

113. Smith et al., *Letters of Delegates*, 23:549.

114. Ibid., 23:545.

115. Ibid.

116. Peter S. Onuf argues in, *Statehood and Union: A History of the Northwest Ordinance* (Bloomington: Indiana University Press, 1987) and "Liberty, Development and Union: Visions of the West in the 1780s," *William and Mary Quarterly*, Third Series, XLIII (April 1986), that a consensus concerning the future of the West existed among political leaders in the United States. The land ordinances, he states, particularly the Northwest Ordinance are expressions of this common viewpoint. "Only by rapidly developing the frontier economy and integrating it into the national economy," he notes, "could the West be preserved for the Union, and the

union itself be preserved." (*Statehood*, p. 4) I believe, however, that southerners were neither as nationalistic nor as unified as Onuf contends.

Chapter Three

A Nationalist Viewpoint

As southerners debated the western question, their discourse gradually changed from one based purely on economic considerations to one articulating a more political point of view. All agreed that the West was the key to unlocking a glorious future for the United States, provided the United States could retain possession of it. Political rumblings in Kentucky and in the Cumberland settlements of North Carolina did not portend an easy time ahead for political leaders in the South, or in the nation. If through their own collective ineptitude the Atlantic seaboard states should happen to lose the West to a foreign nation or to an independence movement, southerners realized that the political repercussions for the South and the nation would be enormous. If western political instability did not give southerners enough to worry about, they also had to ensure that the development and settlement of the West proceeded at a nonthreatening pace to either section of the nation. By 1788, many southerners had started to realize the seriousness of their ongoing debate with northerners concerning the western territory. The issue was no longer only over which section of the country should reap the financial rewards of westward expansion. It was also over which section of the country could, through its control of the instruments of government, best protect its interests in the emerging political union of states.

Southerners did not instantly perceive that they could use a properly groomed and controlled West to protect their interests within the Union. Instead, this realization was a gradual reaction to the political situation confronting them as they attempted to redress what they perceived as the political imbalance of a system favoring the northern states. However, before the South consciously made this political alliance with the West, a small group of southerners worked to prevent the West from becoming merely a source of petty sectional squabbles. They hoped to transform the West into a striking manifestation of national unity and an illustration of southern commitment to the Union. At first, these nationalists experienced few successes, as most southerners centered their attention on their financial relationship with the West. The Jay-Gardoqui negotiations in 1786 became the first great test of this policy. Fortunately for the nationalists, though the Mississippi crisis had the ability to destroy their nationalistic approach to the West, most southerners viewed the crisis as a threat to the financial stability of both sections. At this time, however, a few perceptive southerners began urging their fellow southerners to look seriously at the relationship among the three sections, South, West, and North. Nationalists managed to retain their ascendancy during the Constitutional Convention of 1787, but shortly thereafter, they reversed their position in favor of a sectional approach.

As a young man, James Madison took an interest in the West, an interest that he retained throughout his life. He derived some of his curiosity from his family's limited activities in Kentucky land speculation. However, unlike many southerners, Madison flirted only briefly with the time-worn practice. He had hoped to amass quickly a small fortune and become financially independent. Then, with his future free from monetary concerns, Madison hoped to throw himself body and soul into his one true love—politics. Unfortunately, his land dealings in Kentucky in 1780 and 1781 produced little income, and he remained dependent on his family for funds. Still, the experience, which began just as Madison entered Congress for the first time in March 1780, increased his financial knowledge about the West. Madison's familiarity with western finances, coupled with the increased knowledge that he gained from his new congressional colleagues' preoccupation with the West, helped show the Virginian that Americans differed in their opinions about the West. Later events that year would confirm his conclusions. [1]

In October 1780, the Continental Congress reaffirmed its instructions to John Jay, the country's minister to Spain, regarding the terms of a possible alliance with Spain. Within those instructions were the explicit requirements that he neither relinquish the right of the United States to navigate the Mississippi River to its mouth nor cede any land lying east of that river to Spain. Within weeks of finalizing and communicating to Jay his instructions, Congress found itself readdressing those same two points. Georgians, concerned about the defensive posture of their state against the British military, sought to loosen Jay's instructions in order to make it easier for him to negotiate an alliance with Spain. Other delegates, concerned about rumors of European mediation of the war based on *uti possidetis*, the principle that territory obtained during war remains with its possessor at the end of the war unless specifically stipulated in a treaty, eventually bowed to the Georgians' request. Thus, out of fear and panic, Congress approved the relinquishment of the right of the United States to the navigation of the Mississippi River to its mouth.

The controversy, which would last for only a few months during a period of intense uneasiness within the country, revealed a division among southerners concerning the wisdom of such a move. It also, more importantly, demonstrated a growing awareness among a few southerner leaders of the future importance of the Mississippi River to the region and to the country. James Madison, representing Virginia in Congress, vehemently opposed any modification of the instructions. Madison believed that Congress's October 1780 instructions to Jay, in which he was intimately involved, were the correct expression on this issue.

In February 1780, Massachusetts delegate James Lovell outlined the Spanish demands for an alliance in a letter to Samuel Adams. First, he told Adams, Spain demanded an explicit western boundary with the United States. Second, Spain demanded the exclusive navigation of the Mississippi River. Third, Spain demanded the return of East and West Florida. Finally, Spain demanded land east of the Mississippi River. On this last point, the French minister, the chevalier de la Luzerne, from whom Congress had learned this information, hinted that the United States should acquiesce in the Spanish demand, accepting as its western boundary the 1763 proclamation line. The Spaniards, he told the congressional committee assigned to meet with him, sought this line as the boundary, since "these States have no Right to those Lands not having possessed them nor having a Claim in the Right of the Sovereign whose Govt. we have abjured."[2] Four days later, in a letter to Henry Laurens, Lovell stated that the United States "must absolutely refuse" this last demand.[3]

American resolve remained strong throughout the summer of 1780. A dispatch from Jay dated 26 May, however, threatened to undermine the American determination to resist Spanish encroachment in the West. On 14 August, Congress read Jay's letter, in which the American minister requested some clarification of his instructions.[4] Confident that Spain would "finally be content with equitable regulations" regarding the Mississippi River, he asked Congress whether it would accept any Spanish regulation of contraband on the river. In closing, he stated: "I wish that as little possible may be left to my discretion, and that as I am determined to adhere strictly to their [Congress's] sentiments and directions, I may be favored with them fully and in season."[5]

On 21 August, the Committee for Foreign Affairs, to which Jay's letter had been directed, recommended that Congress create a three-man committee to deal with the issue. Congress immediately established such a committee and assigned three delegates to it: Virginian Joseph Jones, Delawarean Thomas McKean, and Georgian George Walton.[6] The next day, as if to frustrate Congress on this issue, the delegates from Virginia introduced their instructions concerning the navigation of the Mississippi River.[7] The Virginia legislature, on 5 November 1779, had directed its delegates to Congress to "obtain an express stipulation in favour of the United American States, for the free navigation of the river Mississippi to the sea, for the purposes of trade and commerce."[8] Congress immediately referred the instructions to the Jones-McKean-Walton committee.[9]

Reaction to Jay's request seemed muted. The day after Congress read Jay's letter, Willie Jones and Whitmel Hill, delegates from North Carolina, informed their state's governor, Abner Nash, of the receipt of dispatches from Jay. They expressed concern that the Mississippi question might "prove a stumbling Block; but we hope the Difficulty will be surmounted."[10] Five days later, Hill sounded more somber in a letter to Thomas Burke, writing that Jay's plan to offer Spain concessions concerning contraband "is a matter of doubt."[11] Rhode Island delegate Ezekiel Cornell, however, seemed confident that Congress would "not willingly agree to" the Spanish demands.[12]

Cornell's confidence in Congress was affirmed on 4 October. That day, delegates unanimously approved the Jones-McKean-Walton committee's instructions to Jay, directing him to "adhere to his former instructions respecting the right of the United States of America to the free navigation of the river Mississippi into and from the sea; which right, if an express acknowledgment of it cannot be obtained from Spain, is not by any stipulation on the part of America to be relinquished."[13] Congress also instructed Jay to adhere to the boundaries that Congress had already determined for the United States, which were based on treaty rights that Great Britain obtained from Spain in 1763. In addition, Congress, well aware that Spain might regain control of East and West Florida, directed Jay to secure rights of navigation for rivers flowing from Georgia into West Florida in exchange for U.S. recognition of Spain's right to both Floridas. Finally, in an attempt to appease the Spanish government on the Mississippi question, Congress directed Jay "to enter into such equitable regulations as may appear a necessary security against contraband."[14] Madison wholeheartedly agreed with Congress's actions.[15]

Two days later, New Hampshire delegate John Sullivan and New York delegate James Duane moved that Congress appoint a committee to explain its 4 October decision. This committee, they moved, should write a letter to Jay outlining the reasoning of Congress for its inflexibility on the issue of the Mississippi River and territory lying to the east of said river. Congress subsequently appointed three members, Chairman James Madison, John Sullivan, and James Duane.[16] The composition of the committee is informative. Irving Brant notes in his Madison biography that Virginia at this time had the support of the New York and New England delegations, whose members worried that if they were to agree to any compromise on the issue of the Mississippi River, Virginia and the other southern states would abandon their respective states' boundary claims.[17]

Madison's letter to Jay was a commentary on the principles underlying Congress's instructions to its minister in Madrid. The main thrust of the letter was the right of the United States to navigate the Mississippi River and to place its western boundary at that river. Taking a nationalist stand, which would at times support his state's western land claims, Madison conceded nothing to the Spanish government. He began by pointing out that Britain obtained possession of the territory by virtue of its treaty with France in 1763. The British king subsequently assumed, in the name of the people, sovereignty over the land. When the American colonists declared their independence, that sovereignty over the land "devolved to them in consequence of their resumption of the Sovereignty to themselves."[18]

With Congress's approval of Madison's instructions to Jay on 17 October, the issue had seemingly come to an end. However, on 18 November, the Georgian delegates would reopen the question by moving that Congress approve new instructions to Jay. Worried that the League of Armed Neutrality might force a peace on Europe based on *uti possidetis* and that such a peace might have adverse repercussions for their state, the Georgians requested that Congress instruct Jay to cede to Spain navigation of the Mississippi River and "a tract of territory, to begin upon the eastern bank of the said river, where the southern line of Georgia Strikes it, running along the said line Eastwardly to the river Mobile, and thence Northwardly to Cape Anthony on the said river," provided Spain granted the United States a subsidy or loan and pledged not to seek peace until the United States was ready.[19] Congress postponed a decision on this motion until 5 December.[20]

The Georgians' motion, while unexpected, was not surprising. By late 1780, the military and economic affairs of the United States were in precarious conditions. British troops controlled large sections of Georgia and South Carolina and threatened other areas in the South. The value of Continental currency was depreciating rapidly, and the United States was in dire need of an infusion of hard currency to stem inflationary tendencies in the economy. In addition, rumors were circulating that the League of Armed Neutrality intended to dictate peace terms to Britain and France, and these terms would leave parts of Georgia and South Carolina as British colonies.[21]

Madison, however, was surprised by the Georgians' move. He had thought that the issue would remain dormant until Congress received a reply from Jay.[22] Following the introduction of the Georgians' motion, Theodorick Bland, Madison's fellow Virginian in Congress, asked Madison to join him in seeking clarification from their state's government. Madison refused. Bland apparently considered such sacrifices on the part of the United States "necessary," since "it might contribute not only to relieve our present necessities, but promise us peace and a firm establishment of our Independence."[23] Like Maryland delegate John Hanson, Bland assumed that the United States would eventually reacquire the lost right once "our Citizens Settled on its Banks and Water."[24] Madison thought otherwise.

"In this important business, which so deeply affects the claims & interests of Virginia & which I know she has so much at heart, I have not the satisfaction to harmonise in Sentiment with my Colleague," he wrote his friend Joseph Jones. Congress, he predicted, would see the wisdom in not sacrificing the rights of one state without that state's concurrence. The New England states, he warned, should worry about their fisheries if Congress were to act rashly. In addition, Madison noted that Jay, in his last dispatches, had told Congress to remain firm, since he thought he saw some flexibility in Spain's position. Congress, Madison believed, should therefore wait on further dispatches from Jay.[25] Unfortunately for Madison, Congress chose to move quickly on the matter.

On 4 December, Congress received dispatches from Jay and William Carmichael, secretary of the U.S. legation at Madrid. The two men described the situation in the Spanish capital as bleak, noting that "the Mississippi is likely to prove a very serious difficulty."[26] Receipt of this information, according to Madison, seemed to encourage the Georgians in their motion.[27] On 5 December, Congress spent time debating the Georgians' motion, but settled nothing.[28] Three days later, just as Congress prepared to approve the Georgians' motion, an action that seemed inconceivable to Madison just a few days earlier, Madison moved that the motion be postponed until the members of the Virginia delegation had a chance to communicate with their state on this issue. Congress concurred, and Madison had his reprieve.[29]

On 13 December, Madison, along with Bland, apprised Virginian governor Thomas Jefferson of recent events. After blaming the situation on unfavorable intelligence from Spain and "the manner of thinking which begins to prevail in Congress," Madison asked Jefferson to place three items of concern before the legislature.[30] First, does the legislature concur in the opinion that the right to navigate the Mississippi River must be sacrificed in order to obtain an alliance with Spain? Second, what territory within the limits of Virginia on the east side of the river is the legislature willing to yield "to Spain as the price of an Alliance with her"?[31] Finally, what should they do in case "we should be instructed in no event to concede the claims of Virginia either to territory or to the navigation of the abovementioned river and Congress should without their concurrence agree to such concession"?[32] Governor Jefferson placed the letter before the Virginia House of Delegates on 25 December without comment.[33]

Apparently worried that their motion might fail in Congress, the three Georgian delegates—George Walton, William Few, and Richard Howley— sat down and produced a pamphlet outlining their case. On 8 January 1781, Robert Aitken, a Philadelphia printer, published the pamphlet, titled *Observations Upon the Effects of Certain Late Political Suggestions, by the Delegates of Georgia*. Not a philosophical discussion on the merits of the Georgian position, the pamphlet was simply a listing of reasons why Georgia was an essential member of the United States.[34] Its release coincided with a flurry of articles in Philadelphia newspapers on war-related events occurring in the South, particularly in Georgia and South Carolina.[35]

The effect of this pamphlet on the public or delegates is unclear. What is important, however, is that the Georgians attempted to affect congressional opinion by outlining the problems that could ensue if Congress were to continue its adherence to the Virginian position. Madison's nationalist stand, in the Georgians' opinion, meant catastrophe for their state and possibly for the country. In addition, Madison's insistence on his state's charter rights, likewise, meant trouble for both Georgia and the country. Fortunately for the Georgians, the Virginians would bow to public pressure.

On 2 January 1781, the Virginia legislature begrudgingly acceded to the request. The legislature insisted that Virginia had a right to the navigation of the Mississippi River, "co-extensive with our territory," but relented by stating that "the said navigation [to the mouth of the river] be ceded if insisting on the same is deemed an impediment to the treaty with Spain," provided the delegates worked to obtain port facilities within the Spanish territory.[36] Jefferson sent these instructions to the Virginia delegates on 18 January.[37] Two days after receipt of the new instructions, Madison introduced, on behalf of his state, a motion on the navigation of the Mississippi River.[38]

Contained within that motion was the text of a letter to be sent to Jay. While adhering to his instructions, Madison tried to massage the letter in a way that would soften the Virginian decision. First, he conditioned the cession on the basis that it "shall be unalterably insisted upon by Spain."[39] Secondly, he insisted that Jay, in offering the cession to Spain, obtain from the Spanish government a guarantee that the citizens of the United States had the right to navigate the river above the Spanish line of possession, the thirty-first degree of north latitude. Finally, he insisted that Jay "exert every possible effort to obtain" the right of the United States to navigate the river below the thirty-first degree of north latitude and also to acquire port facilities below the line.[40] By a vote of seven to three, Congress approved the letter on 15 February.[41]

Although the Georgians had carried the day, Madison would continue to champion the right of Americans to the navigation of the Mississippi River to its source, including nibbling away at Congress's 15 February decision. For instance, Madison moved on 21 March 1782 that Congress congratulate Jay on his performance as minister to Madrid. Buried beneath the praises in Madison's motion was an acknowledgment that Congress's concession on the Mississippi River was meant to be a timely offer and that if the Spanish government were to continue procrastinating, "the reason of the sacrifice will no longer exist."[42] Madison would incorporate the wording of his motion into a letter to Jay the following month.[43]

Given the conditions under which the Americans found themselves in the fall of 1780, their decision to cede the right of navigation of the Mississippi

River below the thirty-first degree of north latitude to Spain can be viewed as a necessary action in order to secure a military alliance with Spain. The Georgians and others, including Madison's Virginia colleague Theodorick Bland, truly believed that the future integrity of the country demanded such action. Madison, however, did not believe that such a sacrifice was in the best interest of the country or, for that matter, of his state. A nationalist, Madison concluded that the West had the potential to disrupt old political alliances. To eliminate this source of sectional tension, Madison believed that politicians needed to disassociate the West from each section, North and South. Madison hoped that removing the West from sectional considerations would lead politicians to use the resources of the West to benefit the entire nation.[44]

While a member of the Virginia delegation to the Continental Congress, Madison helped ensure the passage in 1784 of the Virginia act of cession by maneuvering around a variety of obstacles that northern representatives had placed before it. Early in the negotiations, Madison realized that certain states were jealous of the western claims of his state. To counter Virginia's dominant political position, these states began advocating the admission of Vermont into the Union as a way to gain strength in Congress. "The true secret," Madison noted to Edmund Pendleton, president of the Virginia Supreme Court of Appeals, "is that the Vote of Vermont is wished for as an auxiliary agst. the Western claims of Virga."[45] Madison believed, however, that the political leaders in the northern states had not formed a unified coalition in support of statehood for Vermont. Even though the landless states—Delaware, Maryland, New Hampshire, New Jersey, Pennsylvania, and Rhode Island—fervently desired Vermont as an ally in Congress to counter the western claims of the landed states—Connecticut, Georgia, Massachusetts, New York, North Carolina, South Carolina, and Virginia—Madison reasoned that the rise of the West as a political question drove Maryland and Pennsylvania into the arms of the landless states. "The general policy and interests of these two States are opposed to the admission of Vermont into the Union," Madison wrote, "and if the case of the Western territory were once removed, they would instantly divide from the Eastern States in the case of Vermont."[46] Thus, the debate convinced Madison about the divisive power of the West. As a result, he resolved to find a way of undermining what he saw as a dangerous force.

Although Madison directed most of his attention to securing satisfactory terms for the cession of Virginia lands north of the Ohio River, he still wanted to detach the West from partisan politics. He seldom addressed himself to the question of anticipated benefits from the ceded lands. When he did, however, he spoke of national benefits. Heading his list of benefits was the revenue that the national government would receive from the sale of its western lands—money that the national government could use to eliminate the national debt. As a member of the committee "to consider the means of restoring and supporting public Credit," Madison supported a call for the cession of all western lands to the national government as a means of "hastening the extinguishment of the debts . . . and of establishing the harmony of the U. States."[47] Cession of the western lands, in conjunction with a temporary import duty and state fiscal contributions to Congress based on population instead of land valuation, became for Madison the answer to the most pressing problem facing the country—the danger generated by North-South sectionalism.[48] Congressional rejection, however, meant in his mind the "melancholy proof that narrow & local views prevail over that liberal policy & those mutual concessions which our future tranquility and present reputation call for."[49]

Because Madison was capable of breaking out of sectional parochialism with its emphasis on short-term economic gains, he was unlike many of his neighbors—men who were afraid of or indifferent to westward migration yet who at the same time championed internal improvements. The Virginian's powerful vision permitted him to see all the issues involved in the western question—the economic and political development of the West and its effect on the Atlantic seaboard states; the fears and anxieties of southerners pitted against the hopes and dreams of the western migrant; and above all else, the Mississippi River and its guaranteed ability to affect positively or negatively all western issues.

In 1784, Spain closed the mouth of the Mississippi River to American commerce in an attempt to slow down American expansion into the trans-Appalachian West. For Madison, the question of American access to the Mississippi River remained a critical element in his evolving western policy. In August 1784, he wrote his close friend Jefferson, who was in Paris as United States minister to France, a letter outlining his position on the Mississippi River. As early as 1782, Madison had expressed his opinion that American navigation of the Mississippi was essential for the future advancement of the United States. He believed that for several reasons Spain could never permanently enforce its 1784 ban against American navigation of the river. First, as he explained to Jefferson, Spanish officials would eventually realize that the thousands of western inhabitants sending their goods down the Mississippi River would need a place to store and sell their goods. New Orleans was the logical choice, and Madison refused to consider the possibility that Spanish officials were so naive that they could not foresee a time when New Orleans would be "one of the richest and most flourishing Emporiums in the world."[50] Secondly, Madison argued that the nations of Europe, aware that the trans-Appalachian West was a fertile area just waiting for enterprising entrepreneurs to tap its riches, would exert a considerable amount of pressure on Spain to open the Mississippi River to American navigation and, ultimately, to European trade.[51]

If, on the other hand, the Spanish government did not open the river, Madison believed Americans would not migrate in large numbers to the West. Instead, they would remain on the Atlantic coast, developing their own manufactured products and competing with the Europeans in marketplaces throughout the world. He also foresaw that should Americans turn to manufacturing, they would place less land under cultivation. With fewer American farmers producing fewer crops, the prices for such items as corn, hemp, indigo, lumber, rice and tobacco would rise affecting not only American but also European consumers.[52] These latter predictions did not worry Madison, however, for he optimistically believed that the "rights of humanity" would prevail over corrupt Spanish counselors, and Spain would grant Americans access to the river.[53] Pragmatically, Madison knew that Europeans wanted the United States to remain an agricultural nation and believed that European rulers would persuade the Spanish crown to open the Mississippi River to American commerce.

Even though American access to the Mississippi River would enhance the economy of the West, Madison noted that the Spanish opening of the river would not have the same effect on the Atlantic seaboard states. Although western migration would relieve those individuals who remained behind from the burden of an overpowering debt, he nevertheless predicted that the same western migration would force them to deal with a variety of problems, some potentially more devastating than just an unmanageable debt. They would have to contend with "the danger to the Confederacy from multiplying the parts of the Machine, by the depopulation of the country, by the depreciation of their lands and by the delay of that maritime strength which must be their only safety in case of war."[54] Madison also reasoned that if the Spanish government opened the Mississippi River to the commerce of the western interior and New Orleans became the commercial capital of the West, merchants in New York, Pennsylvania, and Virginia would have to satisfy themselves with minor roles in western economic development and never reap the financial benefits that such a lucrative trade might have brought to them. Likewise, Virginia would lose its position as the premier tobacco-growing state, for western migrants would take the knowledge of tobacco cultivation with them. On the bright side, Madison did note that if Virginia were to lose its premier status among the tobacco-growing states, it could console itself by the "disburden of the slaves," who, he expected, would follow the tobacco west.[55]

Seven months later, Madison reiterated his points to the marquis de Lafayette, whom he hoped to enlist as a powerful ally in the Spanish negotiations.[56] "You have not erred," he wrote, "in supposing me out of the number of those who have relaxed their anxiety concerning the navigation of the Mississippi."[57] Those who do, Madison noted, "frame their policies on both very narrow and very delusive foundations."[58] He then quickly moved to deflect the position that Lafayette had taken in a previous letter that the settlement of the West would eventually create a natural division between the Atlantic seaboard states and the western areas of the country. Turning the argument around, he asked "how much will the connection be strengthened by the ties of friendship, of marriage and consanguinity? Ties which it may be remarked, will be even more numerous, between the ultramontane and the Atlantic States than between any two of the latter."[59] Refusing to accept Lafayette's position that western expansion would harm the Union, he spoke of the benefits that the navigation of the Mississippi River would bring to the United States and the American people in general:

> Upon this navigation depends essentially the value of that vast field of territory which is to be sold for the benefit of the common Treasury: and upon the value of this territory when settled will depend the portion of the public burdens of which the old States will be relieved by the new. Add to this the stake which a considerable proportion of those who remain in the old states will acquire in the new by adventures in land either on their own immediate account or that of their descendants.[60]

Besides, as Madison argued, how could the United States allow the closure of the Mississippi River and remain true to its national existence?[61]

In a similar vein, Madison chided as foolish those who emphasized internal improvement projects as a way to draw the commerce of the West permanently to the Atlantic seaboard states. Admitting that the proposed James River and Potomac River projects would have the immediate effect of solidifying the economic and political relationship of Virginia with the West, Madison believed that southerners could not divorce the Mississippi River from the western question.[62] "I can not believe that many mind[s] are tainted with so illiberal and short sited a policy," he remarked in a letter to Jefferson.[63] Southern parochialism, both economic and political, was an obstacle that Madison desperately sought to overcome.

In late 1784, Madison helped fellow delegate Joseph Jones draft an extradition bill and maneuver it through the Virginia General Assembly.[64] For some time, Virginia had been having difficulty with its western settlers. With little regard for the treaty guarantees of the state to the Indians, settlers had started moving onto treaty land, which often belonged to Indian tribes at peace with Virginia. The settlers' proclivity for armed attacks against the Indians as well as their "licentious & predatory" intrusion into Spanish territory also alarmed the lawmakers.[65] Virginians naturally assumed that the Indian tribes would not remain docile forever and would sooner or later retaliate against the western settlers. An Indian war would be a serious event, but Virginians feared something considerably more ominous—hostilities between Americans and Spaniards, like those occurring at Natchez.[66]

When Thomas Green, a resident of the Natchez district, petitioned the Georgia General Assembly to create a county out of the district, assembly members happily complied. Despite the general awareness that Spain also claimed this area, they created Bourbon County on 7 February 1785. They appointed four justices—Nathaniel Christmas, William Davenport, Thomas Green and Nicholas Long—to organize the parts of the county not occupied by Spain. In June, Green reached Natchez before his fellow justices and promptly set about organizing the county. Besides raising the anger of the Spanish commandant, Green's actions antagonized many of the residents who did not want to come under the control of Georgia. When Esteban Miro, the Spanish governor, requested Green's presence at New Orleans, Green left for Indian country with his plans for Bourbon County still not fully implemented. When his fellow justices arrived in Natchez during the summer, they found the district divided into anti-American and pro-American factions, with the Spanish commandant cracking down on the pro-American supporters. Eventually, Spanish officials evicted the three men from the district, and Georgia gave up its plans to organize the area, which eased tensions between the United States and Spain.[67]

Madison was acutely aware of the political delicacies of law and order in the western settlements. In late 1784, he had participated in a debate in the Virginia house on the question of disturbances in Kentucky and had helped Joseph Jones draft two resolutions on the issue. The 3 November resolutions, generally attributed to Jones, addressed the duality of the problem—respect for the laws of man and respect for the laws of nature. The first resolution sought to quell the western lawlessness by calling for the imposition of "speedy and exemplary punishment" upon "every person doing injury to the subjects of Spain or the Indians in that quarter."[68] The second resolution tried to allay any apprehensions that the first resolution might have caused among westerners. In essence, it was a reaffirmation of the commitment of Virginia to the belief that the western inhabitants had a natural right to navigate the Mississippi River to its mouth. Seeking to eliminate western anxieties, this second resolution directed the Virginia congressional delegation "to move that honorable body [Congress] to give directions, (unless the same have already been given to the American ministers in Europe) to forward negotiations to that end, without loss of time."[69]

In supporting the resolutions, Madison continued his nationalistic approach to western problems. Unlike some Virginians, including Jefferson, who would have allowed troublesome westerners "to be chastised by the Spaniards"[70] but would not have allowed the national government to concede American rights to the territory around Natchez, Madison knew that the United States had to placate Spanish fears if it wanted access to New Orleans without war.[71] Thus, Madison's 26 November preamble to the extradition bill, which faced intense opposition, expressed his belief in the ability of the country to achieve its legitimate rights in an orderly and legal manner: "Whereas it is the desire of the good people of this Commonwealth in all cases to manifest their reverence for the law of Nations, to cultivate amnity and peace as far as may depend on them between the United States and foreign powers, and to support the dignity and energy of the federal Constitution."[72]

After revisions, the controversial bill passed the Virginia House of Delegates by a vote of 44 to 43.[73] It contained an extradition provision, requiring "the governor, with the advice of the council of state," to apprehend and turn over to authorized officials any individual who illegally entered any "jurisdiction of any civilized nation on amity with the United States," committed a crime, and subsequently fled to Virginia.[74] In October 1785, Congress saw the wisdom in the Virginia resolutions and passed a similar expression of nationalism and conciliation.[75]

Through early 1786, Madison had been fashioning a strong nationalistic response to the West. On 31 May 1786, however, he received a letter from James Monroe that threatened to erode his nationalistic position. Monroe, a Virginia delegate to Congress, informed Madison that John Jay had requested Congress to appoint a committee to oversee his negotiations with Diego de Gardoqui. Monroe correctly speculated that the "object was to relieve him [Jay] from the instruction respecting [the] Missisipi."[76] Monroe, as chairman of the committee of instructions, had directed Jay on 25 August 1785 to negotiate a commercial treaty with Spain that did not cede the American right to the complete navigation of the Mississippi River.[77] Now, Jay wished to rid himself of these burdensome instructions. When southerners learned of the substance of the Jay-Gardoqui negotiations, a number of them, including Charles Pinckney of South Carolina and William Grayson of Virginia, vehemently opposed it.[78] For a while, Monroe had even suspected Jay of negotiating "dishonestly."[79] The ensuing struggle in Congress to modify Jay's instructions illustrated how deeply the Mississippi occlusion question had divided southerner from southerner and northerner from northerner.[80]

Following his initial disbelief, Madison spoke of the harm that the prospective treaty would do to the country. He could not fathom that any person would harbor a thought of surrendering American rights to the Mississippi River, while at the same time guaranteeing to Spain its claims east of the river. If Congress accepted the treaty, Madison believed that those members voting for it were actually sacrificing the goodwill of France and its military might for a treaty with an impotent nation from which the United States had nothing to fear. Likewise, he believed that should the United States accept the terms of the proposed agreement, it would be sacrificing its western residents and "the richest fund we possess" to satisfy the desires of another part of the nation.[81] Although Madison remained fully confident that Congress would reject the measure, it was this one final point that caused him the greatest trepidation.

Since his retirement from Congress in 1783, Madison had been busy trying to convince Virginia and its transmontane residents that Congress was a national body intent on preserving the rights and ensuring the interests of each region of the nation. The occlusion issue, however, threatened to create a sectional controversy between northern and southern members that could undermine Madison's plans for creating a stronger national union. Southerners would not graciously grant Congress greater powers if their opponents in the crisis, the numerically dominant northern states, had already used current congressional powers for their own benefit. Likewise, Madison knew that the West would not stand still and allow the northern states to negotiate the removal of its economic lifeline. Even though Madison cautiously proclaimed that Congress would never ratify the proposed treaty as Jay and Gardoqui had drafted it, he lacked the confidence to predict that members of Congress would want to change the sectional tone of the debate. If no one sought to alter the sectional tone of the discussions, he believed "an augmentation of federal authority" would be an unattainable goal. [82]

During this period Madison feared for the continuation of the Union. He thought that the limited powers of the national government, which did not include the right to regulate commerce or the right to raise revenue through taxation, hindered the economic development of the infant nation. The only way to save the nation was to grant the national government these powers and more. Yet, somehow Madison hoped to persuade those people who were already wary of increasing the powers of the national government that they needed to make such a move. When supporters of the concept started questioning the wisdom of such action, Madison's task became even more difficult. [83]

It did not take Madison long to find the source of that doubt—the Jay-Gardoqui negotiations, which in his mind had caused certain individuals to place their personal desires above the needs of the nation. "Many of our most federal leading men," he lamented, "are extremely soured with what has already passed." [84] Patrick Henry, whose term as governor of Virginia had just expired, was one person whom Madison once considered a "Champion of the federal cause." [85] The occlusion controversy, however, made him, Madison noted, a "cold advocate, and in the event of an actual sacrifice of the Misspi. by Congress, [he] will unquestionably go over to the opposite side." [86] Henry, along with a very tepid James Monroe, was among a small number of southerners who believed that a separate southern confederacy, including the West, might be the answer to all their problems. [87] Madison, however, refused to accept this solution and chose to fight for the Union by ensuring that the nation retained not only possession of the West but also the allegiance of westerners.

Madison brought his fight for a nationalistic position on the West to Richmond, where, as a new member of the General Assembly, he hoped to persuade members to adopt a strong rebuttal to the actions of Jay and his supporters in Congress. More importantly, Madison wanted to prevail on members to endorse the reforms that he and his fellow commissioners from five states meeting in Annapolis, Maryland, in September had recommended, namely the calling of another convention to consider steps necessary "to render the constitution of the Federal Government adequate to the exigencies of the Union."[88] Madison doubted his ability to prevail on the latter matter if members allowed the Mississippi question to dominate the legislative agenda, for he knew that legislators' anxieties over the Mississippi question would weaken their support for a strong national government.[89] In their eyes, the affair illustrated how a national government invested with strong constitutional powers might use its authority to act contrary to the wishes of a perceived majority of its citizens.[90] Still, when Massachusetts farmers under the leadership of Daniel Shays rebelled against oppressive taxes in the fall of 1786, Virginia legislators quickly discarded their reservations and selected seven delegates, including Madison,[91] to the convention that Congress in late February 1787 had reluctantly called "for the sole and express purpose of revising the Articles of Confederation."[92] With his primary objective secured, Madison turned his attention toward formulating the Virginia response to the Mississippi question.

Madison drafted three resolutions that the House of Delegates debated and unanimously passed on 29 November 1786. The resolutions, which were actually instructions to the Virginia delegates to Congress, reaffirmed the American right to the Mississippi River. They also affirmed that the national government had the duty to protect the interests of all its members and to avoid the "sacrifice of the rights of any one part, to the supposed or real interest of another part."[93] For Congress to do so, in Madison's opinion, would represent a "direct contravention of the end for which the foederal government was instituted, and an alarming innovation of the System of the Union."[94] Furthermore, congressional acceptance of Jay's negotiations would not only evoke "the just resentments and reproaches of our Western Brethren" but also erode "that confidence in the Wisdom, Justice and liberality of the foederal Councils which is so necessary at this Crisis, to a proper enlargement of their authority; and finally, as tending to undermine our repose, our prosperity, and our Union itself."[95] Lastly, the house instructed the delegates to oppose any measure that would surrender the right to navigate the Mississippi River.[96] In the senate, a few members resented the tone of the resolutions but supported the measures, for as Madison noted, "they certainly express in substance the decided sense of this Country at this time on the subject."[97]

Having acquired the Virginia legislature's endorsement of his position, Madison took his fight to Congress as the newest delegate from Virginia. Arriving in New York on 9 February 1787,[98] Madison learned, to his surprise, that few delegates actually knew the substance of Jay's negotiations with Gardoqui.[99] Intent on ending this paucity of information, Madison and William Bingham, director of the Bank of North America and also a newly elected member of Congress, called on the Spanish minister at his home.[100] Gardoqui startled them with the disclosure that he and Jay had ended their negotiations in October 1786 and that he intended to depart for Spain shortly. The one aspect of their conversation that most alarmed Madison was Gardoqui's stand on the opening of the Mississippi River. Madison noted that the Spanish minister would not even consider the American position; instead, he confidently proclaimed that Spain intended to deny permanently American access to New Orleans and, thus, the Mississippi River.[101] In Congress, Madison on 4 April managed to maneuver members into requesting the text of the proposed treaty from Jay.[102] Once they had read it, enthusiasm for the proposal began to wane until only a few states—Connecticut, Massachusetts, New Hampshire, and New York—supported the "obnoxious project."[103]

As Madison headed for Philadelphia to attend the convention, he probably could not help but give a heavy sigh. He knew that he had succeeded in silencing, at least for the moment, the sectional tones of the western debate and had again placed the discussion within a national context. He had successfully removed from congressional consideration a treaty that probably would not only have driven western settlers from the Union but also would have created a powerful anti-convention movement in the South. Madison also managed to show skeptics that a national government, even one as weak as the Confederation government, could operate in an impartial manner overseeing the interests of the various sections. Whereas Madison was happy to announce that "the Spanish project sleeps," he could not fail to see the serious damage it had already done.[104] Patrick Henry had become a powerful opponent of the federal convention. The former governor of Virginia had refused a seat in the upcoming convention, Madison believed, in order that he might keep himself free to criticize or commend the work of the convention according to its actions on the Mississippi question.[105] Like a growing number of people across the South, Henry knew that the political strength of the South within any government was directly tied to the West. Thus, he did not intend to stand idly by and allow a small group of men to decide arbitrarily the fate of the West within the Union.[106]

Madison's next challenge lay in the creation and defense of a new form of government, one in which he hoped to remove the West as a source of sectional tension. Madison did not foresee that the events surrounding the ratification of the Constitution would force him to readjust his thinking about the West and the political relationship between it and the South.

NOTES

1. Ralph Ketcham, *James Madison: A Biography* (New York: The Macmillan Company, 1971), 95–100, 144–48.

2. James Lovell to Samuel Adams, 8 February 1780, in *Letters of Delegates to Congress*, eds. Paul H. Smith et al. (Washington, DC: Library of Congress, 1988), 14:397. Congressional committee members issued their report on their conference with Luzerne on 2 February 1780. It was at this conference that Luzerne outlined the Spanish position. "Communications of the Honorable the French Minister to a Committee of Congress at a Second Conference," *The Revolutionary Diplomatic Correspondence of the United States*, ed. Francis Wharton (Washington, DC: Government Printing Office, 1889), 3:488–90.

3. James Lovell to Henry Laurens, 12 February 1780, in Smith et al., *Letters of Delegates*, 14:413.

4. *Journals of the Continental Congress, 1774–1789*, ed. Worthington C. Ford et al. (Washington, DC: Government Printing Office, 1910), 17:727.

5. Jay to Congress, 26 May 1780, in Wharton, *Revolutionary Diplomatic Correspondence*, 3:725.

6. *Journals of the Continental Congress*, 17:754.

7. Ibid., 17:755.

8. "Resolution Instructing Delegates in Congress, on Treaty with Spain to stipulate for Free Commerce of Mississippi," in *The Statutes at Large: Being a Collection of All the Laws of Virginia from the First Session of the Legislature, in the Year 1619*, ed. William W. Hening (Richmond: J & G. Cochran, 1822; repr., Charlottesville: Published for the Jamestown Foundation of the Commonwealth of Virginia by the University Press of Virginia, 1969), 10:537.

9. *Journals of the Continental Congress*, 17:755.

10. North Carolina Delegates to Abner Nash, 15 August 1780, in *Letters of Delegates to Congress*, eds. Paul H. Smith et al. (Washington, DC: Library of Congress, 1988), 15:587.

11. Whitmel Hill to Thomas Burke, 20 August 1780, in *The State Records of North Carolina*, ed. Walter Clark (Goldsboro, NC: Nash Bros., Book and Job Printers, 1898), 15:57.

12. Ezekiel Cornell to William Greene, 22 August 1780, in *Letters of Delegates*, 15:615. Both Irving Brant and Paul Chrisler Phillips refer to an episode, possibly occurring in September 1780, in which Maryland delegate Daniel of St. Thomas Jenifer, a spokesperson for the Illinois-Wabash Company, attempted to have Congress instruct Jay to recede from his previous instructions concerning U.S. positions on the Mississippi River and western territory. Congress defeated the motion. Francois, marquis de Barbé-Marbois, the French chargé d'affaires, placed a summary of this event in one of his letters to Luzerne, but, as Phillips and Brant note, it cannot be independently confirmed through congressional sources. Irving Brant, *The Fourth President: A Life of James Madison (Indianapolis and New York: The Bobbs-Merrill Company, 1970)*, 67; Irving Brant, *James Madison* vol. 2, *The Nationalist: 1780–1787* (New York: The Bobbs-Merrill Company, 1948), 2:74–78, passim; Paul Chrisler Phillips, *The West in the Diplomacy of the American Revolution* (Urbana: The University of Illinois Press, 1913; reprint, New York: Johnson Reprint Corporation, 1967), 178.

13. *Journals of the Continental Congress*, ed. Worthington C. Ford et al. (Washington, DC: Government Printing Office, 1910), 18:900. Ketcham attributes the instructions to Jones. Ketcham, *James Madison*, 95.

14. *Journals of the Continental Congress*, 18:900–2.

15. James Madison to Joseph Jones, 10 October 1780, in *The Papers of James Madison*, eds. William T. Hutchinson, William M. E. Rachal et al. (Chicago: The University of Chicago Press; Charlottesville: University of Virginia Press, 1962), 2:186.

16. *Journals of the Continental Congress*, 18:908.

17. Brant, *Fourth President*, 68. Brant attributes this alignment to Barbé-Marbois.

18. "Draft of Letter to John Jay, Explaining His Instructions," in Hutchinson et al., *Madison Papers*, 2:128-129. Madison's instructions printed in the *Journals of the Continental Congress* contain minor punctuation and capitalization differences from the manuscript contained in *The Papers of James Madison*. *Journals of the Continental Congress*, 18:935–47.

19. "Georgia Delegates' Proposed Resolutions," in *Letters of Delegates to Congress*, eds. Paul H. Smith et al. (Washington, DC: Library of Congress, 1989), 16:349–50.

20. *Journals of the Continental Congress*, 18:1121.

21. These concerns are discussed in several sources, including footnotes 3 and 4 in *Papers of Madison*, 2:196–97, John Hanson's 30 October 1780 letter to Charles Carroll, in Smith et al. *Letters of Delegates*,16:285, and Madison's 25 November 1780 letter to Joseph Jones, in Hutchinson et al. *Madison Papers*, 2:202-3.

22. Madison to Joseph Jones, 25 November 1780, in Hutchinson et al., *Madison Papers*, 2:202.

23. Theodorick Bland to Thomas Jefferson, 22 November 1780, in Smith et al., *Letters of Delegates*, 16:375.

24. Ibid. For Hanson's view see John Hanson to Charles Carroll, 30 October 1780, in Ibid., 16:285.

25. Madison to Joseph Jones, 25 November 1780, in Hutchinson et al., *Madison Papers*, 2:203.

26. Madison to Jones, 5 December 1780, in Ibid., 2:223.

27. Ibid.

28. *Journals of the Continental Congress*, 18:1121. Brant alludes to a vote occurring in Congress on the Georgians' proposal. It reportedly lost by one vote. Virginian delegate Bland reportedly spoke in favor of the motion, but he still voted against it. The *Journals of the Continental Congress* do not mention such a vote having occurred. See Brant, *James Madison*, 2:85.

29. *Journals of the Continental Congress*, 18:1131–32; James Madison, "Navigation of the Mississippi," in *Niles' Weekly Register*, 26 January 1822, p. 347. Madison contacted Hezekiah Niles to clarify inaccuracies contained in David Ramsay's *History of the American Revolution*, vol. 2, pages 300 and 301. Ramsay had stated that it was the Virginia delegation that had proposed that Jay's instructions be amended.

30. Virginia Delegates in Congress to Thomas Jefferson, 13 December 1780, in Hutchinson et al., *Madison Papers*, 2:242.

31. Ibid.

32. Ibid.

33. Jefferson to Benjamin Harrison, 25 December 1780, in *The Papers of Thomas Jefferson*, ed. Julian P. Boyd (Princeton: Princeton University Press, 1951), 4:238.

34. George Walton, William Few, and Richard Howley, *Observations Upon the Effects of Certain Late Political Suggestions, by the Delegates of Georgia* (Philadelphia: Robert Aitken, 1781; reprint, *Letters of Delegates to Congress*, eds. Paul H. Smith et al., Washington, DC: Library of Congress, 1989): 16:561–66. The transcript bears the handwriting of Walton, but it is signed by all three delegates. See notes, Smith et al, *Letters of Delegates*, 16:560.

35. See for instance the *Philadelphia Pennsylvania Journal and Weekly Advertiser's* 3 January 1781 article on the destruction of plantations in South Carolina and its 10 January and 8 February 1781 articles on American military activity in Georgia and South Carolina. The *Philadelphia Pennsylvania Gazette and Weekly Advertiser* carried similar articles. See 31 January, 14 February, and 28 February 1781.

36. "Resolution respecting the Navigation of the Mississippi," in Hening, *Statutes at Large*, 10:538.

37. Jefferson to the Virginia Delegates in Congress, 18 January 1781, in Boyd et al., *Jefferson Papers*, 4:398.

38. Virginia Delegates to Thomas Jefferson, 30 January 1781, in Smith et al., *Letters of Delegates*, 16:650. For a discussion of when the instructions were submitted to Congress, see footnote 1, "Virginia Delegates Proposed Instructions," 1 February 1781, Ibid., 16:661.

39. *Journals of the Continental Congress*, ed. Worthington C. Ford et al. (Washington, DC: Government Printing Office, 1912), 19:152.

40. Ibid., 19:152-53.

41. The states that voted in favor of the letter were: Delaware, Georgia, New Hampshire, Pennsylvania, Rhode Island, South Carolina, and Virginia. The states that voted against it were: Connecticut, Massachusetts, and North Carolina. The vote of New York divided one to one, so

it did not count. Maryland and New Jersey had only one delegate present, with each voting "aye." However, their votes are recorded as asterisks rather than as "aye" in the final tally. Ibid., 19:154. Wharton's *Revolutionary Diplomatic Correspondence* presents the vote as nine to three, with New York as divided. *The Revolutionary Diplomatic Correspondence of the United States*, ed. Francis Wharton (Washington, DC: Government Printing Office, 1889), 4:258–59.

42. *Journals of the Continental Congress*, ed. Worthington C. Ford et al. (Washington, DC: Government Printing Office, 1914), 22:142.

43. Ibid., 22:207.

44. Ketcham, *James Madison*, 95–100, 144–48.

45. Madison to Edmund Pendleton, 23 April 1782, in *The Papers of James Madison*, eds. William T. Hutchinson, William M. E. Rachal et al. (Chicago: The University of Chicago Press; Charlottesville: University of Virginia Press, 1965), 4:178.

46. "Observations Relating to the Influence of Vermont and the Territorial Claims on the Politics of Congress," 1 May 1782, in Ibid., 4:201.

47. "Report on Restoring Public Credit," [6 March 1783], in *The Papers of James Madison*, eds. William T. Hutchinson, William M. E. Rachal et al. (Chicago: The University of Chicago Press; Charlottesville: University of Virginia Press, 1969), 6:312.

48. Ibid., 6:312–13.

49. Madison to Edmund Randolph, 11 March 1783, in *Letters of Members of the Continental Congress*, ed. Edmund C. Burnett (Washington, DC: Carnegie Institution of Washington, 1934), 7:69.

50. Madison to Jefferson, 20 August 1784, in *The Papers of James Madison*, eds. William T. Hutchinson, William M. E. Rachal et al. (Chicago: The University of Chicago Press; Charlottesville: University of Virginia Press, 1973), 8:105.

51. Ibid.

52. Ibid., 8:107–8.

53. Ibid., 8:104.

54. Ibid., 8:108.

55. Ibid.

56. Madison to Jefferson, 7 September 1784, in Ibid., 8:113.

57. Madison to Lafayette, 20 March 1785, in Ibid., 8:250.

58. Ibid.

59. Ibid., 8:251.

60. Ibid.

61. Ibid.

62. Madison to Jefferson, 9 January 1785, in Ibid., 8:226.

63. Madison to Jefferson, 27 April 1785, in Ibid., 8:269.

64. "Preamble and Portion of an Extradition Bill," [26 November 1784], in Ibid., 8:154.

65. Madison to Jefferson, 9 January 1785, in Ibid., 8:227.

66. Ibid. Joseph Jones described the bill as a way "to prevent our people transgressing agst. the Spaniard[s] which they are disposed to do from all accounts." Jones quoted in footnote 1, in Ibid., 8:154.

67. Kenneth Coleman, *The American Revolution in Georgia, 1763–1789* (Athens: University of Georgia Press, 1958), 261–64; Gilbert C. Din, "War Clouds on the Mississippi: Spain's 1785 Crisis in West Florida," *The Florida Historical Quarterly*, 60 (July 1981), 51–76.

68. "Resolution on Western Law Enforcement and Mississippi Navigation," [3 November 1784], in Hutchinson et al., *Madison Papers*, 8:124. For the attribution see footnote 1, in Ibid., 8:125.

69. Ibid., 8:125.

70. Jefferson to David Hartley, 5 September 1785, in *The Papers of Thomas Jefferson*, ed. Julian P. Boyd (Princeton: Princeton University Press, 1953), 8:483.

71. Madison to Monroe, 8 January 1785, in Hutchinson et al., *Madison Papers*, 8:220.

72. "Preamble and Portion of an Extradition Bill," [26 November 1784], in Ibid., 8:154.

73. Footnote 1, in Ibid.

74. *An Act Punishing Certain Offences Injurious to the Tranquility to this Commonwealth*, in *The Statutes at Large: Being a Collection of All the Laws of Virginia from the First Session of the Legislature, in the Year 1619*, ed. William W. Hening (Richmond: J & G. Cochran, 1823; repr., Charlottesville: Published for the Jamestown Foundation of the Commonwealth of Virginia by the University Press of Virginia, 1969), 11:471–72.

75. *Journals of the Continental Congress*, 1774-1789, eds. Worthington C. Ford et al. (Washington, DC: Government Printing Office, 1933), 29:829–30.

76. Monroe to Madison, 31 May 1786, in *The Papers of James Madison*, eds. William T. Hutchinson, William M. E. Rachal et al. (Chicago: The University of Chicago Press; Charlottesville: University of Virginia Press, 1975), 9:68.

77. *Journals of the Continental Congress*, 29:657–58; *Journals of the Continental Congress*, 1774–1789, eds. Worthington C. Ford et al. (Washington, DC: Government Printing Office, 1934), 31:595–96.

78. "Charles Pinckney's Speech," 10 August 1786, and "Charles Thomson's Notes on Debates," 16 August 1786, both in *Letters of Delegates to Congress*, eds. Paul H. Smith et al. (Washington, DC: Library of Congress, 1996), 23:446–57, 485.

79. Monroe to Jefferson, 16 July 1786, in *Letters of Delegates*, 23:404.

80. See Timothy Bloodworth to Richard Caswell, 16 August 1786, in Smith et al., *Letters of Delegates*, 23:474.

81. Madison to Monroe, 21 June 1786, in Hutchinson et al., *Madison Papers*, 9:82–83.

82. Madison to Jefferson, 12 August 1786, in Ibid., 9:96–97.

83. Madison to James Madison, Sr., 1 November 1786, Madison to Washington, 7 December 1786, and Monroe to Madison, 3 September 1786, all in Ibid., 9:154, 200, 113; Monroe to Patrick Henry, 12 August 1786, in *The Papers of James Monroe: Selected Correspondence and Papers, 1776–1794*, ed. Daniel Preston (Westport, Connecticut: Greenwood Press, 2006), 2:331–34; John Marshall to Arthur Lee, 5 March 1787, in *The Papers of John Marshall*, eds. Herbert A. Johnson et al. (Chapel Hill: University of North Carolina in association with the Institute of Early American History and Culture, Williamsburg, Virginia, 1974), 1:205.

84. . Madison to Washington, 7 December 1786, in Hutchinson et al., *Madison Papers*, 9:200.

85. Ibid.

86. Ibid.

87. John Marshall to Arthur Lee, 5 March 1787, in Johnson et al., *Marshall Papers*, 1:205; Monroe to Patrick Henry, 12 August 1786, in Smith et al., *Letters of Delegates*, 23:465.

88. *Documents Illustrative of the Formation of the Union of the American States*, ed. Charles C. Tansill (Washington, DC: Government Printing Office, 1927), 43.

89. Madison to Washington, 7 December 1786, in Hutchinson et al., *Madison Papers*, 9:200.

90. Timothy Bloodworth to Governor Richard Caswell, 29 September 1786, in *Letters of Members of the Continental Congress*, ed. Edmund C. Burnett (Washington, DC: Carnegie Institution of Washington, 1936), 8:474; William Grayson's comments on the matter are contained in Charles Thomson, "Minutes of Proceedings," 16 August 1786, in Ibid., 8:429.

91. *An Act for Appointing Deputies from this Commonwealth to a Convention proposed to be held in the city of Philadelphia in May next, for the purpose of Revising the Federal Constitution*, in *The Statutes at Large: Being a Collection of All the Laws of Virginia from the First Session of the Legislature, in the Year 1619*, ed. William W. Hening (Richmond: J & G. Cochran, 1823; repr., Charlottesville: Published for the Jamestown Foundation of the Commonwealth of Virginia by the University Press of Virginia, 1969), 12:256–57.

92. *Journals of the Continental Congress*, 1774-1789, eds. Worthington C. Ford et al. (Washington, DC: Government Printing Office, 1936), 32:71–74.

93. "Resolutions Reaffirming American Rights to Navigate the Mississippi," 29 December [November] 1786, in Hutchinson et al., *Madison Papers*, 9:182. While no evidence exists to determine who was the author of the resolutions, biographers of Madison, including Irving Brant in *James Madison: The Nationalist*, 2:399, and Ralph Ketchum in *James Madison*, 179, have concluded that Madison did draft the resolutions.

94. "Resolutions Reaffirming American Rights to Navigate the Mississippi," 29 December [November] 1786, in Hutchinson et al., *Madison Papers*, 9:182.

95. Ibid., 9:183.

96. Ibid.

97. Madison to Washington, 7 December 1786, in Ibid., 9:199-200.

98. Madison to Eliza House Trist, 10 February 1787, in Ibid., 9:259.

99. Madison to Jefferson, 19 March 1787, in Ibid., 9:319.

100. *American National Biography*, s.v. "Bingham, William;" "Notes on Debates," 13 March 1787, in Hutchinson et al., *Madison Papers*, 9:309.

101. "Notes on Debates," 13 March 1787, in Hutchinson et al., *Madison Papers*, 9:309-11.

102. *Journals of the Continental Congress*, 32:152; Madison began the process on 30 March by requesting that "the Secy. of F. Affrs. [Foreign Affairs] to lay before Congs. [Congress] the State of his negociation with Mr. Gardoqui." "Notes on Debates," 30 March 1787, in Hutchinson et al., *Madison Papers*, 9:341.

103. Madison to Jefferson, 23 April 1787, in Hutchinson et al., *Madison Papers*, 9:400.

104. Madison to Jefferson, 19 March 1787, in Ibid., 9:319.

105. Ibid.

106. Henry Mayer, *A Son of Thunder: Patrick Henry and the American Republic* (New York: Franklin Watts, 1986), 350–51.

Chapter Four

The West and the New Constitution

When the southern delegates to the federal convention at Philadelphia, Pennsylvania, took their seats for the first time on 25 May 1787, they brought with them a variety of opinions on the West. Some of these men formed their views from first-hand experiences of life in the West. Washington, who had seen parts of the West during the French and Indian War, had travelled as far west as Pittsburgh in 1784 in an effort to oversee his lands in the area.[1] William Few, a member of the Georgia delegation, had grown up in the North Carolina back country and had lost a brother in the Regulator movement in 1771. When financial misfortunes forced his family and later him to relocate in Georgia, he quickly immersed himself in local politics, becoming surveyor-general of Georgia and Indian commissioner during the Revolutionary War.[2] Others, such as William Blount and Hugh Williamson, both of North Carolina, and George Mason of Virginia had invested heavily in lands in the West and had an economic stake in western advancement. Others, such as the Virginian Richard Henry Lee, had consistently championed the West as an economic resource for the Atlantic states. And a few southerners, like James Madison, with his network of friends and associates keeping him informed of western activities, had embraced the West as a national treasure.

Rumors of westerners' unhappiness possibly manifesting itself in acts of violence against American interests disturbed the delegates as they met in Philadelphia. The friendly policy of Spain to residents in the Natchez region of Mississippi elicited warnings that while the United States continued to wallow in indecision "she [Spain] will secure the hearts of a great people now settling on the western waters."[3] The political void existing in the French Broad region of North Carolina (the state of Franklin) evoked praise for the "peace, good order, and contentment in the Cherokee towns" when compared to the communities of "their white neighbours."[4] This same corre-

49

spondent, noting that the events in the West necessitated the federal convention, sent his blessing to the delegates: "May the Governor of the universe inspire them with wisdom and unanimity."[5] In Kentucky, a few political leaders had begun directing the popular outcry against Spain's closing the Mississippi River into a popular movement to separate the district from Virginia and ultimately the Union.

By March, this rising level of discontent in the West had caught James Madison's eye. If the Atlantic states continued to act as if nothing were wrong and failed to eliminate the source of frustration felt by settlers, Madison predicted the loss of the West or, at the least, a political headache for the United States. Westerners, he reasoned, would either open communications with British officials in the West or seize the vacant lands and offer generous bounties to lure settlers "and in all respects play the part of Vermont."[6] Yet, despite a general knowledge of western events present among delegates and the possession of strong opinions on the subject of the West among a few of them, the issue of the West seldom emerged as a major point of contention during the course of their debates.

Until William Paterson of New Jersey presented his plan of representation in Congress on 15 June, southern delegates had remained silent on the issue of the West. Small states, including New Jersey and Delaware, objected to James Madison's Virginia Plan because they feared the power that the large states presumably would gain from its population-based system of representation. The small states, with Paterson as their spokesman, believed the large states might use their dominant position in the Union to promote their own welfare and neglect the interests of the smaller states. The New Jersey plan, with each state represented equally in Congress, quelled the fear of the smaller states.[7] When Paterson announced his plan, Madison, as expected, objected quite strenuously to it, for the New Jersey plan undermined his system of a strong central government. While illustrating the inherent flaws in the New Jersey plan, Madison introduced the West into the debate for the first time. "The prospect," he told the delegates, "of many new States to the Westward was another consideration of importance."[8] The population in the new states, he reminded the proponents of the New Jersey plan, would be smaller than in the Atlantic seaboard states, and "if they shd. [should] be entitled to vote according to their proportions of inhabitants, all would be right & safe."[9] Playing to the western biases of many of the delegates, Madison tried to show how truly vulnerable their interests would be under the New Jersey plan: "Let them have an equal vote, and a more objectionable minority than ever might give law to the whole."[10]

Madison's words of warning also rang true for some southerners. Like their counterparts in the small states who feared losing control of their interests to the large states, a few southerners feared a system of government that allowed westerners to subvert the dominant position of the Atlantic states within the Union. Hugh Williamson, speaking on the subject of congressional salaries, reminded his fellow delegates that the new western states "would be poor" and their residents incapable of paying a large share of taxes.[11] These new states, he believed, "would have a different interest from the old States."[12] Thus, he reasoned a new system of government should not force the old states "to pay the expences of men who would be employed in thwarting their measures & interests."[13] Later, the North Carolina delegate restated the issue when he warned members that the "new States from the Westward" might burden the old states with excessive taxes.[14] The great distances between these new western states and their Atlantic coast markets, he told the convention, created a dangerous situation for the Atlantic states. It reduced the value of western produce, which, in turn, increased the need of the western states to find other sources of revenue for their development. Thus, he argued, the new states "would consequently be tempted to combine for the purpose of laying burdens and consumption which would fall with greater weight on the old States."[15]

Likewise wary of western dominance, Pierce Butler, a popular political leader representing the South Carolina back country, believed the delegates should incorporate into the new government "some balance . . . between the old & New States."[16] To accomplish this goal, Butler suggested that the convention adopt a system of representation based on property—"the only just measure of representation."[17] Finding security in Butler's statements, John Rutledge, also of South Carolina, voiced a similar fear of western domination and proposed that both wealth and population form the basis of representation in Congress. Why, he asked, should a region hopelessly lacking the necessary resources "to contribute in proportion to their numbers" to the general welfare of the nation displace the Atlantic states within the Union?[18] It was ridiculous, he believed, to allow such an eventuality to happen. To ensure that the western states never displaced the dominant position of the Atlantic states, Rutledge offered a resolution creating a national census of population and wealth, from which "'the Legislature shall proportion the Representation according to the principles of wealth and population.'"[19] Not all southerners were willing, however, to place the West on a "different footing" than the Atlantic states.[20] Hugh Williamson, seeing nothing wrong with representation based on wealth, believed that in all fairness "if their [westerners'] property shall be rated as high as that of the Atlantic States, then their representation ought to hold like proportion."[21] If Congress, however, should decide to adjust representation between the old Atlantic states and the new western states, the North Carolinian did not think that his fellow delegates should rate the property of westerners equally with that of the Atlantic states.

Madison, who introduced the western question into the debates to eliminate the New Jersey plan from discussion, suddenly found himself repeatedly defending the West against distrustful southerners and northerners. Gouverneur Morris of Pennsylvania, who apparently believed in an inherent inferiority of westerners, emphasized that "if the Western people [should] get the power into their hands," they would destroy the interests of the Atlantic seaboard states.[22] Madison, mindful of the proud nature of the western migrants, argued that the Atlantic seaboard states had to treat the new states rising in the West "as equals & as brethren."[23] Seeing no reason why the Atlantic states should fear the West, he held that the convention must strengthen the western settlers' ties to the new government. If it failed to do so and instead adopted a policy of discrimination against the West, the nation would lose the abundant resources of the West.

> He thought also that the hope of contributions to the Treasy. from them had been much underrated. Future contributions it seemed to be understood on all hands would be principally levied on imports and exports. . . . Whenever the Mississpi should be opened to them, which would of necessity be ye. case as soon as their their [sic] population would subject them to any considerable share of the public burdin, imposts on their trade could be collected with less expense & greater certainty, than on that of the Atlantic States. In the meantime, as supplies must pass thro' the Atlantic States their contributions would be levied in the same manner with those of the Atlantic States.[24]

Because the West offered much to the nation, Madison steadfastly believed "that the Western States neither would nor ought to submit to a union which degraded them from an equal rank with the other States."[25]

George Mason of Virginia, a stockholder in the defunct Ohio Company and large investor in Kentucky lands, soon joined Madison in defense of the West.[26] Although he later objected to the centralization of power under the Constitution and its lack of a bill of rights, Mason nevertheless defended the western right to equal representation within the Union. "Ought we to sacrifice what we know to be right in itself, lest it should prove favorable to States which are not yet in existence?" he asked his fellow delegates.[27] "If the Western States are to be admitted into the Union . . . they must, he wd. [would] repeat, be treated as equals, and subjected to no degrading discriminations."[28] Like Madison, he viewed the apparent state of poverty in the West as a temporary condition. Fully confident of western agricultural potential, he predicted that the western states would eventually "be both more numerous & more wealthy than their Atlantic brethren."[29] Surprisingly, Mason's statement marked one of the few times in the convention that southerners expressed their expectations about the West and its place within the Union.

Southerners were sensitive to any method of representation in the lower house that would perpetuate the minority status of their region within the Union.[30] They fully expected the population of the South, in association with the West, to increase in the future and repeatedly strove in the convention to create an equitable system of representation. When Massachusetts delegate Elbridge Gerry moved on 14 July "that in order to secure the (liberties of the) States already confederated" the number of representatives from new states should never exceed the number of representatives from states that originally ratified the constitution, only one southern state, Maryland, voted for the measure, which failed by a vote of four to five with one state (Pennsylvania) divided.[31] George Mason wholeheartedly supported his southern colleagues in their actions. Earlier he had been unhappy with a proposal to create a sixty-five-seat house, a house in which the South would have only twenty-nine seats.[32] He later objected even more to a house whose members determined when and whether it should be reapportioned. Looking into the future, Mason foresaw a time when the original makeup of the house "would cease to be the Representatives of the people."[33] "As soon as the Southern & Western population should predominate," Mason predicted that the northern members "would never yield to the majority, unless provided for by the Constitution."[34] Mason, however, failed to detail the type of relationship that the West and the South should have when this not too distant event occurred.

Curiously, southerners never took the bait offered by Pennsylvanian Gouverneur Morris concerning westerners and the Mississippi River. On at least three separate occasions, Morris intimated that westerners, and in turn their supporters in the South, would precipitate a war with Spain for control of the Mississippi River and the northern states would have to go along with the decision.[35] As such, Morris preferred that the original thirteen states retain greater power under the new constitution. Upon completion of his remarks, a southerner would immediately rise to address the convention and then would, surprisingly, proceed to disregard Morris's more inflammatory statements by addressing the issue at hand—fair representation for the West in the Union. However, Madison, the southerner who spoke after Morris's third hostile remark, could not hide his irritation with the Pennsylvanian. "At the same time that he recommended this implicit confidence to the Southern States in the Northern Majority," Madison retorted, "he was still more zealous in exhorting all to a jealousy of Western Majority. To reconcile the gentln with himself, it must be imagined that he determined the human character by the points of the compass. The truth was that all men having power ought to be distrusted to a certain degree."[36] As far as the West was concerned, Madison believed that once residents had access to the Mississippi River, their share of the public burden would increase and objections against their place within the Union would decrease.[37]

Once the delegates to the federal convention completed the difficult task of drafting a constitution and presenting it to the Confederation Congress, southerners quickly began lining up either to lend their voices in support of a document creating a "form of government that is perfectly fitted for protecting liberty and property" or to oppose a document "which might some day lead 'to the utter subversion of our sacred freedom.'"[38] Despite the many compromises during the convention, including ones reached on commerce, slavery, and representation in Congress, the southerners had managed to preserve two key elements needed for a future southern and western political alliance—the equality of the West in the Union and the required reapportionment of the House of Representatives (and thus the Electoral Congress) every ten years.

By the time Virginia met in convention to discuss the federal charter, three southern states had already ratified the document—Georgia on 2 January 1788, Maryland on 2 April 1788, and South Carolina on 23 May 1788. Seldom did the issue of the West arise in their ratification debates. In Georgia, rumors of Indian wars erupting on the frontier greeted the delegates as they arrived in Savannah. With Congress under the Articles of Confederation providing the state with little help in controlling the Creeks and Cherokees, most of the Georgian delegates saw the new plan as the answer to this most vexing problem and voted for the document with little debate.[39] To the north, in South Carolina, where supporters of the Constitution were in the majority and passage was a foregone conclusion, debate was a mere formality.[40]

In Maryland, Luther Martin, who had attended the federal convention and had refused to sign the document, objected to the inability of the proposed government to erect new states from existing states without the approval of the parent legislature. The son-in-law of a noted Maryland frontiersman, Michael Cresap, Martin echoed the historic stand of his state against the large landed states.[41] "Let it not be forgotten," he told legislators when he briefed them on the federal convention, "that a great part of the territory of these large and extensive States . . . [was] acquired by the common blood and treasure, and which ought to have been the common stock, and for the common benefit of the Union."[42] The landed states, he predicted, would not willingly divide themselves into smaller states. Instead, armed with the power of the new Constitution, they would call on Maryland "to assist, with her wealth and her blood, in subduing the inhabitants of Franklin, Kentucky, [and] Vermont . . . and in compelling them to continue in subjection to the States which respectively claim jurisdiction over them."[43] Even more hideous than this "act of injustice," was the fact that "they [the larger, landed states] shall have superiority of power and influence over the other States."[44]

Although all of the southern states wrestled with the difficult question of accepting a new form of government, only in one state, Virginia, did western concerns become a central issue in the ratification discussions of many of its residents. Only in Virginia, a state that boasted of having, not coincidentally, the largest number of western residents, did the future of the West become a critical issue in the debate and a formidable challenge to the ratification hopes of the Federalists.[45] Expressing the inconvenience that he and other friends of the Constitution felt, George Washington noted that if only western concerns "could have remained as silent, & glided as gently down the Stream of time for a few years," then they could have achieved his idea of sound policy easier.[46]

As the two opposing forces in Virginia began to survey opinions in the state, it became clear to most Virginians that Kentucky, with its fourteen delegates, held the balance of power at the upcoming ratifying convention.[47] Patrick Henry, George Mason, William Grayson, and James Monroe, the leaders of the Antifederalist forces in Virginia, understood early the situation and attempted skillfully to use the potential surrender of the Mississippi River as a means to kill the document.[48] Taking advantage of the anxiety in Kentucky over the Mississippi River, the opponents of the "New Plan" tried to instill in the minds of many Kentuckians "that the surrender of the Mississippi would probably be among the early acts of the new congress."[49]

Returning to New York after the federal convention, Madison felt confident that Virginians supported the new Constitution. Removed from the ongoing debate in the state on the new plan, he based his optimistic outlook on letters from trusted friends, which understated the level of discontent and, as a result, hindered his comprehension of the effectiveness of the Antifederalists' campaign.[50] By January 1788, however, Madison had begun to worry, expressing his anxieties over Henry's drive "at a Southern Confederacy" in a letter to Edmund Randolph.[51] Still, Madison remained cautiously optimistic:

> I believe on good ground that N. Carolina has postponed her Convention till July, in order to have the previous example of Virga. Should N. Carolina fall into Mr. H---y's [Henry's] politics which does not appear to me improbable, it will endanger the Union more than any other circumstance that could happen. My apprehensions of this danger increase every day. . . . I have no information from S. Carolina or Georgia, on which any certain opinion can be formed of the temper of those States. The prevailing idea has been that both of them would speedily & generally embrace the Constitution. It is impossible however that the example of Virga. & N. Carolina should have an influence on their politics. I consider every thing therefore as problematical from Maryland Southward.[52]

Two days after penning the letter to Randolph, Madison wrote *The Federalist Number Thirty-eight*. In that paper, he added a twist to his continued theme of the West "as a mine of vast wealth to the United States."[53] The Confederation Congress, Madison argued, had finally managed in 1787 "to render it [the West] productive" through the creation of temporary governments, the appointment of officers and the drafting of the terms under which the territories would enter the Union as states.[54] Despite the silence of the Articles of Confederation on the issue of new states, Madison marveled at how few people had sounded the republican alarm. "A great and independent fund of revenue is passing into the hands of a single body of men, who can raise troops to an indefinite number, and appropriate money to their support for an indefinite period of time."[55] Although not angry with these actions of Congress, for "I am sensible they could not have done otherwise," Madison, as he had skillfully done in the constitutional convention against Paterson's New Jersey plan, used the West to eliminate opposition to a stronger national government.[56] Recent congressional action, he declared, illustrated the "alarming proof of the danger resulting from a government which does not possess regular powers commensurate to its objects."[57]

As the time of the ratifying convention drew near, Federalists in Virginia tried to erase the image of a new government gladly handing the Mississippi River to the Spanish government. To help the Virginia Federalists, Hugh Williamson of North Carolina, told Madison to reconstruct the debates of the federal convention, for it would "certainly enable you to say that there is a Proviso in the new Sistem which was inserted for the express purpose of preventing a majority of the Senate or of the States . . . from giving up the Mississippi."[58] Seeking to "counteract efforts . . . for turning their jealousy on the subject of the Mississippi, against the proposed change in the foederal System," Madison informed George Nicholas of his intention to write several influential Kentuckians and inform them of the foolishness of their actions.[59] Only the new government, he reiterated, could "promise in any short time such arrangements with Spain as Kentucky must wish for."[60]

When Virginians in April 1788 selected their delegates to the ratifying convention, Madison hesitantly, "though not absolutely,"[61] viewed it as a victory for the Federalists, especially since the "divided" Kentucky delegates remained the key element in the struggle.[62] Madison's early confidence proved fleeting, however, as news arrived telling of the Kentucky delegation's unfriendly position on the new Constitution.[63] Alarmed by the Antifederalist composition of the Kentucky delegation, George Nicholas, himself a future Kentucky resident, asked Madison to express in writing his reasons for believing "that their navigation so far from being endangered, will probably be promoted by the adoption of the new government."[64]

Madison, who wholeheartedly agreed with Nicholas's assessment, wrote a letter to his friend in which he listed his reasons why the new Constitution did not damage the western position within the Union. A "more intimate and permanent Union," Madison stressed, increased the mutual bonds between sections, destroying the "exclusive regard" of the Atlantic seaboard states to their "own interests" and helping to "accelerate the population & formation of new States there [in the West]."[65] Besides, Madison noted, as the new government made it easier for settlers to move west, it would be creating a new group of western "advocates"—men who had friends and relatives living in the West—who would see that the new government did nothing to harm the "concerns" of the western country.[66] Even when he added the dependency of the government on its western lands to extinguish the national debt, Madison still knew that these safeguards were not enough to ease the qualms of the Antifederalists. Their repeated descriptions of a northern-dominated Senate voting to abandon American rights to the Mississippi River had turned many Kentuckians against the Constitution.[67]

Continuing, Madison stressed how foolish was the idea that western interests were safer under the Articles of Confederation than under the "New Plan." "The form of the new system will," Madison repeatedly told Nicholas, "present greater obstacles to the measure than exists under the old."[68] First, Madison noted, members of the Confederation Congress served one-year terms whereas senators under the new plan would serve six-year terms. If the first Senate election should produce a body in favor of western interests, Madison noted that it would be two years at the earliest before the enemies of the West could possibly capture the Senate. Under the Articles of Confederation, the sentiments of Congress changed each year, increasing the likelihood of Congress abandoning the West. "How many chances does such a body present in a period of six years for the turning up of any particular opinion," Madison wrote.[69] Also, he reminded Nicholas that two delegates from each state under the old constitution could "give the vote of the State."[70] If two similar-minded delegates attended a session without the rest of the congressional delegation from their state or with only one additional member, their opinion would be in the majority. "On the very subject of the Mississippi," Madison reflected, "I have seen the opinion of a State in Congress depending altogether on the casual attendance of these or those members of the same delegation, and sometimes varying more than once in the course of a few days."[71] As the proposed constitution would grant each state two senators who would vote separately, Madison proclaimed that it would eliminate this potentially dangerous situation for the West.

Even if the enemies of the West should somehow gain control of the Senate, Madison still saw no reason to despair. He noted two safeguards within the proposed Constitution—the president and the House of Representatives. He confidently predicted that the president, who alone must answer for the deeds of his administration, would "more naturally revolt against a measure which might bring on him the reproach not only of partiality, but of a dishonorable surrender of a natural right."[72] As for the lower chamber of the legislature, control over the purse strings made its tacit approval necessary for most treaties to go "into full effect."[73] And with a membership composed of a "large majority of inland & Western members," Madison argued the House could adequately protect western interests.[74]

When the opening day of the convention finally came, Federalists arrived at Richmond "in the best spirits."[75] Delegates quickly selected as president of the convention Edmund Pendleton, whose conversion on 4 June to the Federalist camp after nearly six months of vacillating foreshadowed good things to come for the supporters of the Constitution.[76] A week into the convention, Patrick Henry raised the fiery issue of the Mississippi River. "In my opinion, the preservation of that river calls for our most serious consideration," he told his fellow delegates.[77] Seven states, he reminded the convention, had in August 1786 gone on record in favor of relinquishing the American claims to the river.[78] With the ratification of the new Constitution, Henry predicted that "those states who have already discovered their inclination that way" would be able to complete their mission.[79] Contrary to the opinions of the Federalists, Henry held that the Articles of Confederation was not a weak document. It possessed, he maintained, the necessary strength to guard southern interests within the Union. "The southern parts of America have been protected by that weakness so much execrated," he told the delegates.[80] Symbolically throwing down the gauntlet, Henry retorted, "Let us hear how the great and important right of navigating that river has been attended to, and whether I am mistaken in my opinion that federal measures will lose it to us forever."[81] Suddenly, western rights and southern political survival became the key issues in the debate for the Antifederalists. The Federalists, however, preferred not to engage in sectional distractions and instead concentrated their remarks on the Mississippi question by asking, "Is this right better secured under the present Confederation than the new government?"[82]

Lose the Mississippi River, the Antifederalist William Grayson told the convention, and "the migration to the western country would be stopped, and the Northern States would not only retain their inhabitants, but preserve their superiority and influence over those of the South."[83] Wise men, Grayson exclaimed, do not give their enemies the means of their own destruction. "In my opinion, the power of making treaties, by which the territorial rights of any of the states may be essentially affected, ought to be guarded against every possibility of abuse."[84] The northern states, Grayson reminded delegates, were "willing to relinquish that great and essential right. For they consider the consequences of governing the Union as of more importance" than all other considerations.[85] Although Massachusetts supported the Ordinance of 1787, he noted that it also lowered the price of land to $1 per acre in Maine as a way "perhaps . . . [to keep] the population on that side of the Continent, in contradistinction to the emigration to the westward of us."[86]

Adopting the new constitution, Henry told the delegates, would not only deny to the people living in the West their "dearest right" but also destroy the South in the process.[87] "Unless you keep open the Mississippi," Henry argued,

> you never can increase in number. Although your population should go on to an infinite degree, you will be in the minority in Congress; and although you should have a right to be the majority, yet so unhappily is this system of politics constituted, that you will ever be a contemptible minority. To preserve

the balance of American power, it is essentially necessary that the right of the Mississippi should be secured.[88]

Gazing into the future, Henry beheld a powerful South "situated contiguously to that valuable and inestimable river."[89] Do not destroy the source of the future southern greatness, he urged the delegates, by adopting a constitution harmful to western settlement. He pleaded with the delegates not to be fooled: "The honorable gentleman has said that the House of Representatives would give some curb to this business of treaties respecting the Mississippi—This is to me incomprehensible."[90] How could this happen, he noted, if the checks and balances of the constitution remained in place? And if they proved to be "mere cobwebs . . . [then] "what kind of constitution . . . can this be? he asked."[91] For Henry, the future greatness of the South, as well as that of the nation, depended on the growth of the West, provided the South did not place itself under the proposed constitution.

Holding little hope for the South under the proposed federal constitution, James Monroe pleaded with his fellow delegates to reject the document drafted at Philadelphia. The northern states, Monroe announced, were jealous of the future "influence and power" of the South and stood ready to abandon the American right to the Mississippi River to stop southern advancement.[92] Only the Articles of Confederation prevented them, he argued, from executing their plan. Warning the convention, Monroe predicted that the northern states "would not fail of availing themselves of the opportunity, given them by the Constitution, of relinquishing that river, in order to depress the Western Country, and prevent the Southern interest from preponderating."[93]

George Mason spent less time on the issue of the West than his colleagues. Predicting dire times for western landholders, Mason, a speculator in western lands himself, warned that if the convention adopted a constitution without amendments, "20,000 families of good citizens in the North-West District, between the Alleghany mountains and the Blue Ridge, will run the risk of being driven from the lands" that the Virginia legislature had granted them.[94] Mason believed the Indiana Company, which claimed ownership of this land could, through the federal courts, gain undisputed title to a large tract of land lying between the Little Kanawha River and the southern boundary of Pennsylvania.[95] As the Grand Ohio Company, the Indiana Company had received title to this land from the Indians in the 1768 Treaty of Stanwix. The company, however, had failed to obtain royal confirmation of the grant before the outbreak of the American Revolution. It was reorganized as the Indiana Company in 1776, and company officials unsuccessfully sought recognition of its claim in the Virginia legislature and in Congress.[96] Mason, who feared a favorable decision for the company in the federal courts, predicted that the "peasants will be . . . reduced to ruin and misery, driven from their farms, and obliged to leave their country."[97]

Unlikely, thought Edmund Pendleton, as he stood to respond to Mason's gloomy prediction. Like most Federalists, Pendleton believed that the inherent weaknesses of the Articles of Confederation were stifling western growth. "We shall have also a much better chance," he told fellow delegates, "for a favorable negotiation [of the Mississippi River], if our Government be respectable, than we have now."[98] "How shall we retain" the right to navigate the Mississippi River? asked John Marshall.[99] "By retaining that weak Government which has hitherto kept it from us?" he wondered.[100] Congress and the states, Madison noted, could continue to pass resolutions to retain the river, but "it is not resolutions of this sort, which the people of this country wish for. They want actual possession of the right, and protection in its enjoyment."[101] "As to the navigation of the Mississippi, it is one of the most unalienable rights of the people," noted George Nicholas, and it "can only be secured by one of two ways. By force or by treaty. As to force, I apprehend that the new government will be much more likely to hold it than the old. It will be also more likely to retain it be by means of treaties."[102]

To serve western needs adequately, Federalists insisted that the country had to erect a new government. Certainly no outside force would guarantee American rights to the river. Antifederalists, Edmund Randolph reminded his fellow delegates, inform us "that France has guarranteed to us the possession of that river. *We* need not trouble ourselves about it . . . [yet] I appeal to what the French ambassador said, in 1781, in Congress, that America had no right to the Mississippi."[103] Only a strong system of government, Pendleton emphasized, would provide the means for the United States to safeguard its rights against unfriendly nations.[104]

Whereas the Antifederalists saw the new government quickly discarding American rights to the Mississippi River, Federalists insisted that the new government protected American usage of the river from a hostile minority. "To justify the conclusion, that the Mississippi may be given away by five states," Nicholas noted that the Antifederalists had to rely on a series of improbable events, the most improbable being southern "senators whose states are most interested in being fully represented, will be those who fail to attend" the session dealing with the relinquishment of the Mississippi River.[105] Besides, with public officials in Pennsylvania and New Jersey committed to the retention of the Mississippi River, Randolph argued "there will . . . be a majority in favor of the Mississippi: a majority that does not depend on the doctrine of chances. There will be 14 senators against 12, admitting the States to remain as they are."[106]

Federalists, taking their cues from Madison, also argued that the "President is a very great security" against the loss of the river.[107] Noting his allegiance to the people and not to the "local interests which the members of Congress may have," they assured their Antifederalist colleagues that he would not dare disregard the wishes of his constituents.[108] If he should, "he will be degraded. . . . He will be absolutely disqualified to hold any place of profit, honor, or trust. . . . From the summit of honor and esteem he will be precipitated to the lowest infamy and disgrace."[109] And even if the president and Senate wanted to relinquish the American rights to the Mississippi River, Federalists argued, as did Madison, that members of the House of Representatives would serve as "a considerable check on the Senate and President."[110]

"To make a treaty to alienate any part of the United States, will amount to a declaration of war against the inhabitants of the alienated part, and a general absolution from allegiance," pronounced Edmund Randolph.[111] Those inhabitants, Federalists pointed out to their critics, had left homes located not just in the South. "Emigrations from some of the northern states," Madison noted, "have been lately increased."[112] If the northern states persisted in their attack on the right to the Mississippi River, they would not hurt only westerners. They would also injure their former citizens, who "will leave behind them all their friends and connections as advocates for this right."[113]

Persist in the misguided notion that the Articles of Confederation were strong enough to retain American rights to the Mississippi River, Federalists warned Antifederalists, and risk the loss of the entire West. "If this navigation be given up, the country adjacent will also be given up to Spain; for the possession of the one must be inseparable from the other."[114] No competent government would gladly consent to its own destruction, a situation which, noted Randolph, would act as "a sufficient check on the general government."[115] Madison added his voice to the chorus saying that the northern states would be foolhardy to turn over the Mississippi River to Spain. With the northern states stressing the carrying trade as their "natural province, how can it be so much extended and advanced" if they cause the United States to lose the Mississippi.[116] With no access to markets, people would stop moving into the West, the only region of the country "so capable of improvement and great extension" of the agricultural output of the United States.[117]

Throughout the debate, Federalists seldom wavered from the position that the West was a great national resource, helping all regions of the country prosper. Predicting a rapid settlement of the fertile lands of the West, they envisioned American ships filled with western crops. Also, as more and more people headed west, they envisioned greater contributions to the national treasury. "Kentucky will have taxes to pay," the Federalists reminded delegates.[118] Likewise, the navigation of the Mississippi River "will be to the interest of all the States, as it will increase the general resources of the united community" through imposts.[119] Federalists, however, failed to view westward expansion as a serious potential source of conflict between the southern and northern states, although Madison, in speaking of the composition of the House of Representatives, noted that in the years to come the South would be the most populous region in the nation, "if we include the western country."[120] Few Federalists were willing to embrace William Grayson's vision of the West as a battle ground between the southern and northern states. Grayson, like Henry, worried about the future of the South in a government deemed hostile to southern political interests. "I look upon this," he told his fellow delegates, "as a contest for empire. Our country is equally affected with Kentucky."[121] Continuing, he linked the navigation of the Mississippi River with westward expansion:

> If the Mississippi be shut up . . . there will be no new states formed on the western waters. This will be a government of seven states. This contest of the Mississippi involves this great national contest—That is, whether one part of the continent shall govern the other. The Northern States have the majority, and will endeavor to retain it. This is, therefore, a contest for dominion—for empire.[122]

Despite Grayson's ominous words, the convention narrowly voted for the Constitution. After dispensing with Henry's motion for drafting a list of amendments and presenting them to the states before voting on the Constitution, the convention ratified the Constitution by a vote of eighty-nine to seventy-nine.[123] Of the fourteen delegates from Kentucky, ten voted "nay"; three voted "aye"; and one abstained.[124] After ratifying, the delegates appointed a committee to draft a list of amendments that the Virginia representatives would present to Congress for its consideration. The committee, which included the most vocal spokesmen on both sides of the issue—Grayson, Henry, Madison, Mason, Monroe and George Nicholas—offered only one amendment dealing with the Mississippi River and the West.[125] The seventh recommended amendment stipulated that "no treaty ceding, contracting, restraining, or suspending, the territorial rights or claims of the United States . . . or navigating the American rivers, shall be made, but in the case of the most urgent and extreme necessity."[126] The amendment further spelled out that only on the "concurrence of three fourths of the whole number of the members of both houses respectively" could such an act go into effect.[127]

The ratification debate revealed the Federalists' commitment to the West. Antifederalists, who envisioned a closer political relationship between the West and the South, forced the Federalists to proclaim at least their loyalty to the West. The Federalists, believing the Constitution a document of national unity, failed to foresee, however, a time when in the hands of northerners, the Constitution could be used to frustrate southern political and economic interests. They also lacked the foresight to see that in the event of northern political or economic assaults on the South, they could use the West to protect southern interests in the Union. Madison still clung to his vision of the West as a national resource. Once the Federalists, particularly Madison, began the process of organizing the new government, the words of William Grayson—"whether one part of the continent shall govern the other"—suddenly began to seem prophetic.

NOTES

1. Robert Francis Jones, *George Washington: Ordinary Man, Extraordinary Leader* (New York: Fordham University Press, 2002), 96.
2. William Few, "Autobiography of Col. William Few of Georgia," *Magazine of American History*, VII (November 1881), 343.
3. *Savannah Gazette of the State of Georgia*, 26 April 1787.
4. *Annapolis Maryland Gazette*, 12 July 1787.
5. *Ibid.*
6. James Madison to Thomas Jefferson, 19 March 1787, in *Letters of Members of the Continental Congress,* ed. Edmund C. Burnett (Washington, DC: Carnegie Institution of Washington, 1936), 8:561. Frank Harmon Garver, in "The Attitude of the Constitutional Convention of 1787 toward the West," *The Pacific Historical Review*, 5 (December 1936), 349–58, mentions several peripheral points, including the admission of new states and the guarantee of a republican form of government for new states.
7. *The Records of the Federal Convention*, ed. Max Farrand (New Haven: Yale University Press, 1911), 1:242.
8. Ibid., 1:322.
9. Ibid.
10. Ibid.
11. Ibid., 1:372.
12. Ibid.
13. Ibid.
14. Ibid., 1:446.
15. Ibid.
16. *American National Biography*, s.v. "Butler, Pierce;" Farrand, *Records*, 1:542.
17. Farrand, *Records*, 1:542.
18. Ibid., 1:582.
19. Ibid.
20. Ibid., 1:560.
21. Ibid.
22. Ibid., 1:583. Morris believed that men living in the West were not as "equally enlightened" as men living in the Atlantic seaboard states. See Ibid.
23. Ibid., 1:373.
24. Ibid., 1:584–85.
25. *The Records of the Federal Convention*, ed. Max Farrand (New Haven: Yale University Press, 1911), 2:454.
26. Pamela C. Copeland and Richard K. MacMaster, *The Five George Masons: Patriots and Planters of Virginia and Maryland* (Charlottesville: University Press of Virginia, 1975), 147–49.
27. Farrand, *Records*, 1:578.
28. Ibid., 1:578–79.
29. Ibid., 1:579.
30. On 10 July, Rufus King stated that, as far as he was concerned, "[n]o principle would justify the giving them the majority." Farrand, *Records*, 1:566.
31. Farrand, *Records*, 2:3.
32. Farrand, *Records*, 1:566.
33. Ibid., 1:586.
34. Ibid.
35. Morris uttered his remarks on 5 July, 10 July, and 11 July 1787. See Ibid., 1:533, 567, 583.
36. Ibid., 1:584.
37. Ibid., 1:585.
38. . [Remarks on the New Plan of Government, by Hugh Williamson, to the Freemen of Edenton and the County of Chowan in North Carolina], *New York Daily Advertiser*, 27 Febru-

ary 1788; Quoted in John P. Kaminski, "Controversy Amid Consensus: The Adoption of the Federal Constitution in Georgia," *Georgia Historical Quarterly*, 58 (Summer 1974), 246.

39. E. Merton Coulter, ed., "Minutes of the Georgia Convention Ratifying the Federal Convention," *Georgia Historical Quarterly*, 10 (September 1926), 223–27; Kaminski, "Controversy Amid Consensus," 257; Kenneth Coleman, *The American Revolution in Georgia, 1763–1789* (Athens: University of Georgia Press, 1958), 270–71.

40. Pauline Maier, *Ratification: The People Debate the Constitution, 1787–1788* (New York: Simon & Schuster, 2010), 250.

41. *American National Biography*, s.v. "Martin, Luther."

42. Luther Martin, "The Genuine Information Delivered to the Legislature of the State of Maryland, relative to the Proceedings of the General Convention, held at Philadelphia, in 1787, by Luther Martin, Esquire, Attorney-General of Maryland, and one of the Delegates to the said Convention," 29 November 1787, in *The Records of the Federal Convention*, ed. Max Farrand (New Haven: Yale University Press, 1911), 3:226.

43. Ibid.

44. Ibid., 3:227.

45. The West, in the form of the Mississippi question, appeared several times during North Carolina's ratifying convention, but personal attacks against members and a profound distrust of the concept of a strong central government dominated the debates. See Richard R. Beeman, *Plain, Honest Men: The Making of the American Constitution* (New York: Random House, 2009), 404, and Eli Merritt, "Sectional Conflict and Secret Compromise: The Mississippi River Question and the United States Constitution," *The American Journal of Legal History*, 35:2 (April 1991), 163-64.

46. Washington to Madison, 22 October 1787, in *The Papers of James Madison*, eds. William T. Hutchinson, William M. E. Rachal et al. (Chicago: The University of Chicago Press; Charlottesville: University of Virginia Press, 1977), 10:204.

47. Madison to Rufus King, 13 June 1788, and Madison to John Brown, 27 May 1788, both in *The Papers of James Madison*, eds. William T. Hutchinson, William M. E. Rachal et al. (Chicago: The University of Chicago Press; Charlottesville: University of Virginia Press, 1975), 9:133, 60.

48. John Mason Brown, *The Political Beginnings of Kentucky: A Narrative of Public Events bearing on the History of the State up to the time of its Admission into the American Union* (Louisville: John P. Morton and Company, Printers to the Filson Club, 1889), 106. The potential loss of the Mississippi River was by far the biggest, but not the only, reason why Kentuckians opposed the Constitution. Other reasons included concern over the federal government's calling out the militia and leaving areas vulnerable to Indian attack and the distance from Kentucky to the site of the Supreme Court. See Charles G. Talbert, "Kentuckians in the Virginia Convention of 1788," *Kentucky Historical Society Register*, 58 (July 1960), 188–89.

49. Edmund Randolph to Madison, 27 December 1787, in Hutchinson et al., *Madison Papers*, 10:346.

50. Robert Allen Rutland, *The Ordeal of the Constitution: The Antifederalists and the Ratification Struggle of 1787–1788* (1965; reprint, Norman: University of Oklahoma Press, 1983), 186.

51. Madison to Randolph, 10 January 1788, in Hutchinson et al., *Madison Papers*, 10:355.

52. Ibid., 10:356.

53. Ibid., 10:370.

54. Ibid., 10:371.

55. Ibid.

56. Ibid.

57. Ibid.

58. Hugh Williamson to Madison, 2 June 1788, in Farrand, *Records*, 3:306–7.

59. Madison to George Nicholas, 8 April 1788, in *The Papers of James Madison*, eds. William T. Hutchinson, William M. E. Rachal et al. (Chicago: The University of Chicago Press; Charlottesville: University of Virginia Press, 1977), 11:12.

60. Ibid.

61. Madison to Jefferson, 23 April 1788, in Ibid., 11:28.

62. Ibid., 11:29. Earlier, Madison expressed similar sentiments to John Brown. See Madison to John Brown, 9 April 1788, in Ibid., 11:16–17.

63. Brown to Madison, 12 May 1788, in Burnett, *Letters of Members*, 8:733.

64. George Nicholas to Madison, 9 May 1788, in Hutchinson et al., *Madison Papers*, 11:40–41.

65. Madison to Nicholas, 17 May 1788, in Ibid., 11:45.

66. Ibid., 11:46.

67. Ibid., 11:46–47.

68. Ibid., 11:46.

69. Ibid., 11:47.

70. Ibid.

71. Ibid., 11:47–48.

72. Ibid., 11:48.

73. Ibid.

74. Ibid., 11:49.

75. Madison to Rufus King, 4 June 1788, in Ibid., 11:76.

76. Ibid.

77. *The Documentary History of the Ratification of the Constitution*, eds. John P. Kaminski and Gaspare J. Saladino (Madison: State Historical Society of Wisconsin, 1990), 9:1051.

78. Those states were Connecticut, Massachusetts, New Hampshire, New Jersey, New York, Pennsylvania, and Rhode Island. See *Journals of the Continental Congress*, 31:595.

79. Kaminski, *Documentary History*, 9:1051.

80. Ibid.

81. Ibid.

82. *The Documentary History of the Ratification of the Constitution*, eds. John P. Kaminski and Gaspare J. Saladino (Madison: State Historical Society of Wisconsin, 1993), 10:1249.

83. Ibid., 10:1192.

84. Ibid.

85. Ibid., 10:1243.

86. Ibid., 10:1244.

87. Ibid., 10:1245.

88. Ibid.

89. Ibid., 10:1246.

90. Ibid., 10:1247.

91. Ibid., 10:1235.

92. Ibid.

93. Kaminski, *Documentary History*, 9:1161.

94. Ibid.

95. Ibid.

96. Otis K. Rice, *The Allegheny Frontier: West Virginia Beginnings, 1730–1830* (Lexington: The University Press of Kentucky, 1970), 63, 121–27.

97. Mason's fears proved well-founded. In *William Grayson et al. v the Commonwealth of Virginia*, Virginia denied the suability of a state in a federal court and refused a summons to appear before the high court, as shareholders in the Indiana Company had sought through the courts the nearly 3,000,000 acres that they thought they had received from the British government but the Virginia legislature had denied them in 1779. In light of *Chisholm v. Georgia* (1793), Virginia officials, along with similarly minded lawmakers from such states as Georgia, worked for the adoption of the Eleventh Amendment, which prohibited a non-resident from suing a state. A successful suit might have also reopened Richard Henderson's claim to large tracts of land in Kentucky. Following the amendment's adoption in 1795 and certification of adoption in January 1798, the Supreme Court dismissed the lawsuit in February 1798 for lack of jurisdiction. See Clyde E. Jacobs, "Prelude to Amendment: The States before the Court," *The American Journal of Legal History*, 12:1 (January 1968), 30–32.

98. Kaminski, *Documentary History*, 10:1200.

99. Kaminski, *Documentary History*, 9:1117.

100. Ibid.

101. Kaminski, *Documentary History*, 10:1242.
102. Kaminski, *Documentary History*, 9:1129–30.
103. Kaminski, *Documentary History*, 10:1253.
104. Ibid., 10:1254–55.
105. Ibid., 10:1249.
106. Ibid., 10:1254.
107. Kaminski, *Documentary History*, 9:1130.
108. Ibid.
109. Ibid., 9:1130–31.
110. Ibid., 9:1131.
111. Kaminski, *Documentary History*, 10:1254.
112. Ibid., 10:1208
113. Ibid.
114. Ibid., 10:1254.
115. Ibid.
116. Ibid., 10:1239.
117. Ibid.
118. Kaminski, *Documentary History*, 9:1131.
119. Ibid.
120. Kaminski, *Documentary History*, 10:1241.
121. Ibid., 10:1259.
122. Ibid.
123. Ibid., 10:1479, 1538, 1540.
124. Lowell Hayes Harrison and James C. Klotter, *A New History of Kentucky* (Lexington: The University Press of Kentucky, 1997), 59.
125. Kaminski, *Documentary History*, 10:1541.
126. Ibid., 10:1554.
127. Ibid.

Chapter Five

The Fight for the Potomac

With the battle over the federal Constitution finished, James Madison left Richmond for New York to resume his seat in the Confederation Congress. He and his fellow Federalists in Virginia had waged a tough campaign against a potent Antifederalist resistance. Their margin of victory had been slim, yet Madison felt confident that the political wounds opened by the ratifying debate would soon be healed and that most opponents of the Constitution would support the new government. Yet, he mused that a couple of the leading Antifederalists "betray the effect of the disappointment, so far as it is marked in their countenances."[1]

In New York, Madison found his fellow delegates busily at work. With the requisite number of states having ratified the Constitution, they began the process of "putting the [new] Government into operation" at an as yet undetermined location.[2] In August, Congress started wrestling with the difficult question of where the new Congress should convene. Although northern delegates divided over the issue, with delegates from Delaware, New York, and Pennsylvania championing cities within their own states, Madison knew that this division within northern ranks was not great enough to allow a southern city to capture the honor. When Baltimore received seven votes during the early balloting, Madison admitted to being somewhat surprised, but he knew its moment in the limelight would be short lived. After Congress convened in Baltimore, he predicted that northern members would quickly vote to move the site to a more northerly location.[3]

As he listened to the tone of the debate, Madison began to worry about its implications for the South. Obviously, he noted, it would give a "great handle . . . to those who have opposed the new Govt. on account of the Eastern preponderancy in the foederal system."[4] This fact seemed of little concern to Madison, however, for he thought he saw a more "serious aspect" in congressional actions for the South and the West.[5] The Potomac River, Madison thought, provided an excellent site for the capital of the United States. Its central location was geographically accessible to all residents of the nation, and like George Washington and Thomas Jefferson, he saw the river as the only practicable avenue of communication with the entire West, north and south of the Ohio River. Writing to Jefferson, he explained his uneasiness with the congressional proceedings: "It will be certainly of far more importance under the proposed than the present system that regard should be had to centrality."[6] With westerners still suspicious of the Atlantic states and scrutinizing every action of Congress to make sure that no "seeming advantage" went to the northern states, Madison continued to worry about the western attachment to the Union.[7] "There is even good ground to believe that Spain is taking advantage of this disgust [with the northern states] in Kentucky and is actually endeavoring to seduce them from the union," he secretly informed Jefferson in France.[8]

Madison's anxieties increased further when the Confederation Congress referred to the new federal Congress Virginia's request to make Kentucky a state.[9] Suddenly, it started to appear to some southerners that the South and the West might have some difficulties in the new nation. As the Confederation Congress debated the Kentucky question, North Carolina delegate James White noticed "the eastern States seem[ed] much at a loss to decide," reasoning that they were "jealous of any additional influence to the Southward."[10] Writing from Richmond, Edmund Randolph informed Madison that many people around the Virginia capital looked on recent congressional actions "with suspicion . . . and in truth a fear, that her [Kentucky] admission may be unnecessarily delayed."[11] White predicted that if the southern states continued to allow the "partial views" of the northern states to overpower other considerations, "affection, fear or interest will not long hold [Kentucky] dependent on the Atlantic States."[12]

Although Madison refused to accept the growing perception in the South that the Kentucky episode revealed the "preponderancy" of the northern states in the nation and their willingness "to profit of that advantage," he felt frustrated by his failure to stop the momentum building to make New York the permanent capital.[13] His frustration grew in large part from the action of South Carolina in the affair. Edward Carrington of Virginia had proposed an amendment, which Madison seconded, designed to change the site for the convening of the First Congress from New York to a "more central [location] than the present seat of Congress."[14] When South Carolina, because of its close financial relationship with New York, joined New York and the New England states in killing Carrington's motion and thus ensuring the selection of New York, Madison became incensed.[15] Nevertheless, he remained committed to his nationalist stance and refrained, even though he believed otherwise, from publicly labeling the episode a northern conspiracy designed to deprive the South and the West of a centrally located capital.[16] The episode, however, caused Madison to remember the dire warnings of the Virginia Antifederalists. This "display of locality . . . ," he noted, "portends the continuance of an evil which has dishonored the old [government], and gives countenance to some of the most popular arguments which have been inculcated by the Southern antifederalists."[17]

Despite his pronouncements to the contrary, the issue of the temporary capital clearly distressed Madison. "It violates too palpably," he confided in a letter to Washington, "the simple and obvious principle that the seat of public business should be made as equally convenient to every part of the public."[18] This principle, he added, was particularly important "on account of the catholic spirit professed by the Constitution."[19] Yet, despite his concern for the people's rights, Madison worried more about the potential harm the issue might do to the West's relationship with the Atlantic states:

> It seems to be particularly essential that an eye should be had in all our public arrangements to the accommodation of the Western Country, which perhaps cannot be sufficiently gratified at any rate, but which might be furnished with new fuel to its jealousy by being summoned to the sea-shore & almost at one end of the Continent. There are reasons, but of too confidential a nature for any other than verbal communication, which make it of critical importance that neither cause, nor pretext should be given for distrust in that quarter of the policy towards it in this.[20]

Such a pretext, Madison reminded Washington could easily arise in the first Congress. When the new Congress under the federal Constitution convened for the first time, Madison knew it would face a difficult task, making "all the great arrangements under the new system."[21] He also knew that if Congress did not convene in a central location, critics could charge it with favoritism. "It may perhaps be," he told Washington, "the more necessary to guard agst. [against] suspicions of partiality in this case."[22]

During the constitutional convention and the Virginia ratifying debate, Madison had remained the dedicated nationalist, unwilling to accept any aspect of the sectionalist argument. For Madison, the West remained a national treasure, its land to be used for the benefit of the nation and its inhabitants to be equal members of the American Union. Even the Mississippi occlusion crisis had failed to dampen seriously Madison's nationalistic fervor. The upcoming debate over the location of the temporary capital, however, would reveal a subtle, yet significant, change in Madison's political outlook. When Madison apparently embraced sectionalism and supported the southern efforts to rescind congressional instructions to John Jay in 1786, he did so largely because he feared the disastrous affect that the loss of the Mississippi River would have on the future of the United States. With the controversy over the location of the temporary capital, Madison began to redefine his allegiances, placing greater emphasis on the South and its role in the nation than on the nation itself.

Congressional selection of New York as the temporary capital ended, for the moment, Madison's efforts to bring the permanent capital to the Potomac River. Writing to his father, James Madison, Sr., Madison called the selection of New York "a very unreasonable thing for the Southn. & Western parts of the Union."[23] Whereas he believed "the best face must be put on it," he knew the controversial issue would soon make another appearance.[24] "I take it for granted that the first Session will not pass without a renewal of the question, and it will be attended with all the unpleasing circumstances which have just been experienced."[25] Madison unhappily predicted, however, that Congress would not be able to decide quickly on the location for the permanent capital. "This temporary period must continue," he predicted, "for several years, perhaps seven or eight, and within that period all the great business of the Union will be settled."[26] Realizing that "New York will never be patiently suffered to remain even the temporary seat of Govt. by those who will be obliged to resort to it from the Western and South. parts of the Union," Madison nevertheless called for calm.[27] Southern congressmen during this temporary period had to proceed cautiously and work in unison to forestall northern attempts to maneuver Congress into making a hasty decision on the location of the permanent capital before the anticipated southern and western political coalition had time to develop. This temporary period in New York, Madison believed, would allow "the Western & S. Western population . . . [to] enter more into the estimate."[28] "If [a choice is] speedily made[, Congress] will not be sufficiently influenced by that consideration [the growth of the West]," Madison confidentially told Washington.[29] On this delay, Madison based his "hope in favor of the banks of the potowmac."[30]

Despite all attempts to paint an optimistic picture, the debate over Kentucky statehood and the temporary capital showed Madison that the northern states probably would use their influence within the new government to achieve their own aims. In Congress, proponents of a central location could not convince northern delegates that a central location for the temporary capital was essential for the infant government. By unduly inconveniencing or hurting the most southern and western members of the nation, southerners argued the new government would lack the appearance of impartiality and create a situation that might result in the loss of southern delegates to Congress. "People from the interior parts of Georgia, S.C.[,] N.C[.,] Va. & Kentucky will never patiently repeat their trips to this remote situation, especially as the legislative sessions will be held in the winter season," Madison told Washington.[31]

Watching the affair from Richmond, Edmund Pendleton noted that the people had already begun to make "taunts on the occasion, as the first instance of Eastern Partiality and influence, which Opposition [Antifederalists] foresaw would pervade & wholly direct the new Government."[32] Upset with the South Carolina vote for New York, Pendleton pessimistically retorted that the northern states would "always find means to engage such [southern] assistance."[33] Echoing Madison, he commented that "nothing . . . can make the new Government wear a more inauspicious aspect, than the appearance of favor to one part of the Society over others, a full and Equal diffusion of its Powers to the whole, is what all had a right to expect from the Ruler."[34]

Madison's arguments for a central location possessed little influence with northern congressmen. Discounting the need for impartiality, the northern congressional delegations forced Madison and a majority of the political leaders in the South to discard their nationalist opinions about the West and to accept the Antifederalists' position on the need to engineer a political coalition between the South and the West. As with Madison, this shift was subtle. Yet, even before the nation had inaugurated its new government, southerners had started to create the impression that they were the champions of the West and the people to whom westerners should attach their political future.

An unnamed traveler journeying "through those parts of the United States bounding on the Ohio and Mississippi" in early 1788 acknowledged the westerners' firm attachment to the Mississippi River.[35] "Any man," he wrote, "that should attempt to recommend a cession of that nature upon any consideration whatever, would, if amongst them, be made to repent dearly for his temerity."[36] Political leaders in Virginia and North Carolina knew the accuracy of this statement. In November 1787, the Virginia House of Delegates passed a resolution similar to Madison's resolution of November 1786. The new resolution reaffirmed Virginians' right to navigate all rivers and streams contained within the Virginia commonwealth. Clearly, Virginians meant the Mississippi River. Yet, before a House committee could draft instructions for the Virginia congressional delegation outlining how they should present the resolution, the session ended, and the Virginia delegates never received a copy of the resolutions.[37]

Lawmakers in North Carolina took a similar step during the final days of their 1787 legislative session when they passed a resolution supporting the right of westerners to navigate the Mississippi River and instructed the North Carolina congressional delegation to place the resolution before Congress.[38] In Congress, North Carolinians coordinated their efforts with their counterparts from Virginia, who, according to North Carolina congressman Hugh Williamson, "are also instructed respecting the Mississippi, but they are disposed not to bring forward that business before we are ready to support them."[39] In July 1788, events, however, forced the North Carolina delegation to present the resolutions of their legislature before Congress.

On the return of Diego de Gardoqui to the United States in July 1788, John Jay reopened commercial negotiations with the newly arrived Spanish minister. It soon became apparent to Jay that Gardoqui wanted the United States to agree to suspend its claim to the Mississippi River, which "appeared to him [Jay] at that Time adviseable."[40] Fearing that Jay had possibly exceeded his instructions, the North Carolina congressional delegation on 14 July moved that Congress adopt a strongly worded resolution attesting to American rights to navigate the Mississippi River.[41] Two months later, on 16 September, Congress passed three resolutions, two public and one secret.[42] Referring to the allegation contained in the North Carolina motion "that Congress are disposed to treat with Spain for the surrender of the claim to the navigation of the River Mississippi," Congress "Resolv'd That the said report not being founded in fact, the Delegates are at liberty to communicate all such circumstances as may be necessary to contradict the same and to remove misconceptions."[43] After dispelling the North Carolina criticism, Congress then "Resolv'd, That the free navigation of the River Mississippi is a clear and essential right of the United States, and ought to be considered and supported as such."[44] Finally, Congress secretly ordered Jay to end all negotiations with Spain regarding the Mississippi River, believing such negotiations now fell under the purview of the new federal government.[45]

Most Virginians expressed satisfaction with the measure. Monroe, who was preparing to take his seat in the Virginia House, thought the action of Congress "right" and believed that it might even "have some influence on the new govt."[46] Unaware of the secret resolution, he expressed some concern that the resolutions seemed to indicate only a temporary change in policy "and this I think equally pernicious as it may affect the form of the confederacy."[47] Conversely, Madison viewed the resolutions as a possible solution to a ticklish situation. Coming on the heels of congressional postponement of the question of statehood for Kentucky, Madison hoped that the resolutions would "have a salutary effect on the temper of our western Brethren."[48] In late September, he still remained deeply concerned that the recent congressional affront to Kentucky might push its residents into the waiting arms of Spain. "I anticipate," he wrote to Kentuckian John Brown, "every political calamity from the event . . . [that will] be viewed in all quarters as no less unnecessary that [than] it certainly is critical and hazardous."[49] In Paris, Jefferson also felt "pleased" to learn of the congressional vote of 16 September. "I had before seen with great uneasiness," he noted, "the pursuit of other principles which I could not reconcile to my own ideas of probity or wisdom, and from which, and my knolege of character of our western settlers, I saw that the loss of that country was a necessary consequence. I wish this return to true policy may be in time to prevent evil."[50] Echoing Jefferson's concern, Madison believed the resolutions reflected "the real opinions which prevail on the subject."[51]

Congressional actions, however, did not impress everyone living in the South. Edmund Pendleton regarded the resolutions as "balmy."[52] He noted that they inclined "to give Repose to those concerned, and impose silence on such as caring nothing about it."[53] Continuing, he warned that certain people "used the Subject as an engine of Opposition."[54] Pendleton, perhaps, was addressing his caustic remarks to western land speculators, who certainly stood to suffer financially if Spain gained control of Kentucky. Just what he meant by "engine of Opposition," however, remains unclear.

For one western land speculator in Congress, Hugh Williamson, the resolutions marked an important turning point in the attitude of the nation toward the West. He believed that the West had been an aberration for many northerners—something they saw but did not understand. Even though they noticed the steady stream of settlers heading west, they failed to comprehend the magnitude of that migration and what it meant for the nation. Their insistence on subordinating western needs and concerns to their own interests, Williamson believed, reflected their ignorance of what was actually happening in the region west of the Appalachian Mountains. "The subject is now much better understood," he informed North Carolina governor Samuel Johnston."[55] "[T]he late Increase of Settlers in the western Country has been so rapid beyond all their Ideas of probability that they are now fully agreed with us that Nature and the fitness of Things must have their due Operation."[56]

Since 1786, when the South united in support of the West against northern attempts to abandon the Mississippi River, southerners had viewed the issue as one of natural rights. Although always vigilant in their watch over the West, they hoped that someday the people who held the balance of power would accept their opinions. In April 1787, the North Carolina delegation laid before Congress a report on the Spanish confiscation of a person's property while traveling on the Mississippi River. "It will propably be productive of some good to our Western Citizens," they noted in their report to Governor Caswell.[57] The affair, they believed, illustrated "in a General point of view our entire claim to the Navigation of the Mississippi and the prospects of the citizens there [which are] founded on this their right."[58] Continuing, they hoped that the unfortunate episode would "eventually lead . . . Congress to the adoption of some uniform line of policy with Spain."[59] The congressional resolutions of 16 September, coming within two years of the southern stand on behalf of the West, showed southerners that their defense of the West had been correct and their struggle to pass the resolutions justified, despite "the wounds given to some & the pretext given to others."[60]

As the nation prepared for the inauguration of a new government in March, rumors of discontent in the West caused the applause for the latest congressional stand on the Mississippi River to diminish quickly.[61] Whereas the resolutions helped sooth rattled nerves, they did not eliminate overnight the animosity that many westerners felt toward northerners. In January and February 1789, an article copied in Virginia and North Carolina newspapers reported "that many of the principal people of [Kentucky] . . . are warmly in favor of separation from the union."[62] It further noted that the Spanish minister had concluded talks with leading Kentucky residents and that the Spanish minister had assured them that "on such a declaration . . . Spain would cede to them the free navigation of the Mississippi, and give them every support and encouragement in their power."[63] Calling the reports "pregnant with mischief to America" and "serious in its consequences, to the peace and existence of the Atlantic States," the writer of the article demanded that Congress immediately address the issue.[64]

Although a few western leaders attempted to work quietly with Spanish officials to create a better economic situation for their region, westerners never wanted to become Spanish subjects. Residents of the Cumberland settlement only hinted of Spanish intrigues in Tennessee to pressure North Carolina politicians into ratifying the Constitution and ceding Tennessee to the federal government.[65] In Kentucky, residents listened to James Wilkinson's arguments for attaching themselves to Spanish Louisiana but decided that in the long run they were better off remaining in the Union. Still, despite the overwhelming commitment of Americans to the United States, a few were willing to renounce their citizenship for Spanish lands. In 1789, George Morgan of New Jersey, a land speculator, publicly launched a grand project to settle a huge expanse of territory located on the western bank of the Mississippi River.[66] Spain, through its American agent Morgan, offered each American settler who immigrated to the Mississippi tract a bounty of $20, a homestead and the right to retain "certain immunities as free men."[67] As bits and pieces of the scheme gradually became known to the public, southerners started keeping "a watchful eye . . . on the machinations of Spain."[68]

"I find [the affair] much more important than I at first apprehended," commented John Dawson, a Virginia congressman.[69] Pointing to the fertile lands available in the Spanish settlement of New Madrid, he predicted that immigration to this new colony promoted by Morgan would be "very great."[70] He also believed that this alarming loss of Americans presented government officials with a compelling reason for the United States to insist on American rights to travel on the Mississippi River. Once these former United States citizens acquired the right to navigate the great waterway, Dawson believed that they would oppose any Spanish attempts to grant the same rights to any other nation, particularly the United States.[71] When the disposition of their former neighbors now living in New Madrid became known to those settlers living on the American side of the river, Dawson feared that they would rebel "against the United States, a separation will ensue, and commercial and other treaties will be formed between Spain and the Western Anglo-Americans for their mutual advantage and security."[72]

Although not so pessimistic as Dawson, Madison also worried about the Spanish drain of American settlers in the West. He informed Washington that "circumstances point out the conduct which the New Govt. ought to pursue with regard to the Western Country and Spain."[73] Despite expecting the Spaniards to fail in their western endeavor, Madison considered the Morgan affair an example of the Spanish policy of "making the Mississippi the bait for a defection of the Western people."[74]

The actions of Spain also reminded southerners that an uneasy relationship still existed between the West and the Atlantic states. In North Carolina, Governor Samuel Johnston listened helplessly as rumors of alliances between Spain and western residents reached him at Edenton. While calling such plans "monstrous and absurd," he admitted that his government lacked the means to end the Cherokee raids in the West, which happened to be a major complaint of the inhabitants in the region.[75] Yet, despite his awareness of western conditions, he still wondered "how could Americans among whom, the Rights of Mankind are so well understood, submit to be under the Dominion of Laws dictated by any one man upon Earth . . . or to gratify the avaricious or arbitrary views of a wicked Minister?"[76] Upon reflection, he concluded that it was impossible: "I think more honourably of the Inhabitants of the Western Waters than to suffer the smallest degree of pain on that account."[77] Likewise, Madison comforted himself in the knowledge that although "some of the leaders in Kentucky are known to favor the idea of connection with Spain[,] . . . [most westerners] are as yet inimical to it."[78] "Their future disposition," he informed Jefferson, "will depend on the measures of the new Government."[79]

A few southerners, however, viewed Morgan's colonizing efforts as being beneficial to the United States. From Culpepper, Virginia, John Strode questioned the sanity of people paying Morgan "1/8 of a Dollar/Acre" for land that Spain was willing to grant free of charge.[80] Despite questioning Morgan's motives, Strode saw a possible opportunity for the United States to expand its territorial limits. Although unsure as "to what State or Nation they are here after to belong," he believed that "local circumstances [would] unavoidably decide" the outcome.[81] The prospect of the people deciding where to place their loyalties, however, did not alarm him. "I believe that the boundary Line between Spain and the United States of America, cannot long Remain where it is," he cryptically informed Madison.[82] Thomas Jefferson, while still in Paris, also received the news with some excitement. Although admitting that the project slowed the pace of western settlement and "weakens somewhat the United States for the present," he noted that "it begins our possession of that country considerably soon[er] than I had expected, and without a struggle till no struggle can be made."[83]

By the time the news began arriving in the South that Morgan's settlement had collapsed and that the "adventurers are returned to Kentucky very

Much disgusted," the new federal government had been in operation for nearly five months.[84] Congress had finally achieved a quorum in April, and George Washington, whom the Electoral College elected in February, had taken the oath of office on the last day of that month. As Congress set about organizing itself, its members seldom concerned themselves with western affairs. In early July, Madison reported to his friend George Nicholas, now a resident of Kentucky, that "no question has yet been started by which the disposition of Congress towards the Western Country or of the Senate towards the Mississippi River could be determined . . . nor any defect of attention to the Western interests in general."[85] Not quite as lenient in his assessment of the activities of Congress, John Dawson worried about certain omissions in the proposed list of constitutional amendments. Although pleased that Congress had quickly addressed the major concerns of the Antifederalists, he "wish'd they had been more extensive."[86] He reminded Madison that the delegates at the Virginia ratifying convention had felt the need to propose an amendment calling for "no treaty, ceding, contracting, restraining or suspending the territorial rights of the United States, or any of them" unless the "most urgent and extreme" situation confronted the nation.[87] "Experience, as well as sound policy point out," he informed Madison, "the propriety of the amendment propos'd by this state for rendering more secure our Western territory, & for guarding against the danger of the surrender of the Mississippi."[88]

Congressional disinterest in the West, however, ended in the early fall when the House began its deliberation, in the words of Virginian Richard Bland Lee, of "a great national question"—the location of the permanent seat of government.[89] On 3 September 1789, Lee initiated the debate when he offered to the House for its approval a preamble comprising the "great principles on which the Government is founded."[90] These principles included the right of protection from foreign enemies, the right of domestic tranquility, the right to a perpetual union and the right of the people to expect their government to "promote their common interests."[91] Concluding the preamble, Lee stated that "all these great objects will be best effected by establishing the seat of Government in a station as nearly central as a convenient water communication with the Atlantic ocean, and an easy access to the Western Territory will permit."[92] After a few members, including Thomas Tudor Tucker of South Carolina, voiced their opposition to the preamble as being unnecessary and too constraining, Lee decided to spell out the issue before the House in no uncertain terms:

> The question is to be settled which must determine, whether this Government is to exist for ages, or be dispersed among contending winds. Will gentlemen say these principles ought not to be recognised? Will gentlemen say, that the centre of Government should not be the centre of the Union? Shall it not be a

situation which will admit of an easy communication to the ocean? Will they say, that our Western brethren are to be disregarded? These are the momentous considerations which lead the House to a conclusion. If they are regarded, it will be an alarming circumstance to the people of the Southern States. They have felt these alarms already. It was with difficulty, on another occasion, that their apprehensions on this score were quieted. If this question is decided, without regarding these interests, it will be said, that a Congress is found, who are not disposed to recognize the general principles of the Government. I have come forward with such explicit propositions as the interest of my country dictates.[93]

Lee's words, however, failed to move many of his fellow House members. Although agreeing that "the subject was important, and ought to be decided on fixed and acknowledged principles," Joshua Seney of Maryland believed that the motion already before the House sufficiently safeguarded these cherished rights.[94] On 27 August, Thomas Scott of Pennsylvania had moved that the permanent residence of the national government be conveniently located "as near the centre of wealth, population, and extent of territory" as possible and yet convenient to Atlantic shipping and "having due regard to the particular situation of the Western country."[95] Like Seney, South Carolinian William L. Smith, one of two William Smiths in the First Congress, also objected to the resolution. Calling it an unnecessary "preamble to a preamble," Smith stated that "he did not believe that the events of fixing the seat of government could have the dangerous consequence which alarmed the gentlemen [Lee], of rending the union in pieces."[96] Although he might have felt alone, Lee did have his supporters in the South. Rallying to Lee's defense, Marylander Michael Jenifer Stone argued that the resolution was harmless. "If the principles were just," he remarked, "there was no reason to fear that the extension of them would lead to any improper decision."[97] Likewise, Madison believed the contents of the proposition to be "substantial truths," which "ought to govern our decision on this question."[98] Yet, despite their pleas to reason, Lee's supporters failed to persuade most of their fellow House members, resulting in the defeat of the preamble by a vote of 17 to 34.[99]

With their task now more difficult, most southerners in Congress refused to abandon quietly their position on a central location for the permanent capital. Georgia congressman James Jackson, who would later lead the successful effort to repeal the Yazoo Act in his state's legislature, began the assault against a site on the northerly located Susquehanna River, which Massachusetts congressman Benjamin Goodhue suggested. "I was originally opposed to the question coming forward, and am so still," he told his colleagues.[100] A decision now, he believed, would be inappropriate. Pointing to his home state, he predicted that on the pacification of the Indians, "Georgia will soon be as populous as any State in the Union" and that "calculations ought not to be made on its present situation."[101] Continuing, he reminded his colleagues of the precarious relationship existing between North Carolina and the United States. With North Carolina residents choosing to remain outside the present union of states, Congress needed to avoid any action that might offend the North Carolinians. The selection of a permanent capital at this time, Jackson warned, "may give umbrage to her" and prevent North Carolina from eventually joining the Union.[102] Madison also cautioned delay. "I hope," he remarked, "there is no desire among the gentlemen who have made up their minds on this subject, a subject admitting as great a variety of considerations as any subject that has or can come before us," to bring it to a vote "in a few hours after it has been disclosed."[103] Noting that certain claims regarding the Potomac River "were not well founded," Madison joined his southern colleagues in asking for time to erase the incorrect impressions lodged in the minds of their fellow lawmakers.[104] "I venture to pledge myself for the demonstration, that the communication with the Western Country, by the Potomac, is more certain and convenient than the other," he declared.[105]

In addition to the problem of incorrect information, southerners believed that they saw in the movement to place the seat of government on the Susquehanna River evidence of yet another example of the northern states using their dominant position in the Union to undermine southern interests. Remarking that the House was about to embark on "a step that was not generally liked," Michael J. Stone of Maryland asked his fellow members to "decide the question on more national principles than they seemed yet to be governed by."[106] Thomas Sumter of South Carolina joined Stone in asking the House to discard its sectional biases.[107] Sumter, who actually saw nothing terribly wrong with leaving the capital in New York, hoped that the House would decide the issue in a "way most likely to promote the general interests and harmony of the Union."[108] Jackson, already in a fiery mood, saw no need to mince words in his description of the crisis facing the South. "I am sorry," he stormed, "that the people should learn that . . . the members from New England and New York had fixed on a seat of Government for the United States."[109] "This is not proper language to go out to freemen," he told his audience.[110] He declared:

> Jealousies have already gone abroad. This language will blow the coals of sedition, and endanger the Union. I would ask, if the other members of the Union are not also to be consulted? Are the eastern members to dictate in this business, and fix the seat of Government of the United States? Why not also fix the principles of Government? Why not come forward, and demand of us the power of Legislation, and say, give us up your privileges, and we will govern you? If one part has the power to fix the seat of Government, they may as well take the Government from the other.[111]

With tempers running high, Stone tried to frame the issue in a less confrontational manner. "In fixing the permanent residence," he told the House, "we ought not only to have in view the immediate importance of the States, but also what is likely to be their weight at a future day."[112] "I infer, that the climate, and means of subsistence, will ever operate as a stimulus to promote the population of the Southern, in preference to the Northern States."[113] Continuing, he reflected on how each passing day supported his conclusion: "If we advert to the situation of that part of the western country, called Kentucky, and compare its increase of population since the war, with any part of the eastern States, we shall find men multiplied there beyond any thing known in America."[114] With such a rapidly expanding population, Stone believed that the federal government "should take a position favorable to its convenience."[115] Discounting Spanish intrigues in the West, Stone cautioned his colleagues against adopting a site that could not retain the westerners' allegiance to the Union. The abundant natural resources of the West, he pointed out, allowed people who were "generally bold, enterprising spirits" and who disdained "strict government" from forming a close relationship with all the Atlantic states.[116] "Their interests are more strongly connected with the Southern States than the Southern States are with the Eastern," he told the House.[117] Forming his words into a thinly veiled threat, Stone concluded:

> The advantages of this Government are felt, in a peculiar manner, by the mercantile and commercial States; the agricultural States have not the same strong reasons for maintaining the Union. Hence we may apprehend that the Western Country may be inclined, as it advances its importance, to drop off. The Susquehanna is no bond by which to hold them.[118]

Richard Bland Lee next rose to address the members of the House. The issue, he informed his colleagues, was not merely the location of a permanent site for the capital, it was "whether this Government was intended for a temporary or a lasting one."[119] If the northern states intended the Union to remain forever, the federal government must "be removed to the Potomac," he stated.[120] Lee further reminded his listeners of the difficult time Federalists in Virginia had in adopting the Constitution amid Antifederalist charges of "confederacies of the States east of Pennsylvania."[121] This decision to remove the seat to a site on the Susquehanna River would, he believed, cause those people living south of the Potomac River to lose faith in the government. Attesting to the validity of Lee's statement, Madison noted "that if a Prophet had risen in that body [the Virginia ratifying convention], and brought the declarations and proceedings of this day into view, that I as firmly believe Virginia might not have been a part of the Union at this moment."[122]

Throughout the debate, southern members wondered aloud why representatives from the northern states wanted to rush the House into voting on the measure to place the capital. "What was the conduct of gentlemen?" queried Aedanus Burke of South Carolina.[123] "A league has been formed between the Northern States and Pennsylvania," he cried.[124] Madison expressed a hope that "nothing will be fixed by a hasty determination. I said before, and repeat again, that I wish to make some observations on what has been advanced, for which at present there is not time."[125] Southerners won a minor victory on this point. Shortly after the conclusion of Madison's speech for more time, the House adjourned for the evening without voting on the permanent site.

On Thursday, 4 September, the House reconvened and immediately resumed its debate on the location of the seat of government. Madison was the first, and the principal, speaker from the South. Attempting to redefine the issue, Madison expressed the wish "that all would concur in the great principle on which they ought to conduct and decide this business; an equal attention to the rights of the community."[126] These rights, Madison stated, composed "the basis" of a republican form of government.[127] "No government," Madison told his colleagues, "not even the most despotic, could, beyond a certain point, violate that idea of justice and equal right which prevailed in the mind of the community."[128] Although failing to specify these rights, Madison noted "that there is no one right, on which the people can judge with more jealousy, than of the establishment of the permanent seat of Government."[129] "If the seat of Government," he predicted, "should be fixed on the Susquehanna, every part south of that river, and every part of the United States south of the Ohio, will conceive that the great principles of equal justice have been disregarded."[130] A simple vote, he told the House, would not end the controversy if the majority of the members decided to proceed as they had planned and fix the seat of government on the Susquehanna River. As the West filled with people and as the population center of the nation continued to move west, Madison warned "the cause of discontent [will] continually increase."[131]

Despite the valiant efforts of the Potomac supporters, a majority of the members of the House remained determined to place the national capital on the Susquehanna River. Madison's motion on 4 September to add the words "or Potomac" to the resolution naming the Susquehanna River as the permanent site "passed in the negative."[132] Undaunted, southerners on 7 September resumed their fight with Lee of Virginia moving that the words "North bank of the River Potomac, in the State of Maryland" replace the words "East Bank of the River Susquehanna, in the State of Pennsylvania."[133] The motion failed to carry, receiving twenty of twenty-two southern votes cast, with John Vining of Delaware casting the only northern vote for the amendment. Joshua Seney and William Smith, both from Maryland, voted against the motion.[134] During the debates, Seney had expressed support for the Susquehanna River since its waters touched his state, a situation that would benefit Maryland and its residents.[135] However, before the House cast the final vote on the location of the seat of government, the South managed a minor victory. Michael J. Stone moved that the word "banks" replace the words "right bank" of the Susquehanna River.[136] The motion passed by only one vote, 26 to 25.[137] For some unknown reason, Stone was the lone southerner voting against the motion. Finally, after four days of maneuvering, the House passed the resolution instructing the president to appoint three commissioners to locate a site for the capital on the "banks of the Susquehanna" in the state of Pennsylvania.[138] Again, the only break in the southern phalanx came from Maryland, where just four representatives, George Gale, Joshua Seney, William Smith, and Michael J. Stone, voted for the measure.[139]

Throughout the debate, southerners followed the proceedings of Congress with great interest. From his Potomac plantation home, Henry Lee, who had risen to fame during the American Revolution as "Light Horse Harry" Lee, remarked that those southerners heading west to settle "consider the fixture of the imperial city on the northern banks of the potomac indubitable."[140] The Potomac River provided the necessary link between the West and the Atlantic states and also the reason why some southerners decided to move west. Though many southerners had dreams of settling on the western side of the Appalachian Mountains, they were apprehensive because "the country of their choice was by nature severed from the country of their birth."[141] The Potomac River calmed their fears, providing a feeling of security by establishing an easy means of communication between regions. If westerners should happen to view an act of Congress as a threat to this vital link or sense any hostile feelings from Congress regarding the West, Lee foresaw trouble. The failure of Congress, he said, to place the seat of government on the Potomac River would cause westerners to become filled "with passion indicative of disagreeable consequences to our peace[,] unity & harmony."[142] "In the present unsettled state of the foederal govt.," he told Madison,

> danger is to be apprehended from a decision of the question concerning the permanent seat. Better would it be in my mind to wait a little longer, let the influence & good of the new constitution be felt among the people & let the edge of opposition be blunted. No injury can result from delay, & much mischeif may be done by precipitation.[143]

The tone of Lee's remarks reverberated across Virginia, as Virginians reacted angrily to what they deemed as a "premature" act on the part of Congress.[144] Adam Stephen of Berkeley County, Virginia, warned the House not to ignore the West. "The Western Country," he noted, "is daily moving into greater importance, and . . . in time it will give Law to America."[145] Petitioners from Alexandria and Georgetown reminded northern congressmen that "the safety of all the Atlantic States" required that the commercial inter-course between the two regions continue or "their [the West's] independence and separation from the Union would beget connections highly dangerous to our existence."[146] The insistence on the part of Virginians that Congress take into consideration the future needs of the West stemmed obviously from the expected political gains they hoped would accrue from the shift in the popu-lation center of the nation. They also based their position on a deeply held sense of justice, however. Writing to his son-in-law Charles Lee, Richard Henry Lee wailed against the political "intrigue" surrounding the question of the location of the capital.[147] Political influence, he cried, "will so manage to procure the final issue to be different from what is right."[148] For Adam Stephen, the issue was a test of the impartiality and fairness of the Union. "In the discussion of this Affair," he wrote, "we shall discover whether our Confederacy is well or ill Combined."[149] The "General Interests of the rising empire," he concluded, must have weight in the debate.[150]

With the debate on the resolution at an end in the House, Madison and his fellow southerners prepared themselves for the next battle—the passage of the bill placing the capital on the Susquehanna River. Although confident that the friends of the Potomac could "parry any decision," Madison knew that their actions merely delayed the inevitable.[151] "I see," he told Pendleton, "little hope of attaining our own object, the Eastern States being inflexibly opposed to the Potowmac & for some reasons which are more likely to grow stronger than weaker."[152] The sense of helplessness that had overcome Madi-son had also taken hold of his southern colleagues. The forlorn tone of Madison's words soon found expression in the voices of southerners on the floor of the House when, in late September, the House returned to the ques-tion of the permanent seat of government.

The bill enacting the resolution that the House had passed a few weeks earlier called for the permanent seat of government to be established on the Susquehanna River. Immediately, George Gale of Maryland offered an amendment that, in part, would have required the president to "be satisfied" that the river was navigable from the proposed site of the permanent capital to its mouth before the act became final.[153] No fiery speeches in support of Gale's motion came from southern members. Instead, they called the motion "proper" and "reasonable" and held that the House should adopt it.[154] Why, asked James Jackson, should the federal government commit itself to remove permanently to a site that might make it "secluded from the world and totally cut off from a water communication with the Atlantic?"[155] "It would be prudent," he told members, if the federal government could avoid this pos-sible problem "when they had it in their power to make their own terms."[156] Their arguments, however, failed to persuade a majority of the members in the House, which only voted to require Maryland and Pennsylvania to enact legislation providing for the removal of any "obstructions" found in the river. [157]

When the House returned to the subject four days later, Madison objected to the bill on constitutional grounds. Besides locating the seat of government on the Susquehanna River, the bill authorized Congress to adjourn and reconvene at New York, thus allowing New York to remain the temporary capital. Angered by this new and more subtle maneuver on the part of northern members, Madison informed the House that he had been prepared to accept the Susquehanna River as the site of the permanent capital, [158] for, as he had earlier expressed his views to Edmund Pendleton, "if we are to be placed on the Susquehannah, the sooner the better." [159] What caused Madison to regain some of his former fire was the "irreconcilable" way in which the bill violated "the spirit of the constitution." [160] Congress could not, he declared, permit the president to decide on the question of adjournment. "Any attempt," he told his fellow members, "to adjourn by law, is a violation of that part of the constitution which gives the power [to adjourn and where to adjourn], exclusively, to the two branches of the legislature." [161]

Southerners, however, failed to rally around Madison. Daniel Carroll of Maryland supported Madison and, because of his oath to uphold the Constitution, found himself "under the disagreeable necessity of giving my [Carroll's] dissent to the bill." [162] Most southerners reacted as James Jackson of Georgia did. During the debate on the resolution he had been a vocal supporter of the need for a central location for the permanent seat of government. Now, "he would acquiesce in the decision of the House, conceiving it to be the voice of his country." [163] When the vote came on 22 September, seven southerners—five Marylanders and two Georgians—joined their northern colleagues and voted for the bill. [164] Madison, who voted against the bill, saw the southern defections as an example of the growing "despair" among members who fear of "ever getting any thing better." [165] "My own judgment," he told Edmund Pendleton, "was opposed to any compromise, on the supposition that we had nothing worse to fear than the Susquehannah and could obtain that at any time, either by uniting with the Eastern States, or Pennsylva." [166] Besides, as Madison reminded Pendleton, the bill "is by no means sure of passing the Senate in its present form." [167] Opponents of the measure, he believed, might work "directly or indirectly" to defeat the bill. [168] "In the case of an indirect mode," he predicted that "some other place, will be substituted for Susquehannah, as Trenton or Germantown, neither of which can I conceive be effectively established." [169] Despite his words to the contrary, Madison conceded that "either . . . might get a majority, composed of sincere and insidious votes." [170]

When the Susquehanna bill arrived in the Senate, it received a barrage of attacks from southern senators, including William Grayson and Richard Henry Lee of Virginia, Pierce Butler and Ralph Izard of South Carolina and

..es Gunn of Georgia. Butler immediately moved that the bill be postponed until the next session. Despite the support of his southern colleagues, Butler's motion failed, and the Senate spent four days debating the bill.[171] When the Senate substituted Germantown, Pennsylvania, for a site on the Susquehanna River,[172] Butler became incensed and launched into a personal tirade against Robert Morris of Pennsylvania, author of the amendment.[173] Despite the southerners' efforts, the Senate accepted Morris's amendment by a vote of ten to seven, with all seven southern senators present voting against it on final passage.[174]

When the bill returned to the House on 26 September with the changes, southern congressmen openly declared their opposition to it. Theodorick Bland of Virginia, the first to respond, considered the bill "so materially changed as to warrant the House to postpone its consideration."[175] Postponement was not enough for William L. Smith of South Carolina. He wanted the House to table the bill and avoid an act "injurious to the public interest."[176] Richard Bland Lee, who also urged postponement, believed the bill violated the resolutions that the House had worked so hard drafting.[177] Jackson resented the Senate telling the House that Germantown was "the most proper spot that can be selected."[178] He believed "an alteration in the sentiment of the House, on this ground, would excite serious alarm in the minds of the people; to avoid which consequence;" he likewise moved that the House postpone consideration of the bill.[179] The motion lost by a vote of 25 to 29, with all twenty-three southerners present voting for it.[180]

With time running out in the session, the task of derailing the bill fell to Madison. On Monday, 28 September, the day before Congress adjourned, Madison reminded the House that once Pennsylvania ceded the ten square miles to the United States, Pennsylvania law would cease to function within the boundaries of the district, a situation that, if the land were without occupants, would cause no problems. The proposed area of cession was inhabited, however, and the elimination of civil government in the district might create anarchy. Thus, Madison proposed an amendment declaring "that nothing herein contained shall be construed to affect the operation of the laws of Pennsylvania, within the district ceded and accepted, until Congress shall otherwise provide by law."[181] The tactic worked. A few hours after its passage, the House received word that the Senate had postponed consideration of the amendment until the next session.[182]

The episode left many southerners guardedly optimistic. John Dawson, a long-time friend of Madison who would represent Virginia in the House of Representatives, had anticipated southern maneuvers in the Senate and the eventual outcome in the House. Believing the South had chosen "the best course it could take," he predicted that with the help of North Carolina, which would ratify the Constitution in late November, success was "at a day not far distant."[183] Madison, however, was less sanguine. "I am extremely afraid that the hopes of the Potomac do not rest on so good a foundation as we wish," he told Henry Lee.[184] The episode, he thought, revealed "the antipathy of the Eastern people to the south-western position."[185] Because of this northern revulsion at a southern site for the permanent capital, Madison expected northern representatives to offer daily reasons why the site should remain in their "neighborhood."[186] The only chance the South had, Madison believed, was if "some arrangement with Pennsylvania" could be made during Washington's tenure in office.[187] Confessing to Lee that he was determined not to compromise until all "remaining effort of prudence shall be exhausted," Madison admitted "that some limits as to time must be set to the struggle for what is perfectly right."[188] In the utmost confidence, he revealed to Lee:

> I am extremely alarmed for the Western Country. I have within a few days seen fresh and striking proofs of its ticklish situation. Mr. Brown thinks that the susquehanah would for the present satisfy them on the subject of the seat of Government—and in his own judgement, prefers it to delay. There are others even from Virginia who could with difficulty be prevailed on to contend for the Potomac, with so little chance of success—and against the danger of plans which would be fatal to the harmony, if not the existence of the Union. Several of the more Southern Members tho attached to the object of Virginia, do not view the rival of it, precisely with her eyes. I make these remarks for yourself alone, and to prepare you for a disappointment which I hold to be very possible, but which I shall certainly be among the last to concur in.[189]

During the adjournment of Congress, some southerners continued to think about ways of getting the capital on the Potomac. Daniel Carroll of Maryland thought perhaps a few published papers on the subject would gain public support for the Potomac site.[190] William Grayson, who would die before the South achieved its ultimate goal, concurred with Carroll. "It is clear to me," he told Madison, "that our contest about the Potowmack has been of infinite consequence; she is gaining friends daily, by being brought into view; & I agree with you that we played a great game & staked nothing."[191] In November, Madison outlined to Washington a possible scenario of how Congress would finally resolve the question of the permanent seat:

> An attempt will first be made to alarm N. York and the Eastern States into the plan postponed, by holding the Potowmac & Philada. as the alternative, and if the attempt should not succeed, the alternative will then be held out to the Southern members. On the other hand N.Y. & the E. States, will enforce their policy of delay, by threatening the S. States as heretofore, with German Town or Trenton or at least Susquehannah, and will no doubt carry the threat into execution if they can, rather than suffer an arrangement to take place between Pena & the S. States.[192]

Although Congress reassembled in January 1790, it was several months before the question of the permanent seat of government came before the House. Alexander Hamilton's fiscal policies were the dominant issues for Congress during these intervening months. The opposition that they sparked in the South caused some people, including Henry Lee of Virginia, to believe that the only relief for the South was placing the capital on the Potomac "or we southern people must be slaves in effect, or cut the Gordian knot at once."[193] Perhaps not slaves, but Edward Carrington felt the impotency of the South in national affairs when he expressed his belief that the permanent site would "be placed at the pleasure of Pensylva."[194]

Finally, in May, the issue came before the House. Thomas Fitzsimons of Pennsylvania promptly moved that Congress hold its next session at Philadelphia.[195] Surprisingly, it passed the House with relative ease.[196] Madison, however, remained distrustful of northern congressmen and continued to hold out little hope for the Potomac site.[197] On 11 June, three days after the Senate rejected the House resolution, the House again voted to adjourn to another city.[198] This time members selected Baltimore.[199] Despite this fortuitous move for the South, Madison still considered the chances of a Potomac victory slim.[200] Before the Senate voted on the measure, however, a meeting between Madison and Hamilton at a dinner hosted by Thomas Jefferson helped southerners achieve their ultimate goal.

Although it is conjecture to what actually transpired between Madison and Hamilton at Jefferson's dinner party on 15 June, it is certain that Madison emerged from the meeting still doubting that the South would finally achieve what it had sought for so long—the permanent seat of government on the Potomac River.[201] Two days later, however, these doubts seemed less pronounced. On 17 June, he told Monroe, "It is not improbable that the permanent seat may be coupled with the temporary one. The Potowmac stands a bad chance, and yet it is not impossible that in the vicissitudes of the business it may turn up in some form or other."[202] To Edmund Pendleton, he remarked: "If any arrangement should be made that will answer our wishes, it will be the effect of a coincidence of causes as fortuitous as it will be propitious."[203]

The Senate, in the weeks before the House bill arrived, had been busy trying to reach an agreement on its own version of a bill. The particular bill under Senate consideration emerged from a meeting between Pierce Butler of South Carolina and Rufus King of New York, who agreed that the permanent location of the capital should be on the Potomac River and the temporary location at New York.[204] Butler presented the deal to the Senate in the form of a bill with the names of the two sites left blank.[205] While the Senate was in the middle of debating how the blanks should be filled, the House bill arrived.[206] After first agreeing to its postponement for two weeks, the Senate took up the Baltimore bill on 28 June and again postponed a decision, allowing the final intrigue to begin.[207]

During the intervening two weeks, Pennsylvania, Delaware, Virginia, and Maryland entered into an agreement on the location of the permanent and temporary capitals. As part of this intrigue, most of the members of the Pennsylvania delegation approved on 24 June a plan "'to place the permanent Residence on the Potowmack, and the temporary residence to remain 10 Years in Philada.'"[208] The next day, Charles Carroll of Carrollton informed his Pennsylvanian colleague William Maclay that the plan "was to take Butler's bill, amended so that" their aims would be achieved.[209]

The plan went into operation following the vote on the House bill. While Carroll was in the middle of offering an amendment, Ralph Izard of South Carolina moved that New York be the site of the temporary residence. A heated debate ensued, culminating in a vote on Izard's motion, which passed thirteen to twelve.[210] The next day, the Senate took up the length of time that the capital should remain in New York. After agreeing that it should remain at the temporary site for only ten years, the Senate voted on the entire clause for the temporary residence, rejecting it by a vote of nine to sixteen.[211] Carroll immediately moved that the clause read ten years at Philadelphia but failed in his motion for lack of support.[212]

On 30 June, Carroll employed a new strategy: he tried to get the bill passed to a third reading without the temporary residency clause. He failed. Maclay believed that the Maryland senator's maneuvering was nothing more than a blatant attempt to double cross him and his fellow Pennsylvanians. Following his setback, Carroll asked the Senate to reconsider the Philadelphia motion of the previous day, but Vice President John Adams ruled him out of order. Under the gentle prodding of Maclay, Butler, who happened to support New York in the matter, moved that the bill containing the Philadelphia clause pass to a third reading.[213] However, before the Senate could vote on the motion, supporters of New York, including Butler, nearly succeeded in gaining a two-year stay for the capital in their town.[214] The Senate tied thirteen to thirteen on a motion to allow the capital to stay in New York for two years.[215] After speaking for a long time "on the decent behaviour of the citizens of New York," Vice President Adams cast his tie-breaking vote against the motion.[216] Finally, the Senate voted on Butler's motion, passing it by a vote of fourteen to twelve, with Butler voting for the motion. Now, the bill faced its third reading. With the senator from South Carolina casting the deciding vote, the Senate passed the bill by a vote of fourteen to twelve.[217] Butler remained silent as to why he voted for Philadelphia when he truly favored New York, but his biographer believed that he did it for fear of the South losing the Potomac if the issue of the permanent capital continued unresolved much longer.[218] Butler's colleague in the House, William L. Smith, was not so kind in his assessment of the situation, attributing the

South Carolina senator's actions to a perceived slight by the New Yorkers or a desire to "shew his power or his independe. [independence] in differing from his Colleagues."[219]

On 2 July, the House received word of the passage of the bill in the Senate.[220] During the short debate that followed, Madison was the only member to address himself to the western implications of the legislation, commenting that a site along the Potomac dwarfed even Baltimore as the most desirable location.[221] With the House clearly having exhausted the issues during its first session, members concerned themselves with supporting or opposing the bill. After several failed attempts to change the location from the Potomac, the House passed the bill on 9 July by a vote of 32 to 29. Only five southerners broke rank and voted against the bill: Aedanus Burke, William L. Smith, and Thomas Tudor Tucker of South Carolina and Joshua Seney and William Smith of Maryland.[222] The South Carolinians had supported New York in the contest and were extremely angry at Butler for his Philadelphia vote.[223] The two Marylanders had desired a site on the Susquehanna River during the debates and, perhaps, still believed that it was the best choice. Nevertheless, when all was said and done, the South, with the help of Pennsylvania, had won the battle.

NOTES

1. James Madison to George Washington, 25 June 1788, in *The Papers of James Madison*, eds. William T. Hutchinson, William M. E. Rachal et al. (Chicago: The University of Chicago Press; Charlottesville: University of Virginia Press, 1977), 11:178.
2. Madison to James Madison, Sr., 27 July 1788, in Ibid., 11:208.
3. Madison to George Washington, 11 August 1788, in Ibid., 11:229.
4. Madison to Edmund Randolph, 2 August 1788, in *Letters of Delegates to Congress*, eds. Paul H. Smith et al. (Washington, DC: Library of Congress, 2000), 25:268.
5. Madison to Randolph, 22 August 1788, in Ibid., 25:314.
6. Madison to Thomas Jefferson, 23 August 1788, in Hutchinson et al., *Madison Papers*, 11:239.
7. Ibid.
8. Ibid.
9. Charles Thomson to Samuel McDowell, 3 July 1788, in Smith et al., *Letters of Delegates*, 25:211.
10. James White to Samuel Johnston, 21 April 1788, in Ibid., 25:68.
11. Randolph to Madison, 27 July 1788, in Hutchinson et al., *Madison Papers*, 11:209.
12. James White to Samuel Johnston, 21 April 1788, in Smith et al., *Letters of Delegates*, 25:68.
13. Madison to Randolph, 14 September 1788, in Hutchinson et al., *Madison Papers*, 11:253.
14. *Journals of the Continental Congress, 1774–1789*, eds. Worthington C. Ford et al. (Washington, DC: Government Printing Office, 1937), 34:515.
15. Ibid.; Madison to Randolph, 14 September 1788, in Hutchinson et al., *Madison Papers*, 11:253.
16. Madison to Randolph, 11 August 1788, in Hutchinson et al., *Madison Papers*, 11:228.
17. Madison to George Washington, 24 August 1788, in Ibid., 11:241.
18. Ibid.

19. Ibid.
20. Ibid.
21. Ibid.
22. Ibid.
23. Madison to Madison, Sr., 6 September 1788, in Ibid., 11:248.
24. Ibid.
25. Madison to Randolph, 14 September 1788, in Ibid., 11:253.
26. Ibid.
27. Ibid.
28. Madison to Washington, 11 August 1788, in Ibid., 11:229. Madison expresses similar sentiments to Jefferson. See Madison to Jefferson, 21 September 1788, in Ibid., 11:258.
29. Madison to Washington, 11 August 1788, in Ibid., 11:229.
30. Madison to Washington, 24 August 1788, in Ibid., 11:242.
31. Ibid.
32. Pendleton to Madison, [6 October 1788], in Ibid., 11:275.
33. Ibid.
34. Ibid.
35. *Annapolis Maryland Gazette*, 27 March 1788.
36. Ibid.
37. Editorial note in Hutchinson et al., *Madison Papers*, 11:263.
38. Hugh Williamson to Samuel Johnston, 26 May 1788, in *The State Records of North Carolina*, ed. Walter Clark (Goldsboro, NC: Nash Brothers, Printers, 1907), 21:475.
39. Ibid.
40. "Mr. Jay's Report," 2 September 1788, in United States Department of State, *The Diplomatic Correspondence of the United States of America, from the Signing of the Definitive Treaty of Peace, September 10, 1783, to the Adoption of the Constitution, March 4, 1789. Being the Letters of the Presidents of Congress, the Secretary of Foreign Affairs—American Ministers at Foreign Courts, Foreign Ministers near Congress—Reports of Committees of Congress, and Reports of the Secretary of Foreign Affairs on Various Letters and Communications; Together with Letters from Individuals on Public Affairs* (Washington, DC: Printed by Francis Preston Blair, 1833), 6:253.
41. *Journals of the Continental Congress*, 34:319. Also see Hugh Williamson to Samuel Johnston, 17 September 1788, in Smith et al., *Letters of Delegates*, 25:376.
42. Hutchinson et al., *Madison Papers*, 11:267.
43. Ibid., 11:266–67.
44. Ibid., 11:267.
45. Ibid. Madison reported that upon the congressional passage of the resolutions, Gardoqui considered his mission finished and planned to return to Spain. See Madison to Monroe, 5 November 1788, in Ibid., 11:333.
46. James Monroe to Madison, 26 October 1788, in Ibid., 11:317.
47. Ibid., 11:318.
48. Madison to Washington, 26 September 1788, in Ibid., 11:267.
49. Madison to John Brown, 26 September 1788, in Ibid., 11:266.
50. Jefferson to Madison, 12 January 1789, in *The Papers of Thomas Jefferson*, ed. Julian P. Boyd (Princeton: Princeton University Press, 1958), 14:436.
51. Madison to Brown, 26 September 1788, in Hutchinson et al. *Madison Papers*, 11:266.
52. Pendleton to Madison, 6 October 1788, in *The Letters and Papers of Edmund Pendleton, 1734–1803*, ed. David John Mays (Charlottesville: Published for the Virginia Historical Society by the University Press of Virginia, 1967), 2:546.
53. Ibid.
54. Ibid.
55. Hugh Williamson to Samuel Johnston, 17 September 1788, in Smith et al., *Letters of Delegates*, 25:377.
56. Ibid.

57.   William Blount, Benjamin Hawkins and John B. Ashe to Richard Caswell, 18 April 1787, in *The State Records of North Carolina*, ed. Walter Clark (Goldsboro, NC: Nash Brothers, Book and Job Printers, 1902), 20:677.

58.   Ibid.

59.   Ibid.

60.   Madison to Edmund Pendleton, 20 October 1788, in Hutchinson et al., *Madison Papers*, 11:306.

61.   The lack of a quorum in both houses of Congress postponed the convening of the House of Representatives until 1 April and the Senate until 6 April. George Washington took the oath of office on 30 April. For this first election to Congress, candidates did not align with any political party or faction. For the most part, local concerns and individuals dominated these elections. The labels "Federalist" and "Antifederalist," however, provided an important way by which voters could differentiate the candidates for office. John F. Hoadley, "The Emergence of Political Parties in Congress, 1789–1803," in Lance Banning, ed., *After the Constitution: Party Conflict in the New Republic* (Belmont: California: Wadsworth Publishing Company, 1989), 65.

62.   *Edenton State Gazette of North Carolina*, 26 September 1789.

63.   Ibid.

64.   Ibid.

65.   North Carolina did not ratify the Constitution until 21 November 1789, two months after Congress submitted twelve constitutional amendments to the states for ratification. The lack of a bill of rights had been a major stumbling block in the state's first attempt to ratify in 1788. Forrest McDonald, *We The People: The Economic Origins of the Constitution* (Chicago: University of Chicago Press, 1958), 310–12.

66.   For an overview of Morgan's efforts see William E. Foley, *The Genesis of Missouri: From Wilderness Outpost to Statehood* (Columbia: University of Missouri Press, 1989), 61–63, and Jay Feldman, *When the Mississippi Ran Backwards: Empire, Intrigue, Murder, and the New Madrid Earthquakes* (New York: Free Press, 2005), 26–57 passim.

67.   Madison to Monroe, 5 November 1788, in Hutchinson et al., *Madison Papers*, 11:333.

68.   Ibid.

69.   John Dawson to Madison, 6 January 1789, in Ibid., 11:410.

70.   Ibid.

71.   Dawson to Beverly Randolph, 29 January 1789, *Calendar of Virginia State Papers and Other Manuscripts, From January 1, 1785, to July 2, 1789, Preserved at the Capitol at Richmond*, ed. William P. Palmer et al. (Richmond: R. U. Derr, Superintendent of Public Printing, 1884; reprint, New York: Kraus Reprint Corp. 1968), 4:555.

72.   Ibid.

73.   Madison to Washington, 8 March 1789, in *The Papers of James Madison*, eds. William T. Hutchinson, William M. E. Rachal et al. (Chicago: The University of Chicago Press; Charlottesville: University of Virginia Press, 1979), 12:6.

74.   Madison to Jefferson, 29 March 1789, in Ibid., 12:39.

75.   Samuel Johnston to Daniel Smith, 31 August 1789, in Clark, *State Records of North Carolina*, 21:561.

76.   Ibid.

77.   Ibid., 21:562.

78.   Madison to Jefferson, 29 March 1789, in *The Papers of Thomas Jefferson*, ed. Julian P. Boyd (Princeton: Princeton University Press, 1958), 15:7.

79.   Ibid.

80.   John Stode to Madison, 20 June 1789, in Hutchinson et al., *Madison Papers*, 12:246.

81.   Ibid.

82.   Ibid.

83.   Jefferson to Lewis Littlepage, 8 May 1789, in Boyd et al., *Jefferson Papers*, 15:106.

84.   Benjamin Hawkins to Madison, 27 August 1789, in Hutchinson et al., *Madison Papers*, 12:359. Morgan abandoned his enterprise at New Madrid for several reasons. First, Spain denied him the right to sell land and instead freely granted it to settlers. Second, he worried that Spain would open the Mississippi River to American commerce, eliminating any reason why

Americans would want to migrate to Spanish territory and consequently frustrating his attempts to establish a lucrative agricultural trade with New Orleans. Finally, he hoped to secure a land grant from the new American government being installed in New York in 1789. See Feldman, *When the Mississippi Ran Backwards*, 56.

85.   Madison to George Nicholas, 5 July 1789, in Hutchinson et al., *Madison Papers*, 12:280.

86.   Dawson to Madison, 28 June 1789, in Ibid., 12:264.

87.   Ibid.; *The Documentary History of the Ratification of the Constitution*, eds. John P. Kaminski and Gaspare J. Saladino (Madison: State Historical Society of Wisconsin, 1993), 10:1554.

88.   Dawson to Madison, 28 June 1789, in Hutchinson et al., *Madison Papers*, 12:264.

89.   *Annals of Congress*, 1st Cong., 1st Sess., 868.

90.   Ibid., 868.

91.   Ibid.

92.   Ibid., 868–69.

93.   Ibid., 871.

94.   Ibid., 872.

95.   Ibid., 816.

96.   *Debates in the House of Representatives: First Session, June–September 1789*, vol. 11 of *The Documentary History of the First Federal Congress of the United States of America, 4 March 1789–3 March 1791*, eds. Charlene Bangs Bickford, Kenneth R. Bowling, and Helen E. Veit (Baltimore and London: The Johns Hopkins University Press, 1992), 11:1403.

97.   *Annals of Congress*, 1st Cong., 1st Sess., 872

98.   Ibid.

99.   Ibid., 873.

100.   Ibid., 877.

101.   Ibid.

102.   Ibid.

103.   Ibid., 882.

104.   Ibid., 883.

105.   Ibid.

106.   Ibid.

107.   Ibid.

108.   Ibid., 884.

109.   Ibid., 877.

110.   Ibid.

111.   Ibid.

112.   Ibid., 886.

113.   Ibid.

114.   Ibid.

115.   Ibid., 887.

116.   Ibid., 887–88.

117.   Ibid., 888.

118.   Ibid.

119.   Ibid., 889.

120.   Ibid.

121.   Ibid.

122.   Ibid., 890.

123.   Ibid., 891.

124.   Ibid.

125.   Ibid.

126.   Ibid., 894.

127.   Ibid.

128.   Ibid.

129.   Ibid.

130.   Ibid., 900.

131. Ibid., 901.
132. Ibid., 908.
133. Ibid., 915.
134. Ibid.
135. Ibid., 884, 914.
136. Ibid., 918.
137. Ibid.
138. Ibid., 919–20.
139. Ibid., 920.
140. Henry Lee to Madison, 8 September 1789, in Hutchinson et al., *Madison Papers*, 12:389.
141. Ibid., 12:388.
142. Ibid., 12:389.
143. Ibid.
144. Adam Stephen to Madison, 12 September 1789, in Ibid., 12:398.
145. Ibid.
146. "Broadside from Alexandria and Georgetown Residents, July 6, 1790," in *Legislative Histories: Mitigation of Fines Bill [HR-38] through Resolution on Unclaimed Western Lands*, vol. 6 of *Documentary History of the First Federal Congress of the United States of America, March 4, 1789–March 3, 1791*, eds. Charlene Bangs Bickford and Helen E. Veit (Baltimore and London: The Johns Hopkins University Press, 1986), 6:1785.
147. Lee to Lee, 28 August 1789, in *Letters of Richard Henry Lee*, ed. James Curtis Ballagh (New York: Macmillan Company, 1914), 2:499.
148. Ibid.
149. Stephen to Madison, 12 September 1789, in Hutchinson et al., *Madison Papers*, 12:399.
150. Ibid.
151. Madison to Pendleton, 14 September 1789, in Ibid., 12:402–3.
152. Ibid., 12:403.
153. *Annals of Congress*, 1st Cong., 1st Sess., 929.
154. Ibid., 930.
155. Ibid., 931.
156. Ibid.
157. Ibid., 929, 932.
158. Ibid., 940.
159. Madison to Pendleton, 14 September 1789, in Hutchinson et al., *Madison Papers*, 12:403.
160. *Annals of Congress*, 1st Cong., 1st. Sess., 940.
161. Ibid.
162. Ibid., 946.
163. Ibid., 945.
164. Ibid., 946.
165. Madison to Pendleton, 23 September 1789, in Hutchinson et al., *Madison Papers*, 12:419.
166. Ibid.
167. Ibid.
168. Ibid.
169. Ibid.
170. Ibid.
171. *The Diary of William Maclay and Other Notes on Senate Debates*, vol. 9 of *Documentary History of the First Federal Congress of the United States of America, 4 March 1789-3 March 1791*, eds. Kenneth R. Bowling and Helen E. Veit (Baltimore and London: The John Hopkins University Press, 1988), 9:156.
172. *Annals of Congress*, 1st Cong., 1st. Sess., 88.
173. *Diary of William Maclay*, 9:156–57; Lewright B. Sikes, *The Public Life of Pierce Butler, South Carolina Statesman* (Washington, DC: Rowman and Littlefield, 1979), 64–65. Apparently, Morris was engaged in several intrigues playing opposing groups against each

other in order ultimately to move the seat of government to either Philadelphia or Germantown, for "these places suit his plans of Commerce," Maclay noted. See *Diary of William Maclay*, 9:146.

174. *Annals of Congress*, 1st Cong., 1st Sess., 91.
175. Ibid., 955.
176. Ibid., 956.
177. Ibid.
178. Ibid., 957.
179. Ibid.
180. Ibid., 958.
181. Ibid., 961.
182. Ibid., 962.
183. John Dawson to Madison, 27 September 1789, in Hutchinson et al., *Madison Papers*, 12:423.
184. Madison to Henry Lee, 4 October 1789, in Ibid., 12:425.
185. Ibid.
186. Ibid., 12:426.
187. Ibid.
188. Ibid.
189. Ibid., 12:426–27.
190. Daniel Carroll to Madison, 4 October 1789, in Ibid., 12:428.
191. William Grayson to Madison, 7 October 1789, in Ibid., 12:432.
192. Madison to Washington, 20 November 1789, in Ibid., 12:452–53.
193. Henry Lee to Madison, 4 March 1789, in *The Papers of James Madison*, eds. William T. Hutchinson, William M. E. Rachal et al. (Chicago: The University of Chicago Press; Charlottesville: University of Virginia Press, 1981), 13:90.
194. Edward Carrington to Madison, 30 April 1790, in Ibid., 13:182.
195. *Annals of Congress*, 1st Cong., 2nd Sess., 1678.
196. Ibid., 1682.
197. Madison to Monroe, 1 June 1790, in Hutchinson et al., *Madison Papers*, 13:234.
198. *Annals of Congress*, 1st Cong., 2nd Sess., 1022.
199. Ibid., 1693.
200. Madison to James Madison, Sr., 13 June 1790, in Hutchinson et al., *Madison Papers*, 13:242.
201. For a discussion of the Compromise of 1790 see Kenneth R. Bowling, "Dinner at Jefferson's: A Note on Jacob E. Cooke's 'The Compromise of 1790,'" *William and Mary Quarterly*, Third Series, 28 (October 1971), 629–48, Jacob E. Cooke, "The Compromise of 1790," *William and Mary Quarterly*, Third Series, 27 (October 1970), 523–45, and "Editorial Note," in Hutchinson et al., *Madison Papers*, 13:243-46.
202. Madison to Monroe, 17 June 1790, in Hutchinson et al., *Madison Papers*, 13:246.
203. Madison to Pendleton, 22 June 1790, in Ibid., 13:252–53.
204. Sikes, *Pierce Butler*, 68. William Loughton Smith notes that both South Carolina senators supported New York City as the site of the temporary residence, although he seems to believe that they preferred Baltimore, not the Potomac River, as the permanent site. William Loughton Smith to Edward Rutledge, 28 June 1790, in *Correspondence: Second Session: 15 March–June 1790*, vol. 19 of *Documentary History of the First Federal Congress of the United States of America, 4 March 1789–3 March 1791*, eds. Charlene Bangs Bickford, Kenneth R. Bowling, Helen E. Veit, and William Charles DiGiacomantonio (Baltimore: The Johns Hopkins Press, 2012), 19:1951.
205. *Annals of Congress*, 1st Cong., 2nd Sess., 1017.
206. Ibid., 1025.
207. Ibid., 1026, 1032.
208. *Diary of William Maclay*, 9:302.
209. Ibid., 9:303.
210. Ibid., 9:306; *Annals of Congress*, 1st Cong., 2nd Sess., 1034.
211. *Annals of Congress*, 1st Cong., 2nd Sess., 1035.

212. *Diary of William Maclay*, 9:306; *Annals of Congress*, 1st Cong., 2nd Sess., 1035–36.
213. *Diary of William Maclay*, 9:307; *Annals of Congress*, 1st Cong., 2nd Sess., 1037.
214. *Diary of William Maclay*, 9:307; *Annals of Congress*, 1st Cong., 2nd Sess., 1037–38.
215. *Diary of William Maclay*, 9:307.
216. Ibid.
217. *Annals of Congress*, 1st Cong., 2nd Sess., 1038.
218. Sikes, Pierce Butler, 70.
219. *Correspondence: Second Session: July–October 1790*, vol. 20 of *Documentary History of the First Federal Congress of the United States of America, 4 March 1789–3 March 1791*, eds. Charlene Bangs Bickford, Kenneth R. Bowling, Helen E. Veit, and William Charles DiGiacomantonio (Baltimore: The Johns Hopkins Press, 2012), 20:2369.
220. *Annals of Congress*, 1st Cong., 2nd Sess., 1715.
221. Ibid., 1722.
222. Ibid., 1737.
223. Bickford et al, *Documentary History of the First Federal Congress*, 20:2369.

Chapter Six

A Western Perspective

"I have heard many people say," wrote Robert Nourse as he journeyed west in April 1787, "that it is a comfort, to see other people, in the same situation with themselves, but I cannot think it so, tho' to speak within bounds, there must be Two Thousand Souls, in the same situation, with ourselves."[1] Nourse, whose extended family straddled both banks of the Potomac River along Washington County, Maryland, and Berkley County, Virginia, had undertaken the perilous journey to Kentucky once before in 1779 with his brothers, James and Charles. Their father, James Nourse Sr., had made a similar journey in 1775 with, among others, George Rogers Clark. This time, however, Robert and his brothers were making the trip as settlers and not as explorers.[2]

Reaching Redstone Old Fort on the Monongahela River, the Nourses stopped amid a sea of western immigrants "incamped for, several miles, up and down the River."[3] All were waiting for rain. A dry spring had left the waterway too treacherous for a safe journey to the Ohio River. Eventually, the rain fell, and the brothers continued their journey.[4]

Near Fort Pitt, they happened to observe a family trying to make its way west on roads that rains had turned into muddy quagmires almost impossible to traverse. The sight of this family—a man, his wife, and their one son and six daughters—James Nourse recalled, "would defy any person whose heart was not composed of stone not to have felt" and to have been moved to pity.[5] The family's meager possessions consisted of "a small cart drawn by a very poor horse[,] two pots[,] a frying pan[,] some provisions and a few bedclothes."[6] Reaching a hill, the family started their climb, although their path was muddy and littered with stones. "Before they had advanc'd many steps," Nourse remembered, "the horse stop'd & they were obliged to take out a pot to guard which was left one of the females[.] a few steps higher they found it necessary to take out the other pot[.] in short before they had gained the height the whole family was dispersed the master with the empty cart, the horse gave out and at this time came on a heavy shower of rain."[7] After leaving the luckless family, the brothers eventually reached Kentucky, where James settled in Nelson County, Robert near Russellville and William in Mercer County.[8]

A year earlier, in October 1786, a group of Virginians bound for Kentucky met with a different fate. The McNitt party, named for its unfortunate leader, camped along the eastern bank of Little Laurel Creek in present-day Laurel County, Kentucky. They had safely passed through the Cumberland Gap and the mountainous southeastern region of Kentucky, an area prone to Indian attacks, and felt confident that they no longer needed to worry about Indians. Probably for this reason, McNitt did not post guards for the night. Later, after the happy travelers had gone to sleep, a band of Indians fell on the slumbering Virginians and killed most of the members of the fourteen families journeying west. Only a man, a woman (who later that night gave birth to a girl) and a small child escaped the massacre. A few days later, a burial party from Crab Orchard dubbed the site the "Defeated Camp."[9]

Despite such stories of death and privation, people continued to move west. "The rage for Kentucky is still predominant in this part of the country," stated a correspondent from Winchester, Virginia, in 1789.[10] Winchester, situated along the Great Wagon Road from Philadelphia, had become a popular stop on the westward route to Kentucky.[11] "The number of families which have passed through this town for the last four or five weeks, on their way to that distant region, is almost incredible."[12] "Notwithstanding the depredations of Indian parties in the State of Georgia," wrote a person from Charleston, "the frontier continues greatly to increase in Strength."[13] One optimistic Winchester correspondent wrote that, with the number of people migrating to Kentucky, "they will soon be in a situation to bid defiance to their savage enemies."[14] From his vantage point in Kentucky, Fayette County resident Caleb Wallace observed that despite the "very serious aspect" of Indian affairs in the region, "people are emigrating to the District by [the] thousands."[15]

"Surely you will say," wrote James Nourse to a cousin in Maryland, "there must be some magic charm some unaccountable infatuation which drives poor souls through thick & thin to an imaginary enjoyment of the Western Country, but it is not my Friend only imaginary."[16] "What would I not give," Nourse exclaimed, "to have your company in this country for only a week—I would show you Nature & Natures works in perfection."[17] Indeed, the beauty of the western wilderness acted as a powerful magnet drawing many people to Kentucky and Tennessee.

Whether in the Bluegrass region of Kentucky or along the fertile banks of the Cumberland and Tennessee rivers, settlers marveled at the handiwork of

Mother Nature. In 1790, a young Virginian fell in love with the Kentucky landscape. While traveling with the Kentucky militia as it headed for a rendezvous with General Josiah Harmar at Fort Washington (Cincinnati, Ohio), Hubbard Taylor, the "lawyer cousin" of James Madison, unexpectedly found himself gazing at a land teeming with luscious vegetation. Acting as his father's agent, Hubbard purchased several thousand acres of land near the mouth of the Licking River and immediately started planning the town of Newport. When Hubbard's brother, James, arrived two years later, he too fell in love with the beauty of the area. Immediately returning to Virginia, he packed up his personal belongings, including several slaves and two blooded horses, and moved with his family to Newport, arriving in 1793.[18]

As a people devoted in many ways to agriculture, southerners' interest in the West quite naturally centered on the land—especially on its fertility and availability. Making the overland trip from Maryland, Thomas Dillon, an investor in western lands, arrived in Nashville, Tennessee, with "the expectation of seeing some good land."[19] As it turned out, the land proved to be better than he had anticipated. The startling discovery prompted Dillon to settle shortly on some of his holdings in Davidson County, believing it to be "the best Land Speculation that will occur in our time."[20]

Writing from his home in New Bern, North Carolina, Abner Nash tried to entice a friend into investing in some of his lands on the Mississippi River, which reportedly "exceed[ed] all discussion for fertility of soil."[21] "If you incline," he told Samuel Purviance, "to hold a part of a Large Tract there" expect a valuable reward because "great numbers [of people are] constantly flocking to it."[22] Although speculators like Nash gobbled up huge chunks of western land in the hope of making a sizeable return on their investment, their preeminence in westward expansion belied one fact—it was the individual, an adventurer in pursuit of a dream, who actually moved west, tamed the wilderness and brought to life the many communities that dotted the landscape.

The many people who headed west in the two decades following the American Revolution did so for many reasons—good land was just one western allurement. Advertising his Kentucky lands in a special edition of the *Richmond Virginia Gazette and General Advertiser*, Henry Banks believed that his likely buyers would be "people of moderate circumstances, who incline to provide for their children."[23] Indeed, concern for the economic well-being of their families motivated many people to pull up stakes and head west. Some of the first settlers to pass through the Cumberland Gap and settle in Kentucky did so "in order to provide a subsistence for themselves and their Posterity."[24] John Breckinridge, who shortly after his arrival in Kentucky rose to political prominence becoming state attorney general and United States senator, moved from Virginia to Cabell's Dale in the spring of 1793 because, among other reasons, he could "provide *good* Lands here for my children, & insure them from *want*, which I was not certain of in the old Country, any longer than I had."[25]

Likewise worried about his family, a former classmate of James Madison, John Hoomes of Bowling Green, Virginia, described his contemplated move to Kentucky in 1789 as "a matter of considerable consequence to me, & perhaps of the greatest & lasting importance to my family."[26] A business-man, Hoomes had just visited Kentucky. Impressed by the landscape, he felt confident in saying that "the lands in Kentucky, are richer than any yet found in N. America & that they do produce more of every thing put into them than any yet Settled."[27] However, he remained cautious and doubted whether the district could live up to everyone's expectations. "[N]othing appears to be wanting," he wrote Madison, "but a good market for what the inhabitants will have to Spare."[28] Although Hoomes decided to remain in Caroline County, Virginia, and operate a stage line, many would-be landowners con-sidered this gamble, and other more heartbreaking gambles, well worth the risk.[29]

"Knowing that there is general prejudice against the title of land in that state [Kentucky], which is more general than just," wrote Henry Banks in the *Richmond Virginia Gazette and General Advertiser*, "I am willing to stipu-late in the contract, that a discount, or deduction, shall be made, when any land may be lost, by reason of a defective title."[30] With approximately 250,000 acres of land in Kentucky for sale, Banks knew first-hand just how tangled the question of land ownership really was in Kentucky. And so did "W.N." Writing in the *Lexington Kentucky Gazette*, the Mercer County resi-dent "lamented that the defect of proper titles of many who make sales as well as the want of due care in those who purchase; leads many of the good people of this State into much trouble and uneasiness."[31] John Breckinridge, who had only been in Lexington for three months, stated the situation even more plainly in his letter to his friend Joseph Cabell Jr.: "I would strongly recommend it to you to do it [acquire land], through some person in this Country in whom you can confide, who can examine the titles and quality. Without this Caution, there is possitive certainty of being cheated."[32]

In the late 1770s, Virginia had established three methods of land acquisi-tion in Kentucky—military land warrants, treasury warrants, and settlement warrants. Designed to raise money for the war against Great Britain, the treasury warrant allowed a person to buy land in Kentucky. Likewise a war-time measure, the military land warrant allowed Virginia to offer its soldiers in the American Revolution and its veterans of the French and Indian War Kentucky land as partial payment for their services. Depending on one's rank, a person could receive from 100 acres to 1,500 acres. Finally, for those individuals who trekked across the mountains and settled in Kentucky prior to 1778, Virginia offered free land in the form of settlement warrants. Unfor-tunately for the various warrant holders, Virginia required that they select their land, notify the county surveyor of their selection, pay surveying costs, and finally register their plat and surveyor's certificate with the land office. Of course, the warrant holder had to complete this procedure within a specified period of time, which was subject to change. If the warrant holder managed to complete the process, he often was confronted by an unexpected problem—his land entry overlapped another person's entry. Lacking a solution to this problem, the Virginia legislature made it easy for a person to sue for ownership in the courts, a situation that inevitably created a demand for lawyers.[33]

One person who heeded the call was Henry Clay. In 1792, his mother, Elizabeth Clay Watkins, had followed her second husband, Stephen, to Versailles, Kentucky, where they operated a flourishing tavern and eventually acquired nearly 1,000 acres of land and more than ten slaves.[34] Intent on establishing a "successful" legal career, young Henry Clay, in 1797, moved to Lexington shortly after passing the Virginia bar and quickly established a law practice and brilliant political career.[35] As with farmers, Kentucky and the West gave people with fewer professional opportunities in the Atlantic states a chance at success. "I am satisfied with this Country better than the old," wrote John Breckinridge, "Because my profession [the law] is more profitable."[36] Reportedly, the first professional lawyer to move to Kentucky after the American Revolution was John Brown of Virginia, a student of Thomas Jefferson and a close friend and political confidant of James Madison. Arriving in the summer of 1783, Brown became an important member of a small group of political leaders in the district.[37] In 1794, a young William C. C. Claiborne arrived in Kentucky with the intention of practicing law in the West. Eventually settling in Sullivan County, Tennessee, Claiborne rose through the political ranks becoming a Tennessee congressman in 1797, territorial governor of Orleans in 1803, and governor of Louisiana in 1812.[38]

Whether in pursuit of fertile land or of professional opportunities most people hoped to achieve economic security in the West. A few people, however, thought about moving beyond the mountains for other reasons. William Carmichael, a Maryland friend of Thomas Jefferson caught up in the hustle and bustle of diplomatic life in Europe, longed to return to the United States. Although he died in Madrid before he could fulfill his dream, he intended to sell his Maryland property and move "beyond the Allegany Mountains, where by all forgot I may pass the rest of my days inoffensively for others, doing all the good in my power and vegetating and decaying like the Trees which surround me."[39] Tired for the same reasons, Richard Caswell, with less than twelve months remaining in his term as governor of North Carolina, contemplated retiring to Tennessee. "It is my intention," he informed John Sevier, governor of the "state of Franklin," to visit the Western Waters and "find a place to secure an agreeable private retreat for the remainder of my

Time[.]"[40] Virginian George Nicholas also clung to a similar desire. Exhausted by state politics, Nicholas moved to Kentucky in 1789 to live a life of peace and solitude, determined "never to engage in public business of any kind. I shall make a sufficient sacrafice when I bury myself there without giving up my happiness and content by engaging in a new state of warfare with knaves and fools."[41] Despite his grand dreams, once he arrived, Nicholas quickly immersed himself in the political affairs of the district, particularly the campaign for statehood.[42]

From those people already living in the West, the almost daily influx of new residents evoked a variety of responses. Some people saw it as an opportunity to make money. In the fall of 1783, Robert McAfee decided to dam the Salt River in central Kentucky and erect a tub mill to grind his grain and the grain of his neighbors. The McAfees had arrived earlier that year from Botetourt County, Virginia. Lacking the easy accessibility of an outside market, the farmers in the vicinity of Benson and Frankfort "often came to his mill with packhorses loaded with grain" to have it ground into flour for sale "to emigrants who began to Flood the country."[43] Writing his family back home, a recent immigrant to Kentucky remarked that he had no difficulty purchasing food in the territory. Clothing, however, was a different subject, for he asked his brother to bring "a Bolt of Ozenbriges" with him when he came west.[44]

Generally speaking, westerners welcomed the new arrival and encouraged others to follow him across the mountains. While on a business trip to Charleston, Franklin resident John Sullivan tried to entice William Brown to move west. "There is no part of the Continent where you could live more at your ease than in Franklin," he told his friend. "I would advise you therefore . . . to come Southward by the first opportunity & secure a body of land for yourself on the Tenasee river—There will be work cut out for you in that Country."[45] Writing from Lexington, Thomas Hart enthusiastically tried to persuade a friend to move to Kentucky. After setting aside several reasons possibly keeping his friend from moving, Hart appealed to his friend's purse by stressing the economic potential of Kentucky. "You will say that Money is scarce in your Country," he told his friend, "and that you cannot get clear of your property to any advantage, and I will tell you that it is from them reasons that I wd. [would] recommend you the more strongly to come for money will never be plenty in your Country[.] there is nothing to bring it."[46]

Knowing that letters of encouragement were often not enough, westerners tried to make the journey to their country as pleasant and as easy as possible. In September 1788, "a new and good road 150 miles near than by way of Kentucky"[47] opened from Campbell's Station at the lower end of Clinch Mountain to Nashville.[48] Called Avery's Trace, it reduced the number of days a person had to be on the road. Hoping to make it even more alluring, the Cumberland settlement also provided armed escorts from Campbell's

Station to Nashville.[49] For a long time, many settlers traveling overland followed Boone's Trace into central Kentucky, which had become a well-worn path by the 1790s. In his speech before the Kentucky legislature in 1795, Governor Isaac Shelby showed no concern about the possible overpopulation of his state but instead expressed the belief that "nothing could have a greater tendency to increase the wealth and population of this State, than the making of good roads in every useful direction from this State to the Eastern States."[50] Within a year of Shelby's speech, Kentucky had begun work on the famed Wilderness Road.[51] From his home in Nashville, William C. C. Claiborne expressed the sentiments of many westerners. New arrivals in the territory "have of late years been great," he commented, "but not so much so as we wish it, or from the great advantage the country affords to emigrants we have a right to expect."[52]

In 1795, the general euphoria for emigration from the Atlantic states took a somber turn in Kentucky. "The distresses of our fellow men," wrote "A Friend To The Distressed" in the *Lexington Kentucky Gazette*,

> most always excite the feelings of the compassionate and humane: but there is no situation in the human life, which calls so loudly for assistance, as that of the man, who finds himself in a strange country, without the necessaries of life, to support a large and helpless family. This is the case at this time with hundreds in this State.—They have nearly expended their all, in removing their families to this country this fall, and are here in the midst of strangers, without the means of purchasing even bread for their subsistence.[53]

An unusually bad harvest had caused the price of food to rise in Kentucky. Unfortunately, this unexpected price increase hurt many immigrants, who expected "to purchase them, as cheap as they have always been bought here before this time."[54] Quickly spending what little money they had on food, they found themselves unable to acquire temporary shelter for their families while they looked for permanent places to live.[55]

Calling for the creation of an immigrant aid society, the petitioner declared that it was the duty of every citizen of the state to help the newly arrived during this period of unexpected distress. Public policy demanded it. The crisis, the "Friend" noted, placed in jeopardy the attractiveness of Kentucky to future immigrants. "Every citizen of this State," he wrote, "should do every thing in his power, to make the situation of the present emigrants, as comfortable as possible, as the not doing of it, will be a certain means of checking emigration in [the] future."[56]

The plight of the helpless immigrant in Kentucky underscored a major concern for many political leaders in the West—how to ensure the growth and development of a region where many of their neighbors and friends regularly moved to unsettled lands farther west. As a young boy growing up in Kentucky, Robert B. McAfee watched his father organize a partnership with John Breckinridge, whom his father had known while living in Virginia. Through the services of John Brown, now a United States senator from Kentucky, the two men sought from Congress title to a large tract of land alongside the White River in the Northwest Territory. With only promises from several congressmen, McAfee led a surveying party to the area and spent the summer of 1793 marking more than 30,000 acres. Their plans, however, collapsed when Congress refused to grant them this tract of land, which young Robert "thought was fortunate . . . because they would have probably moved to it."[57]

Just how restless the people actually were is hard to tell. Whatever the rate of migration, it appeared to visitors and residents alike that "the spirit of wandering is in the people; ever they are seeking a paradise and find it nowhere."[58] Daniel Grant, a Methodist minister from Georgia, believed the number of settlers leaving the trans-Appalachian region worthy of mention in a letter to his children. "There is numbers of people lately moved from Kentucky to Georgia," he remarked.[59] Two ministers traveling in Tennessee in 1799 recalled meeting several families "moving back to Georgia, still others to Illinois, or to Natchez."[60]

Early western leaders constantly worried about the depopulation of their country. "The emigration from this country [Kentucky] to that [Spanish territory] is already alarming," wrote George Nicholas in 1789.[61] Nine years later, John Sevier, who had fled the ruins of the "State of Franklin" for Tennessee, echoed Nicholas's concerns. "A great number of people," he declared, "are determined to descend the Mississippi, and . . . I fear one half our citizens will flock over into another government, indeed they are now doing it daily." "Instead of our state in its infancy being encouraged[,] fostered, and matured," Sevier complained, "it appears that measures are calculating to check and destroy the happiness, if not its existence."[62] In 1799, residents of the newly formed Mississippi Territory criticized territorial officials for a government so disliked "in consequence of which, our population is rapidly decreasing, and our inhabitants moving to the Spanish dominions."[63]

For this crisis, early leaders blamed the national government. "Let the General Government take the proper steps to defend the country from the Indians," wrote Nicholas to James Madison.[64] "No people will remain long under a Government which does not afford protection."[65] "It is not now," the newly transplanted Kentuckian declared, "the question whether the settlement in the western Country shall be encouraged but whether such steps shall be taken as will fill the Spanish territory with American Citizens."[66] Worried what the summer of 1794 had in store for the residents of Tennessee, Andrew Jackson commented that the "Indians appear Verry Troublesome[.] [F]rontier Discouraged and breaking and [num]bers leaving the Territory and moving [to] Kentucky."[67] "This Country," he lamented, "is Declining [fast] and unless Congress lends us a more am[ple] protection this Country will have at length [to break] or seek a protection from some other Source." Sometimes, however, the army did more harm than good.[68]

In July 1790, General Arthur St. Clair, governor of the Northwest Territory, and General Josiah Harmar planned a military expedition against the Shawnee and Miami living along the Wabash and Maumee rivers. Considering their orders to be rather vague, they drafted a far-reaching plan calling for a two-pronged attack against the Indian villages. Harmar was to command the main force while Major John F. Hamtramck was to command the smaller force. Kentuckians hoped the general would inflict a crushing blow against an enemy that constantly raided deep into Kentucky. Harmar's force, numbering about 320 officers and federal troops and 1,200 militia from Kentucky and Pennsylvania, departed Fort Washington (Cincinnati) the last week in September. At Nine Mile Run (Ohio), Harmar sent a detachment of 400 men (sixty federal troops and 300 Kentucky militiamen) against what he believed was the lightly defended village of Kekionga. On the morning of 22 October, the detachment attacked, only to be routed by a more disciplined Indian force. About fifty regulars and one hundred Kentucky militiamen died in the engagement.[69]

When the startling news of the defeat arrived in Kentucky, Kentuckians quite naturally grieved at the loss of so many of their men. But once they had time to contemplate the defeat, they knew that it could only mean trouble. While an emboldened enemy made life on the frontier more dangerous, it also made it less attractive to immigrants. "The interest of the country necessarily suffered with our reputation," wrote George Nicholas, "for as emigration is our chief dependance everything that deters emigrants must materially injure us; and it will now be held out to the world that even with the assistance of the regulars we were no match for the Indians."[70] "Emigration," he complained, "is put a stop to."[71]

For some westerners, hostile Indians were only part of their problem. When a group of Tennesseans proposed to settle the area around the Muscle Shoals in 1797, the federal government stepped in and stopped the enterprise. "The prevention of a settlement . . . is a manifest injury done to the whole western country," John Sevier angrily wrote:[72]

> Will the American Congress cramp and refuse to the Western Americans, the great natural advantages, providence has designed for, and placed before them? Will that body suffer the citizens to be drained out of their states, by other nations who will take the advantage of our discords and jealoucies, by granting to emigrants privileges of promoting their natural and useful advantage? God forbid I hope they will not; and I sincerely pray, they will maturely deliberate on the matters and things relative to the interest of the western country, while they have it in their power to keep us United, by granting and extending our just and equitable rights.[73]

"I know fifty families of Dutch," Nicholas told Madison, "who have been repeatedly driven by the Indians from their settlements, and are now living on rented land who are determined unless they can return with safety to their own land to go to the spanish Country where they are offered land and protection without paying for either."[74]

A story such as Nicholas's illustrates just how determined people were to make a life for themselves in the West. Nicholas and other western leaders knew the anger of their neighbors toward a government that they believed cared little for them, and the Spanish government's closing of the Mississippi River made the situation even more volatile. For a time, events seemed to make the southern desire for a western alliance almost impossible to accomplish.

[handwritten marginalia: "what about land north of the Ohio River"]

NOTES

1. Robert Nourse to Joseph Chapline, 24 April 1787, in "Nourse-Chapline Letters," *Register of the Kentucky State Historical Society*, 31 (April 1933), 155.
2. [Introduction,] in Ibid., 152; Otis K. Rice, *Frontier Kentucky* (Lexington: University Press of Kentucky, 1993), 71.
3. Robert Nourse to Joseph Chapline, 24 April 1787, in "Nourse-Chapline Letters," 155.
4. Ibid.
5. James Nourse to Joseph Chapline, 27 May 1788, in Ibid., 157.
6. Ibid.
7. Ibid., 157–58.
8. Introduction in Ibid., 152.
9. McNitt's first name has been lost over time. Even the tombstone marking the site of the massacre just says "McNitt." "McNitt's Defeat," in *The Kentucky Encyclopedia*, ed. John E. Kleber (Lexington: The University Press of Kentucky, 1992), 600; Kentucky State Parks, "History of the McNitt Massacre, Levi Jackson Wilderness Road State Park" (unpublished brochure); Laurel County Historical Society, "The Story of Laurel County" (unpublished brochure); Lloyd G. Lee, *A Brief History of Kentucky and Its Counties* (Berea, KY: Kentucke Imprints, 1981), 367.
10. *Edenton State Gazette of North Carolina*, 12 November 1789.
11. Warren R. Hofstra, *A Separate Place: The Formation of Clarke County, Virginia* (Madison: Madison House Publishers, 1999), 32.
12. *Edenton State Gazette of North Carolina*, 12 November 1789.
13. *Annapolis Maryland Gazette*, 17 December 1789.
14. Ibid., 10 July 1789.
15. Caleb Wallace to James Madison, 12 November 1787, in *The Papers of James Madison*, eds. William T. Hutchinson et al. (Chicago and London: The University of Chicago Press, 1977), 10:249, 250.
16. James Nourse to Joseph Chapline, 27 May 1788, in "Nourse-Chapline Letters," 158.
17. Ibid.
18. Marie Dickoré, comp., *General James Taylor's Narrative* (N.p,: N.d.), Ohio Historical Society Archives/Library Stacks 929.2 T214d, 44, 51–52; *Kentucky: A Guide to the Bluegrass State Compiled and Written by the Federal Writer's Project of the Works Projects Administration for the State of Kentucky, American Guide Series* (New York: Harcourt, Brace and Company, 1939), 246–47; W. H. Perrin, J. H. Battle, and G. C. Kniffin, *Kentucky: A History of the State, Embracing a Concise Account of the Origin and Development of the Virginia Colony; Its Expansion Westward, and the Settlement of the Frontier Beyond the Alleghanies; the Erection*

of Kentucky as an Independent State, and Its Subsequent Development, 8th ed. (Louisville, KY, and Chicago, IL: F A. Battey and Company, 1888), 989.

19. "Thomas Dillion's Account," ed. Samuel Cole Williams, *Early Travels in the Tennessee Country, 1540–1800, with Introductions, Annotations and Index* (Johnson City, TN: The Watagua Press, 1928), 358–60.

20. Ibid.

21. Abner Nash to Samuel Purviance, 19 August 1784, in Purviance Family Papers, 1757 (1776–1920) 1932, Manuscript Department, William R. Perkins Library, Duke University, Durham, NC.

22. Ibid.

23. *Richmond Virginia Gazette and General Advertiser Extraordinary*, 3 August 1791.

24. James Rood Robertson, ed., *Petitions of the Early Inhabitants of Kentucky to the General Assembly of Virginia, 1769 to 1792* (Louisville: John P. Morton & Company, 1914), 36.

25. John Breckinridge to Joseph Cabell Jr., 23 July 1793, in Breckinridge Family Papers, box 9, Library of Congress, Washington, DC.

26. John Hoomes to James Madison, 27 July 1789, in *The Papers of James Madison*, eds. Charles S. Hobson et al. (Charlottesville: The University Press of Virginia, 1979), 12:312.

27. Ibid.

28. Ibid.

29. *The Statutes at Large: Being a Collection of All the Laws of Virginia from the First Session of the Legislature, in the Year 1619*, ed. William W. Hening (Richmond: George Cochran, Printers, 1823; repr., Charlottesville: Published for the Jamestown Foundation of the Commonwealth of Virginia by the University Press of Virginia, 1969), 12:618–19.

30. *Richmond Virginia Gazette and General Advertiser*, 13 March 1794.

31. *Lexington Kentucky Gazette*, 14 July 1792.

32. Breckinridge to Cabell, 23 July 1793, in Breckinridge Family Papers.

33. Patricia Watlington, *The Partisan Spirit: Kentucky Politics, 1779–1792* (New York: Atheneum for the Institute of Early American History and Culture at Williamsburg, Virginia, 1972), 11–17, and Thomas D. Clark, *Agrarian Kentucky* (Lexington: The University Press of Kentucky, 1977), 9–10.

34. Robert V. Remini, *Henry Clay: Statesman for the Union* (New York: W. W. Norton & Company, 1991), 17.

35. "Speech of Henry Clay at the Great Barbecue at Lexington, [Kentucky], June 9, 1842," *Jamestown [New York] Journal*, 14 July 1842. The speech was reprinted in numerous newspapers across the country.

36. Breckinridge to Cabell, 23 July 1793, in Breckinridge Family Papers.

37. Elizabeth Warren, "Senator John Brown's Role in the Kentucky Spanish Conspiracy," *The Filson Club History Quarterly*, 36 (April 1962), 159; Watlington, *Partisan Spirit*, 81.

38. David Ross to Arthur Campbell, 16 April 1794, in Arthur Campbell Papers, The Filson Historical Society, Louisville, KY; *American National Biography*, s.v. "Claiborne, William Charles Coles."

39. William Carmichael to Thomas Jefferson, 3 October 1786, in *The Papers of Thomas Jefferson*, ed. Julian P. Boyd (Princeton: Princeton University Press, 1954), 10: 429; *American National Biography*, s.v. "Carmichael, William."

40. Richard Caswell to John Sevier, 23 February 1787, in *The State Records of North Carolina*, eds. Walter Clark et al. (Goldboro, NC: Nash Brothers, Book and Job Printers, 1902), 20:618. Despite his intentions, Caswell remained in North Carolina, becoming speaker of the state senate, a position he held until his death in November 1789. *American National Biography*, s.v. "Caswell, Richard."

41. George Nicholas to James Madison, 2 January 1789, in *The Papers of James Madison*, eds. Robert A. Rutland et al. (Charlottesville: University Press of Virginia, 1977), 11:408.

42. Lowell H. Harrison and James C. Klotter, *A New History of Kentucky* (Lexington: The University Press of Kentucky, 1997), 61.

43. Robert B. McAfee, "The Life and Times of Robert B. McAfee and Family Connections," *Register of the Kentucky State Historical Society*, 25:74 (May 1927), 113.

44.   David Rowland to Joseph Anderson, 14 August 1788, in David Rowland Letter, Miscellaneous Collection, Filson Historical Society, Louisville, KY.

45.   John Sullivan to William Brown, 24 September 1787, in Record Group 11: General Records of the United States Government: Papers of the Continental Congress (Washington, DC: National Archives and Records Administration), M247, r102, i78, v21, p. 477.

46.   Thomas Hart to [Unknown] Hogg, 24 February 1795, in Edward Vernon Howell Papers, Southern Historical Collection, University of North Carolina Library, Chapel Hill, NC.

47.   *Edenton State Gazette of North Carolina*, 20 October 1788.

48.   For a copy of the North Carolina law establishing the road, see "An Act to Effect the Cutting and Clearing a Road from the Lower End of Clinch Mountain to the Cumberland Settlements, and for Preserving and Granting Safety to the Inhabitants Thereof," *State Records of North Carolina*, ed. Walter Clark (Goldsboro: Nash Brothers, Book and Job Printers, 1905), 24:913–14.

49.   W. E. M'Elwee, "'The Old Road,' From Washington and Hamilton Districts to the Cumberland Settlement," *American Historical Magazine and Tennessee Historical Society Quarterly*, 8 (October 1903), 347–49.

50.   *Lexington Kentucky Gazette*, 28 November 1795.

51.   Ibid., 15 October 1796. Kentucky upgraded the road, making it better suited for wagon and carriage traffic.

52.   *Knoxville [Tennessee] Gazette*, 2 October 1795.

53.   *Lexington Kentucky Gazette*, 19 December 1795.

54.   Ibid.

55.   Ibid.

56.   Ibid.

57.   McAfee, "Life and Times," 123–24.

58.   "Report of the Journey of the Brethren Abraham Steiner and Frederick C. De Schweinitz to the Cherokees and the Cumberland Settlements (1799)," in Williams, *Early Travels in the Tennessee Country*, 507.

59.   Daniel Grant to John Owen Jr., 21 August 1789, in Campbell Family Papers, Manuscript Department, Duke University Library, Durham, NC.

60.   "Report of the Journey of the Brethren," 507.

61.   George Nicholas to Madison, 8 May 1789, in Hobson et al., *Madison Papers*, 12:139.

62.   John Sevier to Andrew Jackson, 26 November 1797, in *The Papers of Andrew Jackson*, eds. Sam B. Smith et al. (Knoxville: University of Tennessee Press, 1980), 1:155.

63.   *Lexington Kentucky Gazette*, 12 September 1799.

64.   Nicholas to Madison, 8 May 1789, in Hobson et al., *Madison Papers*, 12:139.

65.   Ibid.

66.   Ibid.

67.   Andrew Jackson to John McKee, 16 May 1794, in Smith et al., *Papers of Jackson*, 1:49.

68.   Ibid.

69.   Michael S. Warner, "General Josiah Harmar's Campaign Reconsidered: How the Americans Lost the Battle of Kekionga," *Indiana Magazine of History*, 83 (March 1987), 45–55.

70.   Nicholas to John Brown, 13 July 1790 and 31 December [1790], in George Nicholas Letters, 1789–1796, Kentucky Historical Society, Frankfort, KY.

71.   Ibid.

72.   John Sevier to Jackson, 26 November 1797, in Smith et al., *Papers of Jackson*, 1:155.

73.   Ibid., 1:155–56.

74.   Nicholas to Madison, 8 May 1789, in Hobson et al., *Madison Papers*, 12:139.

Chapter Seven

An Unhappy West

In February 1788, a recent traveler to the West described a country "visibly improving" every day. The "hardy emmigrant from the old states," he declared, had taken his ax and transformed the "forests as old as the creation" into "elegant farms." This transformation impressed him, and the visitor confidently predicted that "every circumstance seems to point out that country as the future seat of a great and powerful empire of confederated republics." The people who chose to live in the region bounded by the Mississippi and Ohio rivers, the traveler continued, were "well disposed towards the states on the Atlantic" and possessed "a degree of fondness" for them, but, he interjected, "they cannot hear, with patience, of the Spaniards claiming or demanding an exclusive right to the navigation of the Mississippi—and any man that should attempt to recommend a cession of that nature upon any consideration whatever, would, if amongst them, be made to repent dearly for his temerity."[1]

Few westerners would refute the assessment of the traveler. Yes, they did possess a fondness for their former homes, and yes, they were anxious for the opening of the Mississippi River to commerce, and indeed, they were quite unwilling to enter into any compromise limiting their access to it. What the visitor missed, however, was the marked aloofness of some westerners to the people living east of the mountains. They had become suspicious of these people, not really certain of their impulses toward the West.

Indian raids in Kentucky in the 1780s imposed numerous hardships on the settlers. The raids forced them, at a hint of danger, to abandon their homes and seek protection within various forts and stations, which, as one disgruntled Kentuckian remarked, "serve as Beds to engender Sedition & Discord in, & as excuses for Indolence, Rags & poverty."[2] While looking around for relief from such misery, Kentuckians, as Walker Daniel pointed out, saw "no vigorous & decided steps taken by [the] Government . . . [and were] apt to conclude as the reason, that those in [the] Administration feeling nothing for their sufferings, are consequently indifferent to the Situation."[3]

The failure, or, as an unidentified contributor to the *Knoxville [Tennessee] Gazette* later termed it, the "neglect," of the United States government to confront the Indian situation in a manner acceptable to the people living in the West was just one reason for the all too common belief among many westerners that Congress, and possibly southerners, resented their region.[4] Why else, wrote a subscriber to the *Lexington Kentucky Gazette*, would the government have given four-fifths of Georgia to the Creek tribe unless members harbored some ill feelings toward the West?[5]

Of course, westerners knew, or at least thought they knew, the reason for this resentment: coastal residents feared the influence a growing West would have in the Union. "The day is not far distant," predicted the *Knoxville Gazette*, "when the country west of the Appalachian Mountains will be the most populous part of America."[6] Although his plans for the "state of Franklin" never materialized, its former governor, John Sevier, knew "that the time is not far distant when they [westerners] will become as Consequential In numbers, if not more so, than most of the Eastern states."[7] Writing under the pseudonym, "A Man of Peace," one Kentuckian expressed the feeling more succinctly when he declared "that this country[,] if not crushed by unwarrantable policy, will soon be the Eden of America; and will draw from the barren and inhospitable parts of Eastern America, all its enterprising and industrious inhabitants; And . . . [become] an important branch in the Legislation [Legislature] of America."[8]

At the conclusion of the American Revolution, Kentucky was "a fertile but uninhabited Wild."[9] Although a wilderness, it promised prosperity to those people who dared leave the comfort and safety of their homes east of the Appalachian Mountains. Venturing "into almost impenetrable forests," pioneers had to endure life "without bread or domestic Cattle," eating beneath "the cloud deformed Canopy" only the "Casual supplies afforded by the chace."[10] As they ceaselessly worked to claim their vision of happiness— farms, towns, roads from the wilderness—they discovered that "not in safety we trod."[11] Resenting the pioneers' presence, the original occupiers of the land "thirsted for [our] blood, lurked in our paths and seized the insuspecting Hunter."[12] Harry Innes, attorney general of the western district of Virginia, estimated in December 1787 that since September 1783 hostile Indians had killed approximately 300 settlers, captured at least 50 others and stolen at least 20,000 horses.[13] Despite such dangers and hardships, Kentuckians persevered, transforming a wilderness into a burgeoning community of farmers and entrepreneurs and providing the proper setting for the germination of political parties.

In her examination of pre-statehood politics in Kentucky, Patricia Watlington has uncovered the existence of three rival interest groups, or "parties," operating in the western district by 1785.[14] Although these interest groups claimed broad-based support, they actually had relatively few active members who rallied around a core group of leaders. Self-interest motivated these leaders. It compelled them to enter the political arena in an effort to achieve certain and generally differing goals, which they tried to obtain by rallying a rather lethargic populace to their point of view.

"Partisans" organized early in Kentucky and "at times," according to Watlington, "amounted to nearly half the population."[15] Consisting mainly of landless settlers from Pennsylvania and the Carolinas, they resented the Virginia land law of 1779, which made it difficult, if not impossible, for them to acquire their own land. Their leaders, however, did not face the same problem. Mainly land speculators, Partisan leaders had managed to accumulate large tracts of land in Kentucky.[16] They nevertheless became the spokesmen of the landless settlers because they too resented the Virginia land laws, which consistently hindered their efforts to acquire even more Kentucky land. United by a common dislike, these men worked to ease their situation in the district.[17]

The two remaining political groups first appeared on the scene articulating a united response to the Partisans. Consisting mainly of Virginians, members of the "Articulate Center" held a variety of official and professional positions in Kentucky—attorneys, judges and surveyors—and generally considered themselves the guardians of the Virginia claim to Kentucky. Despite their similar backgrounds, they eventually divided over objectives.[18]

The "court party," whose members included the leading businessmen and legal minds—judges and attorneys—in the district, wanted to preserve their own land claims while at the same time obtaining control of the vacant lands in Kentucky, including those vast expanses of wilderness owned by absentee landholders. They also dreamed of turning an agriculturally dependent Kentucky into a commercially dominant Kentucky. For this reason, they needed the Mississippi River open to their agricultural and manufactured products.[19]

The "country party," on the other hand, wished to preserve the sanctity of all land claims in the district. They feared that if the court party gained political control of a new state, they would loosen many of the existing ties with Virginia. Because of their Virginia roots, most country party members possessed a deep affinity for Virginia and wanted to retain a close relationship with the Old Dominion. As a result, they opposed any measure that would weaken the bond between their district and Virginia.[20]

The issue that came to divide these three emerging political groups was the future relationship of Kentucky with Virginia and the United States. Partisans organized first. Because they blamed Virginia for making it difficult for non-Virginians to acquire land in Kentucky, they supported the idea that Kentucky and the western territory belonged to all Americans under congressional oversight. When Congress, however, tacitly accepted the claim of Virginia to ownership of Kentucky in 1784 (the Virginia cession), Partisans lost their only hope of circumventing the land laws of Virginia. Fearful that statehood would mean higher taxes, Partisans spent the next six years arguing that Kentucky must remain a part of Virginia and not become a state. [21]

When Partisans yielded to the realization that a permanent separation from Virginia would eventually happen, the Articulate Center, whose members consistently had opposed Partisan plans for the district, suddenly found themselves divided over Kentucky separating from Virginia. [22] At first, they only spoke about a legal separation, but as the likelihood of a Partisan victory subsided, a number of men within this group started to redefine their aspirations for Kentucky. They soon adopted the position that a violent, or illegal, separation from Virginia might be necessary. They based their position on a firm belief that the northern states would naturally resent a strong commercial rival in the West and would logically block any agreement between Virginia and Kentucky that would allow Kentucky to enter the Union as a state. Confident that the northern states would act as they had imagined, these "court party" supporters concluded that Kentucky must secede unilaterally from Virginia. Having completed this step, they planned either to ask the United States for statehood or to enter into some type of an arrangement with a foreign country, perhaps Spain. [23]

The talk of a violent separation from Virginia frightened the remaining members of the articulate center. Constituting Watlington's third political group, the country party supported only a peaceful and legal separation from Virginia, which leaders knew would protect the legitimacy of their land claims. Strongly loyal to Virginia and to the United States, they opposed the secession plans of the court party. [24]

Throughout the pre-statehood period of Kentucky history, only one of the three parties consistently viewed the maritime states with suspicion—the court party. During the early stage of development of their faction, court party leaders started clinging to the idea that Kentucky, as a representative of the West, and the maritime states were actually two distinct entities, each with its own economic and political future. The Allegheny Mountains helped foster this feeling of separateness, limiting communication between the sections. The rivers and streams flowing westward from the Alleghenies also dictated that the settler's gaze should turn west rather than east. As far as court party leaders were concerned, the economic future of the region depended on access to the Mississippi River. The repeated attempts of maritime residents to redirect the commercial traffic of the region through their many canal projects only darkened the prospects of a bright future. Convinced that their dreams for Kentucky would never come true as long as the district remained a part of Virginia, court party members became early advocates of separation and access to the Mississippi River was the only issue, they believed, strong enough to secure for them the support of the people of Kentucky.[25]

The Spanish decision to close the Mississippi River to American commerce in 1785 angered many Kentuckians. David Wood Meriwether, a resident of the Beargrass settlement (later to be absorbed by a growing Louisville), bitterly lamented the western country's economic prospects if current reports of Spain opening the river proved to be inaccurate: "With out a Trade I think we shall ever remain poor."[26]

What upset people even more, however, was the startling news that in the early winter of 1786–1787 John Jay, the American secretary of foreign affairs, had spoken with the Spanish minister to the United States, Diego de Gardoqui, about relinquishing American navigational claims to the Mississippi River for a period of twenty-five or thirty years. "The late commercial treaty with Spain," wrote a worried Kentuckian, "has given the western Country an universal shock, and struck its Inhabitants with an amazement."[27] Kentucky chief justice and court party leader George Muter remarked to James Madison that he had "not mett one man, who would be willing to give the navigation up, for ever so short a time, on any terms whatever."[28] The thought of losing the Mississippi River upset district attorney Harry Innes so much that he set down on paper nine reasons refuting "the suggestion of Mr. Jay—'that the Western People had nothing yet to export, & therefore the Cession of the Mississippi would be no injury to them.'"[29]

Patricia Watlington notes that the Spanish action in 1784 to inhibit American expansion in the trans-Appalachian West by closing the Mississippi River gave the court party the issue by which members hoped to persuade Kentuckians to follow their lead and support a call for the separation of the district from Virginia. The nearly universal protest in Kentucky against the Jay-Gardoqui negotiations a year or so later only underscored the importance that Kentuckians placed on access to the Mississippi River. They needed the waterway to unleash the economic potential of the region. When the Atlantic states suddenly seemed willing to bargain away their access to this vital highway, Kentuckians became angry at their American brethren and suspicious of their relationship with them.[30]

An "alarmed Kentuckian" stated the situation bluntly in early December 1786: "To sell us, and make us vassals to the merciless Spaniards, is a grievance not to be borne."[31] "What benefit can you on the Atlantic shore receive from the act?" he asked.[32] Certainly not new markets, for the Spaniards, he reasoned, "can supply all their own markets at a much lower price than you possibly can."[33] Continuing, he asked,

Do you think to prevent the emigration from a barren country, loaded with
taxes and impoverished with debts, to the most luxurious and fertile soil in the
world? Vain is the thought, and presumptious the supposition. . . . Shall the
best and largest part of the United States be uncultivated—a nest for savages
and beasts of prey? Certainly not. Providence has designed it for some nobler
purposes.[34]

As he continued his plea for access to the mighty river, his tone suddenly
grew more serious: "Our situation is as bad as it possibly can be; therefore[,]
every exertion to retrieve our circumstances must be manly, eligible, and
just."[35] These "manly" exertions, he noted, included raising "twenty thousand troops" and driving "the Spanish from their settlements at the mouth of
the Mississippi."[36] He also mentioned the possibility, "if we need it," of
ending their [Kentuckians'] alliance with the United States, a country that is
"as ignorant of this country as Great Britain was of America."[37] He concluded his essay with several words of advice: "These hints, if rightly improved, may be of some service. If not, blame yourselves for the neglect."[38]

On 29 March 1787, court party leaders John Brown, Harry Innes, George
Muter and Benjamin Sebastian declared in an open letter to all western
inhabitants that "this is a subject [the Jay-Gardoqui negotiations] that requires no comment, the injustice of the measure is glaring."[39] Loss of the
navigation of the Mississippi River, they stated, "tends to almost a total
destruction of the Inhabitants of the Western Country."[40] Seeing the talks
between the Spanish minister and the American foreign secretary as tantamount to the end of their world, they and "a respectable number of the
inhabitants of this District [Kentucky]" did, quite naturally, view the negotiations with alarm.[41] They subsequently called for a convention of delegates to
meet the first Monday in May 1787 for the purpose of showing "Congress
that the Inhabitants of the Western Country are united in their opposition . . .
[and] will not tamely submit to an act of Oppression which must tend to a
deprivation of our just Rights & Priviledges."[42] To this end, they charged the
convention with preparing "a spirited but decent remonstrance against the
cession" and with the responsibility of creating a committee of correspondence for the purpose of communicating with other "inhabitants residing on
the western waters [who] are equally affected by this partial conduct of
congress."[43]

The convention convened on schedule in May. Details of the meeting,
however, are sketchy. Watlington notes that the delegates' instructions gave
them broad leeway in remedying the problems facing the district. Court party
members, she believes, hoped to use the convention as a vehicle for with-
drawing Kentucky from Virginia but "could not muster support" for it among
the delegates.[44] The convention ended after only meeting for a few days
ostensibly because delegates believed that the Virginia condemnation of the

Jay-Gardoqui negotiations adequately expressed their outrage and concerns.[45] Although the convention failed in terms of court party objectives, its mere convocation provides convincing evidence that the possibility of losing the Mississippi River alarmed many people in Kentucky and stirred them to action.

While Kentuckians were focusing their attention on the questions of separation and statehood, delegates from the Atlantic states were meeting in Philadelphia and drafting a new plan of government for the nation. When Kentuckians had the opportunity to review the delegates' handiwork, they immediately saw problems with it. John Brown, the lone congressman from the district and cautious supporter of the new plan, noted that Kentuckians held a number of "prejudices against the new Constitution" because of a misguided belief that the new government would make it easier for the Atlantic states to part with the Mississippi River.[46] "I have carefully examined the proposed plan," he told a member of the Kentucky delegation to the Virginia ratifying convention, "as it may affect the District in particular and . . . I have not been able to discover that it contained principles partially injurious to the Interest of Kentucky."[47] As for the past inclination of the Atlantic states to abandon American claim to the Mississippi River, Brown stressed that a "total change of Policy . . . has taken place."[48]

Despite such assurances from leading figures in the district like Brown, some Kentuckians clung to their belief that ratification of the new Constitution meant the eventual loss of the Mississippi River. The Constitution, they argued, would enable the northern states "to carry into effect the proposed treaty with Spain."[49] Past disappointments when dealing with the Atlantic states had conditioned Kentuckians to expect the worst in any dealings between the two regions. It was, Brown stressed, "the ill advised attempt to cede the navigation of that River" that produced the pronounced lack of "confidence of the people in the Western Country in the Justice of the Union."[50] This condition, he lamented, had "laid the foundation for the dismemberment of the American Empire" by causing western inhabitants "to despair of obtaining possession of that Right [complete usage of the Mississippi River] by means of any other exertions than their own."[51] For this reason, Brown feared continued congressional delay in admitting Kentucky into the Union, believing that it would "be productive of Consequences ruinous to the tranquility of that promising Country; or to the importance and dignity of the United States; and perhaps to both."[52]

Although "it is beyond dispute that the question of the navigation of the Mississippi entered largely into the formation of opinion," Kentuckians did have other reasons for rejecting the Constitution.[53] They worried about the judiciary, wondering whether the Atlantic states would grant them easy access to the courts while fearing that the judicial system might be harboring some unknown "danger." They also disliked the idea that their militia might be on duty in another state at the moment of their greatest peril—an Indian uprising.[54]

At their Saturday evening meetings, members of the Danville Political Club, whose members included leading court party activists, carefully examined the new plan of government. They eventually concluded that the Constitution had several serious flaws, including lengthy senatorial terms, the lack of a role for state legislatures in some federal elections, and the absence of restraints on the president's use of the veto. Club members also wanted the role of the militia redefined. Instead of simply granting the president the power to call out the militia "to execute the laws," the club declared that the Constitution should grant the president the authority to use the militia to enforce "*obedience* to the laws of the Union."[55]

Political club members also found several unsettling items in the Constitution that they believed warranted deletion and one omission that they deemed glaring. The federal government, they declared, did not need jurisdiction over the proposed federal city or over all fort, arsenal and dock sites, nor did the federal government need, in their opinion, the useless office of vice president. They also unanimously objected to the twenty-year limitation on the ability of the federal government to end the Atlantic slave trade.[56] Reflecting the antislavery position that William W. Freehling calls "conditional termination," they believed that the federal government should end the trade in human cargo as soon as possible.[57] Finally, prefacing their remarks on the new plan of government, political club members "Resolved, That . . . the Federal Constitution ought to be proceded by a Declaration of Rights" that would prohibit Congress from altering or abridging the Constitution in any manner and void "all laws contrary to the true spirit, intent and meaning of the same."[58]

Court party leaders wasted little time in channeling the general unhappiness of Kentuckians with the proposed Constitution into a united expression of opposition. On 29 February 1788, Harry Innes, George Muter and other court party members released an open letter to the Fayette County court demanding that it call a convention for the purpose of providing voting instructions for the as yet unknown Kentucky delegation to the Virginia ratifying convention. Kentuckians voted the following April for delegates and, to the relief of the members of the court party, selected a delegation overwhelmingly Antifederalist. Court party leaders, as a result, abandoned their call for a convention.[59]

The fourteen Kentuckians who attended the Virginia ratifying convention limited their participation in the great debate between Federalists and Antifederalists. For the most part, the Kentuckians sat and listened to the leading political figures in the state—Patrick Henry, James Madison, George Nicholas, and Edmund Randolph—as they addressed their remarks to them in a manner designed to win their support. In the end, however, the Kentucky delegates voted as their constituencies expected, three for ratification and ten against, with the lone uncast vote reflecting the unexplained absence of Bourbon County delegate Notley Conn.[60]

That fall, Kentuckians representing all three rival interest groups met in convention to discuss the future of their district. They opened their convention on the heels of yet another major disappointment—congressional postponement of the Kentucky statehood application. Instead of rendering a final decision on the question, Congress had referred it to the new Congress scheduled to convene in early 1789. Now, their chances of entering the Union looked bleak, especially in light of the expiration of the Virginia ordinance granting Kentucky statehood. Generally, they were an unhappy group of men. Indeed, several court party members, their patience nearly exhausted, were prepared to support separation if Congress or Virginia rejected their final plea for statehood. James Wilkinson, in fact, had hoped to convince the convention that the time had finally arrived to declare the independence of Kentucky, but he lacked the support of fellow court party members in his efforts to maneuver the convention into such a declaration. Unwilling to take that ultimate step, the delegates spent their time drafting addresses to Congress and the Virginia General Assembly re-emphasizing their position on the Mississippi River and asking for help in obtaining statehood.[61]

In a carefully worded address to Congress that barely concealed their disgust with the Atlantic states, they declared:

> If you will really be our fathers[,] stretch forth your hands to save us. If you would be worthy Guardians, defend our rights. We are a member that would exert every muscle to your service. Do not cut us off from your Body. By every tie of consanguinity and affection, by the remembrance of the blood which we have mingled in the common cause, by a regard to Justice and to policy we conjure you to procure our right. May your Councils be guided by wisdom and justice, and may your determinations be marked by decisions and effect. Let not your beneficence be circumscribed by the Mountains which divide us. But let us feel that you are really our Fathers & assertors of Our Rights. Then you would secure the prayers of a people whose Gratitude would be as warm as their vindication of their Rights will be eternal. Then our connexions shall be perpetuated to the latest times, a Monument of your Justice and a Terror to your Enemies.[62]

Despite their pleas, Kentuckians had to wait nearly four more years before obtaining statehood. During that time, political players on the national scene worked to hold an anxious Kentucky and its western neighbors in the Union and to align the West with the South.

NOTES

1. *Annapolis Maryland Gazette*, 27 March 1788.
2. Walker Daniel to Governor Benjamin Harrison, 21 May 1784, in *Calendar of Virginia State Papers and Other Manuscripts, From January 1, 1782, to December 31, 1784, Preserved at the Capitol at Richmond*, ed. William P. Palmer (Richmond: James E. Goode, Printer, 1883), 3:586–87.
3. Ibid., 3:587.
4. *Knoxville [Tennessee] Gazette*, 4 December 1795.
5. *Lexington Kentucky Gazette*, 15 January 1791. In August 1790, the United States concluded "A Treaty of Peace and Friendship" with the Creek nation. As part of its efforts to diminish the chances of conflict between the Creek and Georgians, the federal government established a permanent boundary between the two groups that limited Georgian settlement to a band of land along the coast. Charles J. Kappler, ed., *Indian Treaties, 1778–1883* (New York: Interland Publishing Inc., 1973), 25–26.
6. *Knoxville [Tennessee] Gazette*, 4 December 1795.
7. John Sevier to Governor Richard Caswell, 28 October 1786, in *The State Records of North Carolina*, ed. Walter Clark (Goldsboro, NC: Nash Brothers, Book and Job Printers, 1907), 22:660.
8. *Lexington Kentucky Gazette*, 17 May 1794.
9. James Mason Brown, *The Political Beginnings of Kentucky: A Narrative of Public Events Bearing on the History of that State up to the Time of Its Admission into the American Union* (Louisville: John P. Morton and Company, Printers to the Filson Club, 1889), 260.
10. Ibid.
11. Ibid.
12. Ibid.
13. G. Glenn Clift, ed., "The District of Kentucky 1783–1787 as Pictured by Harry Innes in a Letter to John Brown," *Register of the Kentucky Historical Society*, 54 (October 1956), 369. Louis B. Wright, in *Life on the American Frontier* (New York: G. P. Putnam's Sons, 1968), 58–72, provides a good general description of frontier life in the trans-Appalachian country.
14. Patricia Watlington, *The Partisan Spirit: Kentucky Politics, 1779–1792* (New York: Atheneum for the Institute of Early American History and Culture at Williamsburg, Virginia, 1972), 232. Not all historians accept Watlington's assertion about early political parties in Kentucky. They, however, seem to accept the idea that "loosely associated factions" operated during this period. See Lowell H. Harrison and James C. Klotter, *A New History of Kentucky* (Lexington: The University Press of Kentucky, 1997), 57, 459.
15. Watlington, *Partisan Spirit*, 52.
16. The Land Law of 1779 granted four hundred acres to those settlers who had occupied their land prior to 1 January 1778, provided they paid a nominal fee, and the right to preempt an additional one thousand acres. Contrary to its intent, the land law facilitated the efforts of speculators who found it much easy to acquire original and preemption claims. Thomas D. Clark, *Agrarian Kentucky* (Lexington: The University Press of Kentucky, 1977), 8.
17. Watlington, *Partisan Spirit*, 46–53, 225–26. Watlington names Arthur Campbell, a land speculator, and Ebenezer Brooks, a doctor and former Presbyterian minister, as partisan leaders. Harrison and Klotter add John Campbell, an Irish immigrant and no relation to Arthur Campbell, and Samuel Taylor, a former Virginia deputy surveyor, to the list. See Harrison and Klotter, *A New History of Kentucky*, 57.
18. Watlington, *Partisan Spirit*, 227.
19. Ibid., 227–29. Watlington's list of court party leaders includes Caleb Wallace and Samuel McDowell, assistant judges; George Muter, chief justice; Harry Innes, attorney general; John Brown and Benjamin Sebastian, attorneys; and James Wilkinson, businessman. Harrison and Klotter also list John Fowler. See Harrison and Klotter, *A New History of Kentucky*, 57.
20. Watlington, *Partisan Spirit*, 229–30. Watlington's list of country party leaders included Humphrey and Thomas Marshall. Harrison and Klotter add Robert Breckinridge, Robert Bullitt, Joseph Crockett, and John Edwards to that list. See Harrison and Klotter, *A New History of Kentucky*, 57.

21. Watlington, *Partisan Spirit*, 226.

22. Ibid., 225–26.

23. Ibid., 228. The "Spanish Conspiracy" remains an important event in the early history of Kentucky, especially in light of the many leading court party members who were active conspirators. It dramatically illustrates the ill will court party members held toward the Atlantic states. Watlington provides an excellent examination of the conspiracy in *Partisan Spirit*, 139–97 passim and 253–60. Surprisingly, Wilkinson's most recent biographer, while placing Wilkinson at the heart of the conspiracy, provides little detail about the conspiracy. See Andro Linklater, *An Artist in Treason: The Extraordinary Double Life of General James Wilkinson* (New York: Walker Publishing Company, Inc., 2009), 85, 87–88, 94–95.

24. Watlington, *Partisan Spirit*, 111.

25. Ibid., 90–97, 228–29.

26. David Wood Meriwether to William Meriwether, 14 September 1785, in David Wood Meriwether Miscellaneous Papers, The Filson Historical Society, Louisville, KY.

27. [Alarmed Kentuckian], 4 December 1786, in Draper Mss. 19CC38 of the Kentucky Papers of the Lyman C. Draper Collection, Wisconsin Historical Society, Madison, Wisconsin.

28. George Muter to Madison, 20 February 1787, in *The Papers of James Madison*, eds. Robert A. Rutland et al. (Chicago and London: The University of Chicago Press, 1975), 9:280.

29. Clift, "District of Kentucky," 370.

30. Watlington, *Partisan Spirit*, 132.

31. Enclosed in a letter from Arthur Campbell to Edmund Randolph, 16 February 1787, in *Calendar of Virginia State Papers and Other Manuscripts*, eds. William A. Palmer et al. (Richmond: R. U. Derr, Superintendent of Public Printing, 1894), 4:243. Campbell does not name the author, but he seemed worried, noting that unnamed individuals had taken "great pains" to circulate the letter, thus "giving them an Air of Seeresy [Secrecy]." Governor Randolph subsequently directed the letter to the attention of the Confederation Congress. Congress also published a letter from Thomas Green to the governor and legislature of Georgia, dated 26 December 1786, that expressed similar sentiments and at times used identical phrasing. It is unclear who forwarded this letter to Congress. See *Journals of the Continental Congress, 1774–1789*, ed. Worthington C. Ford et al. (Washington, DC: Government Printing Office, 1936), 32:194–99. The Draper source speculated that Wilkinson (probably James Wilkinson) was the author of the letter. It does resemble the type of letters Wilkinson was writing about this time. See Wilkinson to Hutchinson, 20 June 1785, in [James Wilkinson], "Letters of James Wilkinson Addressed to Dr. James Hutchinson, of Philadelphia," *Pennsylvania Magazine of History and Biography*, 12 (1888), 56–61.

32. [Alarmed Kentuckian], in Draper Mss. 19CC38.

33. Ibid.

34. Ibid.

35. Ibid.

36. Ibid.

37. Ibid.

38. Ibid.

39. "Circular Letter Directed to the Different Courts in the Western Country," in Brown, *Political Beginnings of Kentucky*, 244.

40. Ibid.

41. Ibid., 243.

42. Ibid., 244.

43. Ibid.

44. Watlington, *Partisan Spirit*, 124.

45. Ibid., 123.

46. John Brown to Matthew Walton, 5 June 1788, in John Brown Miscellaneous Papers, The Filson Historical Society, Louisville, KY. Brown made similar arguments in Brown to James Breckinridge, 21 June 1788, in Breckinridge Papers, University of Virginia, Charlottesville, VA. Also see Robert Breckinridge to James Breckinridge, 2 July 1788, in Breckinridge-Marshall Papers, The Filson Historical Society, Louisville, KY.

47. Brown to Walton, 5 June 1788, in John Brown Miscellaneous Papers.

48. Ibid.

49. Brown to Thomas Jefferson, 10 August 1788, in *Letters of Delegates to Congress*, eds. Paul H. Smith et al. (Washington, DC: Library of Congress, 1998), 25:283.

50. Ibid.

51. Ibid.

52. Brown to Madison, 7 June 1788, in *The Papers of James Madison*, eds. Robert A. Rutland et al. (Charlottesville: University Press of Virginia, 1977), 11:89.

53. Brown, *Political Beginnings of Kentucky*, 106.

54. Charles Gano Talbert, "Kentuckians in the Virginia Convention of 1788," *The Register of the Kentucky Historical Society*, 58 (July 1960), 189.

55. Brown, *Political Beginnings of Kentucky*, 108. Brown lists as members of the club Brown, Innes, McDowell, Muter, and Sebastian. Although Brown did not list Caleb Wallace as a member of the Political Club, Wallace's critique of the Constitution is similar to the Political Club's statement. See Wallace to William Fleming, 3 May 1788, in Fleming-Christian Correspondence, Grisby Papers, Virginia Historical Society, Richmond, Virginia.

56. Brown, *Political Beginnings of Kentucky*, 108–9.

57. William W. Freehling, *The Road to Disunion*, vol. 1 of *Secessionists at Bay, 1776–1854* (New York and Oxford: Oxford University Press, 1990), 121–38 passim; Brown, *Political Beginnings of Kentucky*, 109.

58. Brown, *Political Beginnings of Kentucky*, 107–8.

59. Brown to Madison, 12 May 1788, in Rutland et al., *Madison Papers*, 11:42; Watlington, *Partisan Spirits*, 150; Talbert, "Kentuckians," 187.

60. Talbert, "Kentuckians," 187–93; *The Documentary History of the Ratification of the Constitution*, eds. John P. Kaminski and Gaspare J. Saladino (Madison: State Historical Society of Wisconsin, 1993), 10:1538–41; Watlington, *Partisan Spirit*, 155–56. The fourteen Kentucky delegates were Notley Conn and Henry Lee of Bourbon County, John Fowler and Humphrey Marshall of Fayette County, Robert Breckinridge and Rice Bullock of Jefferson County, John Logan and Henry Pawling of Lincoln County, Green Clay and John Miller of Madison County, Thomas Allin and Alexander Robertson of Mercer County, and John Steele and Matthew Walton of Nelson County. Breckinridge, Bullock and Marshall voted in favor of the Constitution.

61. Harrison and Klotter, *A New History of Kentucky*, 58; Watlington, *Partisan Spirit*, 159, 165, 179. Wilkinson's plans collapsed when John Brown failed to reveal his knowledge of Gardoqui's willingness to offer the use of the Mississippi River to the Kentuckians if Kentucky were to break away from the Union. Andro Linklater, *An Artist in Treason*, 92–95; Watlington, *Partisan Spirit*, 175–78; George Morgan Chinn, *Kentucky: Settlement and Statehood, 1750–1800* (Frankfort: Kentucky Historical Society, 1975), 455–61; and Harrison and Klotter, *A New History of Kentucky*, 58–60.

62. "To the United States in Congress Assembled," in Brown, *Political Beginnings of Kentucky*, 261.

Chapter Eight

And Slavery

Just how great an influence slavery had on a person's decision to settle in the West in the late eighteenth century is hard to measure. Nonslaveholder and slaveholder alike crossed the Appalachian Mountains and settled in the fertile river valleys of Kentucky and Tennessee. For most people, the West meant opportunity and, whether they owned slaves or not, they chose to undergo the arduous journey west to share in that opportunity.

The accounts of some settlers reveal a nonchalant attitude toward the connection between slavery and western settlement. Remembering his move to Kentucky, John Graves recalled that he "came here, Dec. 5 or 6, 1786. . . . [I] had come out the year before, & purchased this place of Elijah & John Craig for my f. [father]. Father, Mother & myself came out w. [with] 30 blacks."[1] Reminiscences like Grave's show just how matter-of-fact slavery and westward migration seemed to some people. This casual attitude, however, belied how truly controversial slavery in the West was for Americans in the late eighteenth century.

The pace of western settlement accelerated at the conclusion of the war against Great Britain. In 1780, the estimated population of Kentucky was 45,000; approximately 10,000 people were living within the boundaries of what would become the present-day state of Tennessee.[2] By the first federal census, more than 73,000 people lived within the district of Kentucky and nearly 36,000 in the two districts of the Territory South of the River Ohio. One decade later, the new states of Kentucky and Tennessee had populations of 220,955 and 105,602, respectively, and the Mississippi Territory, created by Congress in 1798, 8,850 residents. The number of slaves also showed dramatic increases between the first and second censuses. The slave population increased in Kentucky from slightly fewer than 12,500 to more than

40,000 and Tennessee from 3,417 to 13,584. In the Mississippi Territory, slaves constituted nearly 40 percent of the population in 1800.[3]

Slavery and its place in the westward movement of the nation unexpectedly became a topic of political discussion when Congress in early 1784 asked Thomas Jefferson of Virginia, Jeremiah Townley Chase of Maryland and David Howell of Rhode Island to "prepare a plan for [the] temporary government of [the] western territory."[4] Jefferson, who had working on a government for the West since late 1783, completed the task within a few days of the formation of the committee on 3 February 1784.[5] The need for such a plan arose from a request that Congress had made to the states in 1780 asking them to relinquish their claims to land in the West. Virginia, which claimed the entire region north of present-day Tennessee, did so in early 1784, excepting only Kentucky and a large military tract north of the Ohio River. Despite the Virginia cession, Congress still lacked complete title to the West. Connecticut and Massachusetts claimed possession of vast expanses of territory north of the Ohio River. At the same time, Georgia and the Carolinas stubbornly retained their land claims south of Kentucky.[6] Nevertheless, anticipating its eventual ownership of the region, Congress acted in early 1784 to establish a "temporary government of the Western territory."[7]

On 1 March, Jefferson presented Congress his plan for the establishment of territories and their eventual transformation into states.[8] The Virginian included within his blueprint a provision prohibiting slavery in the territory "after the year 1800."[9] The proposal encountered stiff opposition from southern congressmen. On 19 April, Richard D. Spaight of North Carolina moved that the item be deleted from the bill; Jacob Read of South Carolina seconded the motion.[10] Sixteen delegates, including Jefferson and Hugh Williamson of North Carolina, voted in favor of retaining the clause. Seven delegates, all from southern states, voted for its deletion.[11] As Jefferson described the voting to his friend James Madison, the provision

> lost by an individual vote only. Ten states were present. The 4 Eastern states, N. York, Penns'va, were for the clause. [New] Jersey would have been for it, but there were but two members, one of whom was sick in his chambers. South Carolina[,] Maryland, and !Virginia! voted against it. N. Carolina was divided as would have been Virginia had not one of it's [sic] delegates been sick in bed.[12]

Thus, Spaight's motion passed, as its opponents could not secure the seven votes needed for its defeat.[13]

Congress returned to the question of slavery in the territories only once before passage of the Northwest Ordinance in 1787. Rufus King of Massachusetts made the motion in 1785 to prohibit slavery in the "States described in the resolve of Congress of the 23 April, 1784," Jefferson's Ordinance of 1784.[14] Eight states, including Maryland, voted to send it to committee; three states (North Carolina, South Carolina, and Virginia), as well as the lone delegate from Georgia, voted against the measure.[15] When it returned from committee with a fugitive slave clause attached, King, who had added the clause in the hope of winning southern support, suddenly realized that he had alienated many supporters of the original proposal and decided against pursuing the measure further.[16] Two years would pass before Congress would once again entertain a similar motion. This time, however, the outcome was different.

On July 11, 1787, Nathan Dane, who replaced Rufus King in the Massachusetts delegation, introduced his amendment prohibiting slavery to a bill establishing a government for the territory north of the Ohio River.[17] To his surprise, Congress, despite the presence of "only Massachusetts of the Eastern States," accepted the amendment without discussion.[18] Only two individuals, Dane and William Grayson of Virginia, are known to have written letters commenting on the amendment. Dane stated that he presented the amendment after he found "the House favorably disposed on the subject," but he offered no reason for its favorable reception among members, especially southern members.[19] Grayson explained the southern vote in economic terms. The amendment "was agreed to by the Southern members for the purpose of preventing Tobacco and Indigo from being made" in the territory north of the Ohio River.[20] Although Grayson's explanation appears reasonable, some historians have argued that southerners supported the measure because of the inclusion of a fugitive slave clause in the amendment, something lacking nationally at the time. They also stress that the passage of the amendment meant the tacit sanction of slavery south of the river.[21] Whatever their motivation, southern congressmen clearly saw nothing in the amendment to fear. A similar conclusion, however, cannot be drawn from the meeting occurring behind closed doors in Philadelphia.

While Congress in 1787 debated a plan of government for the territory north of the Ohio River, delegates from twelve states were busy forging a new government for the United States. As in the case of congressional action on the Northwest Ordinance, slavery became a topic for discussion at the Constitutional Convention. Unlike members of the Confederation Congress, delegates to the Constitutional Convention did not act with such unanimity.

Alone among the states, Georgia and South Carolina had continued the unrestricted importation of Africans after the American Revolution. Maryland and Virginia had prohibited the practice, whereas North Carolina had simply imposed a duty of between five and fifty pounds on each slave imported into the state based on point of origin. At the convention, the two southernmost states wished to continue the trade; Virginia, Maryland, and the middle Atlantic states wanted to end it. The New England states, in contrast, sought a compromise that would protect their carrying trade.[22]

On 21 August, Luther Martin of Maryland "proposed to vary the sect: 4. article VII so as to allow a prohibition or tax on the importation of slaves."[23] The Committee of Detail, which the convention had instructed to prepare a draft text incorporating all agreements, had written the clause to read: "No tax or duty shall be laid by the Legislature on articles exported from any State; nor on the migration or importation of such persons as the several States shall think proper to admit; nor shall such migration or importation be prohibited."[24] Luther cited three reasons for making the motion. First, he told delegates, the three-fifths clause, which counted five slaves as three free men for the purpose of taxation and apportionment in the House of Representatives, would encourage states to import slaves to increase their representation in the lower house. Secondly, Luther believed that it was "unreasonable" for one section of the nation to protect a practice that "weakened one part of the Union."[25] Finally, the institution, the Marylander declared, "was inconsistent with the principles of the revolution and dishonorable to the American character to have such a feature in the Constitution."[26]

George Mason of Virginia, an outspoken critic of the "infernal trafic" at the convention, was apparently the only member who equated slavery with the West.[27] He envisioned nothing but harm befalling the United States if delegates chose to permit Georgia and South Carolina to retain their trade in slaves. "The Western people are already calling out for slaves for their new lands," he declared, "and [they] will fill that Country with slaves if they can be got thro' S. Carolina & Georgia."[28] Slavery, he told his fellow delegates, "discourages arts & manufactures. The poor despise labor when performed by slaves. They prevent the immigration of Whites, who really enrich & strengthen a Country. They produce pernicious effect on manners. Every master of slaves is born a petty tyrant."[29] As for the United States, Mason predicted nothing but trouble, believing that Heaven punished nations for their wickedness. "By an inevitable chain of causes & effects," he warned, "providence punishes national sins, by national calamities."[30] It was, therefore, "essential" in Mason's view for the new government to have the authority to prevent the further spread of slavery in the United States.[31]

Charles Cotesworth Pinckney and John Rutledge of South Carolina and Abraham Baldwin of Georgia vehemently opposed any ban on the importation of slaves. Pinckney, who believed that the southern states would eventually prohibit the practice if left alone, warned the convention that any "attempt to take away the right as proposed will produce serious objections to the Constitution."[32] "S. Carolina & Georgia cannot do without slaves," he declared.[33] Later, at the South Carolina ratifying convention, Pinckney clarified his position:

> While there remained one acre of swampland uncleared of South Carolina, I would raise my voice against restricting the importation of negroes. I am

thoroughly convinced . . . that the nature of our climate, and the flat, swampy situation of our country, obliges us to cultivate our lands with negroes, and that without them South Carolina would soon be a desert waste.[34]

Baldwin, who said he had attended the convention to decide "national objects alone," pronounced the importation of slaves an issue of "local nature."[35] It was Pinckney's associate who, perhaps, said it best. "The true question at present," Rutledge told the delegates, "is whether the Southn. [Southern] States shall or shall not be parties to the Union."[36]

Eventually, as Pinckney told the assembled group at the South Carolina ratifying convention, a majority of the states decided to commit the question to a "committee of the states . . . and, after a great deal of difficulty, it was settled on the footing recited in the Constitution."[37] Pinckney spoke of the role played by the New England members, who, he said, asked for a time in the future when the trade might be ended "'and we will endeavor, for your convenience, to restrain the religious and political prejudices of our people on this subject.'"[38] George Mason, who refused to sign the Constitution due to its perceived monarchial or aristocratic overtones and its lack of a bill of rights, cast the last week of the convention as a period when the supporters of the Constitution "found they had a decided Majority in their Favour, which was obtained," he maintained, "by a Compromise between the Eastern, and the two Southern States, to permit the latter to continue the Importation of Slaves for twenty odd Years; a more favourite Object with them than the Liberty and Happiness of the People."[39]

During the First Congress, representatives from Georgia and South Carolina continued to protect their peculiar institution from attacks. When memorialists started asking Congress to end slavery, their actions provoked strong responses from men whose states had sought to preserve the practice during the Constitutional Convention. One particular memorial sparked intense debate in early 1790. The Pennsylvania Society for Promoting the Abolition of Slavery asked Congress to restore liberty "to those unhappy men, who alone, in this land of freedom are degraded into perpetual bondage."[40] The society further implored Congress "to step to the very verge of the power vested in you for discouraging every species of traffic in the persons of our fellowmen."[41] Thomas Tudor Tucker of South Carolina immediately challenged the right of the House to hear the memorial, declaring its requests unconstitutional. He further expressed surprise that Benjamin Franklin, "a man who ought to have known the Constitution better," would have signed such a document.[42] The Pennsylvanian had signed the memorial in his capacity as president of the society. Representative Aedanus Burke agreed with his fellow South Carolinian. He described the situation as sorrowful, especially when "petitioners [are] paid more attention to than the Constitution."[43]

Not all southerners reacted negatively to the memorial. Representatives Joshua Seney of Maryland and John Page of Virginia saw nothing wrong with assigning it to a committee, as did James Madison.[44] Madison, speaking late in the debate, admitted that the Constitution restricted Congress from ending the slave trade; "yet there are a variety of ways by which it could countenance the abolition, and regulations might be made in relation to the introduction of them into the new States to be formed out of the Western Territory."[45] Elbridge Gerry of Massachusetts agreed with Madison, adding that Congress could purchase all the slaves using the proceeds from western land sales if it desired.[46] Eventually, the House, by a vote of 43 to 14, decided to commit the memorial to a committee. Only Virginia, among the southern states, had a majority of its representatives vote for commitment.[47]

For the most part, the West was a peripheral issue in the general discourse over slavery. When most residents of the seaboard states addressed the issue of slavery and the West, they spoke of something removed from their every-day lives. Not so with the people who ventured across the Allegheny Mountains to carve out new homes for themselves in the West. Slavery was a real part of their lives, either directly or indirectly. Many slaves had accompanied their masters west; a smaller number had arrived as part of slave traders' gangs of human wares.[48] Some people, however, abhorred slave labor and preferred not to be a part of a slave society. Unlike seaboard residents, when westerners addressed the subject of slavery and its place in the West, they were speaking about something very important—their future.[49]

After many failed attempts at statehood, Kentuckians came together in the spring of 1792 to take the final step before becoming a state. They had been close before, but this time, they had the consent of all the necessary parties. Only the drafting of a state constitution stood in the way of statehood.[50]

In April 1792, forty-five men met in Danville to prepare the document. Small landowners and planters, they mirrored the emerging social structure in Kentucky. Virginia had the largest number of former sons, with more than one-half of the men present. For the most part, however, the delegates appeared to lack the political experience necessary for the task before them. Only a handful of delegates had ever attended college, only two men were lawyers by profession, and fewer than twelve delegates could point to a record of more than one term in the Virginia legislature. Despite their short-comings, they drafted a constitution that defined Kentucky as a state, and slavery formed the basis of that definition.[51]

Slavery had been a part of Kentuckians' earliest discussions about state-hood, and, as the historian Joan Wells Coward has noted, it later "became one of the most important issues in the 1792 convention."[52] In 1788, a "Farmer" wrote the *Lexington Kentucke Gazette* "wishing to hear the opinions of gentlemen on several particulars which have been the subject of debate in some companies where I have been."[53] The lack of discussion about a constitution, "which is of the greatest importance to posterity," had prompted the Farmer's letter to the Lexington newspaper.[54] The Farmer, in particular, wanted to hear comments about whether the constitution should include a clause respecting slavery, for, as the Farmer knew, not everyone who settled in Kentucky supported the practice.[55]

Coward attributes the antislavery sentiment in Kentucky to three groups of people. She notes that settlers who hailed from the New England and northern states generally felt little attachment to the institution, preferring, in some cases, not to associate with it.[56] Daniel Drake, whose family moved to Kentucky from New Jersey in 1788, remembered as a young boy hearing his father and neighbors talk about leaving Kentucky for "The Territory [the Northwest Territory]."[57] Although his father never made the move, Drake did recall the primary reason why his father had contemplated it: "The existence of slavery in Kentucky."[58]

Coward also believes that antislavery sentiments were prevalent among certain settlers from Virginia, such as John Brown and Harry Innes, who had been touched by the "antislavery liberalism" of some of their former state's leading men.[59] Brown, who represented the district in Congress, had started to form his antislavery views as early as 1779.[60] His friend Harry Innes, who was serving as a federal district court judge, had participated in the Political Club's lengthy discussion of the federal Constitution and was a member of the committee that drafted "The Constitution of the United States as amended and approved by The Political Club."[61] Club members had objected to the 1808 Clause, preferring that Congress act sooner.[62] The strongest antislavery impulses in the district, however, came from the churches.

Methodist, Presbyterian, and, to a lesser extent, Baptist ministers in Kentucky were generally opposed to slavery during the late eighteenth century. The Methodist ministers' opposition to the practice stemmed from the antislavery pronouncements of the 1784 Christmas Conference, which officially created the denomination, and their 1780 meeting in Baltimore, during which they pledged to work for gradual emancipation. Unlike their Methodist counterparts, Presbyterian ministers could not point to a particular event or events. Rather, their educational background, steeped in the works of Enlightenment writers, caused them to view slavery as an affront to the natural rights of man. Such formal education was a rarity among Baptist ministers, who often had spent little, if any, time in classrooms. Like the people to whom they ministered, Baptist preachers were divided over slavery, with personal views on morality guiding their decisions on the subject. In the end, voters elected 16 antislavery advocates to the constitutional convention— seven ministers and nine laymen. For a time during the convention, their leader was David Rice.[63]

David Rice had arrived unexpectedly in Kentucky in the fall of 1783. Earlier that year, in the spring, he had toured Kentucky with the intention of moving from Bedford County, Virginia, where he was pastor of the church at Peaks of Otter. The speculative nature of land acquisition in the district, not to mention the uncertainty about land titles, caused the minister to reconsider the move. After returning home, he received a request from residents in the vicinity of Danville to be their pastor. Only after reassuring himself of their sincerity did Rice agree to become their pastor. He arrived with his family at the Forks of Dick's River in late October.[64]

At the convention, Rice confronted an able opponent, George Nicholas. A well-known and respected lawyer from Virginia, Nicholas had joined his friend James Madison during the Virginia ratifying convention in championing the Federalist position against the persuasive oratory of Patrick Henry. Soon after the conclusion of the convention, Nicholas departed for Danville, Kentucky, where he intended to put his legal training to work litigating land title disputes while he managed his sizeable investment in land and slaves.[65] Although the future Kentucky attorney general had foresworn politics when he left Virginia, he could not resist the temptation of participating in the formation of a new government for Kentucky.[66] Even before Nicholas and Rice tangled over the issue of slavery in the convention, the debate on the future of the institution in Kentucky had already become intense.

In the fall of 1791, the *Lexington Kentucky Gazette* started printing a number of letters from individuals offering advice on a future constitution for Kentucky. Several commentators addressed ways to make the state government more accountable to the people, such as granting county committees the "negative upon the bills passed by the Assembly."[67] Others concentrated on upholding individual rights, particularly the right expounded in the bills of rights of some southern states, which declared that "all men . . . [were] born equally free."[68] The newspaper debate proved to be a preview in many ways of the upcoming slavery discussion in the constitutional convention.

A proposal calling for the gradual emancipation of slaves in Kentucky appeared in the *Lexington Kentucky Gazette* in October 1791. Besides leaving blank the date on which "involuntary servitude or slavery" would end in Kentucky, it failed to trace the route that emancipation would take, preferring to leave it to "a future law of the Legislature."[69] Despite these shortcomings, the proposed measure helped to set the parameters of the slavery debate in the newspaper.

Proponents of the practice countered the natural rights position of slavery opponents with their own interpretation of natural rights. "As great a friend as Mr. H.S.B.M. appears to be, to the great rights of mankind," wrote one "disinterested Citizen,"

> yet do his principles thwart and counteract the very the very [*sic*] article of our declaration of rights—This article declares, That all men are by nature equally free and independent, and have certain inherent rights, of which, when they

enter into a state of society, they cannot by any compact, deprive or divest their posterity; namely, the enjoyment of life and liberty, with the means of acquiring and possessing property, and pursuing and obtaining happiness and [unintelligible].—But notwithstanding this noble declaration, he wishes to take away our slaves and so deprive us of this means of acquiring and possessing property.[70]

Another individual writing under the name "Little Brutus" argued the maxim "that no man, or body of men, has a right to deprive me of my honest and legal[ly] acquired property, either in the organizing the Constitution, or in the formation of laws under that Government."[71]

A few months later, "Brutus Senr. [Senior]" rebuked Little Brutus in the newspaper. After admitting that Little Brutus's maxim was "certainly very good," Brutus Senior proceeded to challenge it:

I am born heir to my liberty, according to the origin of laws; but born the property of another according to the doctrine of Brutus; then it follows, that the Convention or Legislature is under an absolute necessity of doing wrong, Brutus or I must be injured; he must lose, perhaps one hundred pounds of his legally acquired property, or I must lose what is dearer to me then [than] ten thousand pounds, my own liberty and that of my family which we were born heirs to. No man can doubt, on which side [of] the question, justice lies.[72]

Once finished with Little Brutus's maxim, the senior Brutus challenged Little Brutus's other reasons for preserving slavery in Kentucky. In his letter, Little Brutus had argued that a prohibition against slavery in Kentucky would deprive the future state not only "of a great source of revenue" but also of a way to ensure that large property owners adequately contribute to the financial well-being of the future state.[73] Brutus Senior's simple response to this line of reasoning was: "Cannot a free man pay his own tax as well as the master can pay the tax of his Slave?"[74] Besides, the writer reminded his readers, "from whose labor does this tax money arise?"[75]

Little Brutus had also warned that the failure of the future state to embrace slavery would seriously "retard . . . [its] opening and culture" and "divert the course of emigration."[76] Just think for a moment, he told his readers, about the cost of labor in a Kentucky without slaves. The image would be so powerful, he concluded, that "no arguments are wanting to enforce the necessity of labourers."[77] Brutus Senior, to the contrary, saw no reason to be alarmed, even after he readily accepted Little Brutus's position that the course of emigration would change in a Kentucky without slavery. "It will invite thousands of honest industrious citizens; while it will shut out only a few who wishes to live at the expence of others. . . . A happy exchange!"[78]

Finally, Brutus Senior could not leave unchallenged Little Brutus's last predicted "evil" for a Kentucky without slavery—"a total change of colour."[79] "Heavens protect us!" he exclaimed.[80] "No, rather than our children or their successors should ever be Mulatoes we will trample all the laws of humanity under foot and sacrifice the rights of thousands to the colour of the skin of our children[']s great grand children[']s children; for what is liberty? . . . The privilege only of a few, far from being a right common to all."[81] "Little is his name," Brutus Senior proclaimed, "and . . . little his ideas, little his reasons, of little use to himself and less to the public."[82]

Similar passion affected the men attending the constitutional convention. "The emancipation of Slaves was a matter much debated in the house," recalled Hubbard Taylor, a delegate.[83] Some of the men in attendance, including the Reverend David Rice, had hoped to secure an immediate end for the institution. "A considerable number of delegates, as well as myself," asserted Taylor, "would have been very glad to have seen a stop put to the ingress of Slaves after a certain point."[84] Instead, the debate was won by George Nicholas and the supporters of slavery.

Nicholas viewed the issue as a legal question first and a policy question second. As a slaveholder, he vigorously defended an individual's right to own slaves, although he was careful to frame his argument in more general terms. "Though we are to form a constitution," he told the delegates, "there are many important points already settled; among them is the right of property. . . . The convention either have a general power to destroy or curtail it, or they have none: If a general power why stop here—divide land—then stock and personal property." "It is a settled principle of all free governments," he reminded the assembled group, "that the nation has no right to deprive an individual of his property unless it is essentially necessary to the public good, and that only after a just compensation has been previously made to him. Liberty consists in a great measure," he explained, "in the exclusive right of property. . . . Those who in any instance destroy this right, tho it is in a case which may appear favourable to personal liberty[,] should consider that by doing it one instance, they break down the barrier which is the security to prosperity."[85]

Later, in a letter to James Madison, Nicholas reiterated his position. "The laws of Virginia," he noted,

> declared them [slaves] property, [and] those laws have obliged the creditor, the orphan and the widow to take them in satisfaction of just demands for money. If then they have either been considered as property by those laws without proper authority, or considerations of public good required that they should no longer be viewed in that light, the country ought to make the owners a compensation.[86]

Rice, on the other hand, refused to look at the issue before the convention simply as a legal question; instead, he argued against the presence of the institution in the new state primarily on moral grounds. "Holding men in slavery," he wrote,

> is the national vice of Virginia; and while a part of that State, we were partakers in the guilt. As a separate state, we are just now come to the birth; and it depends upon our free choice, whether we shall be born in this sin, or innocent of it. We now have it in our power to adopt it as our national crime; or to bear a national testimony against it. I hope the later will be our choice; that we shall wash our hands of this guilt; and not leave it in the power of a future legislature, ever more to stain our reputation or our conscience with it. [87]

Both men also realized that the outcome of their debate would have an effect on future immigration patterns to the state. "Policy obliged us," Nicholas told Madison shortly after the conclusion of the convention, "to do something of the kind, for if we had not we should have received no more valuable emigrants from the five S. [southern] states."[88] Rice, on the other hand, viewed the migration of slaveholders to Kentucky with alarm. The elimination of slavery in Kentucky, he wrote, would keep "out a great and intolerable nuisance, the bane of every country where it is admitted[, while] . . . it would invite useful citizens into our state."[89] "A man," Rice warned the delegates, "who has no slaves, cannot live easy and contented in the midst of those, who possess them in numbers."[90] Eventually, the man must leave. "Thus this country will spew out its white inhabitants; and be peopled with slaveholders, their slaves, and a few, in the highest posts of a poor free man, I mean that of an overseer."[91]

Rice, however, was not present when the convention voted on a motion by Samuel Taylor to delete article nine from the proposed constitution.[92] Nicholas viewed the article, which prohibited the legislature from emancipating slaves without their owners' consent and without providing a "full equivalent in money" in compensation to their owners, not so much as a proslavery statement, but rather as an attempt on the part of the supporters of slavery "to secure" their property from "a proposition . . . declaring that the legislature should provide for a gradual emancipation without saying any thing about an equivalent to the slave holders."[93] On 18 April, a majority of the convention delegates, including James Madison's cousin Hubbard Taylor, chose to retain the article by voting against Samuel Taylor's motion.[94]

Tennessee avoided a similar debate when it became a state in 1796. Slavery had been a part of the Territory South of the River Ohio ever since its establishment in 1790. In its act "ceding to the United States of America certain western Lands," the North Carolina legislature stipulated that "*provided always* that no regulations made or to be made by Congress shall tend to emancipate Slaves."[95] Congress accepted the terms and the land on 2 April

1790.[96] The influx of settlers from slaveholding states during the territorial period helped ensure the proslavery character of the new state.

Migration patterns also helped create the proslavery posture of the Mississippi Territory and mute any debate on the subject. In their memorial to Congress asking for "a Constitution or form of Gov^t," members of the Natchez Permanent Committee reminded Congress that the "great part of the labour in this Country is performed by slaves. . . . From this consideration your Memorialists request that the system of slavery may be continued as heretofore in this territory."[97] Andrew Ellicott, one of the U.S. commissioners surveying the boundary line between the United States and Spanish Florida and an actor in the drama unfolding, approved of their request, noting that, although slavery was "disagreeable to us northern people, it would certainly be expedient to let it continue in this district . . . ; otherwise emigrants possessed of that kind of property, would be induced to settle in [S]panish territory."[98]

Congress was also inclined to allow slavery to continue in the Natchez country despite the efforts of some House members to exclude it from the proposed territory.[99] In the final analysis, a majority of the members of Congress voted in favor of a Mississippi territorial bill with slavery because, as Secretary of State Timothy Pickering explained it to the first governor of the territory, Winthrop Sargent, "almost all the inhabitants are possessed of slaves."[100]

Of the one district and two territories established in the West prior to 1800, only one, Kentucky, experienced any real internal debate on the merits of slavery. For a short time, residents of the district freely and openly debated the impact of slavery on their lives and on their new state. Some wished to rid themselves of it; others wished to retain it. In the end, constitutional considerations in the form of a person's right to property persuaded enough men at the Kentucky constitutional convention to reject its abolishment.

NOTES

1. [Shane, John D.], "Interview with Colonel John Graves, Fayette County, Kentucky," in Draper Mss 11CC121 of the Kentucky Papers of the Lyman C. Draper Collection, Wisconsin Historical Society, Madison, WI.

2. *Historical Statistics of the United States, Colonial Times to 1970, Part Two* (Washington, DC: Government Printing Office, 1975), 2:1168.

3. *Return of the Whole Number of Persons Within the Several Districts of the United States, According to "An Act Providing for the Enumeration of the Inhabitants of the United States," Passed March the First, One Thousand Seven Hundred and Ninety-One* (1791, reprint, New York: Norman Ross Publishing Company, 1990), 51, 56; *Return of the Whole Number of Persons Within the Several Districts of the United States, According to "An Act Providing for the Second Census or Enumeration of the Inhabitants of the United States," Passed February the Twenty Eighth, One Thousand Eight Hundred* (1801; reprint, New York: Norman Ross Publishing Company, 1990), 2P, 2Q, 2R.

4. *Journals of the Continental Congress, 1774-1789*, ed. Worthington C. Ford et al. (Washington, DC: Government Printing Office, 1928), 26:118; "Editorial Note" in *The Papers of Thomas Jefferson*, ed., Julian P. Boyd (Princeton: Princeton University Press, 1952), 6:585.

5. Ford, *Journals of the Continental Congress*, 26:118.

6. Paul Finkelman, "The Northwest Ordinance: A Constitution for an Empire of Liberty," in *Pathways to the Old Northwest: An Observance of the Bicentennial of the Northwest Ordinance: Proceedings of a Conference held at Franklin College of Indiana, July 10–11, 1987* (Indianapolis: Indiana Historical Society, 1988), 2; "Map One," in *The Northwest Ordinance, 1787: A Bicentennial Handbook*, ed. Robert M. Taylor, Jr. (Indianapolis: Indiana Historical Society, 1987).

7. Ford, *Journals of the Continental Congress*, 26:274. Also see "Editorial Note," in Boyd et al., *Jefferson Papers*, 6:585-87, for a general overview of Jefferson's preparations.

8. Ford, *Journals of the Continental Congress*, 26:118.

9. Ibid., 26:119.

10. Ibid., 26:247.

11. Ibid.

12. Thomas Jefferson to James Madison, 25 April 1784, in *The Papers of Thomas Jefferson*, ed. Julian P. Boyd (Princeton: Princeton University Press, 1954), 7:118.

13. Ford, *Journals of the Continental Congress*, 26:247. The bill passed Congress by a vote of ten to one, with all members present voting "aye" except the two delegates from South Carolina, Richard Beresford and Jacob Read. Ibid., 26:279.

14. *Journals of the Continental Congress, 1774–1789*, eds. Worthington C. Ford et al. (Washington, DC: Government Printing Office, 1933), 28:164.

15. Ibid., 28:165.

16. Robert Ernst, *Rufus King: American Federalist* (Chapel Hill: The University of North Carolina for the Institute of Early American History and Culture at Williamsburg, Virginia, 1968), 55.

17. *Journals of the Continental Congress, 1774–1789*, eds. Worthington C. Ford et al. (Washington, DC: Government Printing Office, 1936), 32:313; Alfred W. Blumrosen and Ruth G. Blumrosen, *Slave Nation: How Slavery United the Colonies and Sparked the American Revolution* (Naperville, Illinois: Sourcebooks, Inc., 2005), 203.

18. Nathan Dane to Rufus King, 16 July 1787, in *Letters of Delegates to Congress, 1774–1789*, eds. Paul H. Smith et al. (Washington, DC: Library of Congress, 1996), 24:358.

19. Ibid.

20. William Grayson to James Monroe, 8 August 1787, in Smith et al., *Letters of Delegates*, 24:393.

21. Paul Finkelman, "Slavery and Bondage in the 'Empire of Liberty,'" *The Northwest Ordinance: Essays on Its Formulation, Provisions, and Legacy*, ed. Fredrick D. Williams (East Lansing: Michigan State University Press, 1989), 63; Taylor, *The Northwest Ordinance*, 73.

22. *The Records of the Federal Convention of 1787*, ed. Max Farrand (New Haven: Yale University Press, 1911), 2:370–73; *The Records of the Federal Convention of 1787*, ed. Max Farrand (New Haven: Yale University Press, 1911), 3:254.

23. Farrand, *Records of the Federal Convention*, 2:364.

24. Ibid., 2:183.

25. Ibid., 2:364.

26. Ibid.

27. Ibid., 2:370.

28. Ibid.

29. Ibid.

30. Ibid.

31. Ibid.

32. Ibid., 2:371.

33. Ibid.

34. Ibid., 3:254.

35. Ibid., 2:372.

36. Ibid., 2:364.

37. Ibid., 3:254, 2:366. Seven states (Connecticut, Georgia, Maryland, New Jersey, North Carolina, South Carolina, and Virginia) voted for committing the issue to a committee. Three states (Delaware, New Hampshire, and Pennsylvania) voted against it. See Ibid., 2:369.

38. Ibid., 3:254.

39. Joseph C. Morton, *Shapers of the Great Debate at the Constitutional Convention of 1787* (Westport, CT: Greenwood Press, 2006), 203. George Mason to Thomas Jefferson, 26 May 1788, in Farrand, *Records of the Federal Convention*, 3:305. Gary B. Nash, in *Race and Revolution* (Madison, WI: Madison House, 1990), 41–42, argues that northerners, for economic reasons, refused to support any serious southern attempt at ending slavery in the United States in the 1780s and 1790s. In fact, New Englanders particularly were interested in facilitating the requirement that only a majority in Congress be required to regulate commerce rather than the two-thirds figure that Madison and other southerners favored. This compromise between the New England states and the two southern-most states ensured that both groups received what they wanted. David Waldstreicher, *Slavery's Constitution: From Revolution to Ratification* (New York: Hill and Wang, 2009), 95.

40. *Annals of Congress*, 1st Cong., 2nd Sess., 1240.

41. Ibid.

42. Ibid.

43. Ibid., 1241.

44. Ibid., 1241, 1245, 1246.

45. Ibid., 1246.

46. Ibid., 1247.

47. Ibid. All three Georgians voted against commitment. The Maryland vote was two for commitment and two against; two representatives did not vote. Four South Carolinians voted against commitment; one member did not vote. Eight Virginians voted for commitment; two against. One member did not vote.

48. John Breckinridge was one slave owner who brought his slaves with him to Kentucky from Virginia in 1792. See Gail S. Terry, "Sustaining the Bonds of Kinship in a Trans-Appalachian Migration, 1790–1811: The Cabell-Breckinridge Slaves Move West," *Virginia Magazine of History and Biography,* 102:4 (October 1994), 455. As far as slave traders are concerned, they are harder to uncover during this period, but John Chisholm, who would later become involved in the "Blount Conspiracy," seems to have been involved in slave-dealing activities as early as January 1795. See John Chisholm to Issac Shelby, 24 January 1795, in Draper Mss 11DD53 of the King's Mountain Papers of the Lyman C. Draper Collection, Wisconsin Historical Society, Madison, WI. The consensus, however, among historians is that prior to 1810, most slaves accompanied their owners west. See Steven Deyle, "The Irony of Liberty: Origins of the Domestic Slave Trade," *Journal of the Early Republic* 12:1 (Spring 1992), 61.

49. Richard Callaway's female slave accompanied him to Kentucky in 1775, serving as one of two cooks for Daniel Boone's company of men building the Wilderness Road. See John Mack Faragher, *Daniel Boone: The Life and Legend of an American Pioneer* (New York: Henry Holt and Company, 1992), 112–13. In 1775, the slave Monk Estill accompanied his owner, James Estill, to Kentucky. See William Dodd Brown, ed., "A Visit to Boonesborough in 1779: The Recollections of Pioneer George M. Bedinger," *The Register of the Kentucky Historical Society*, 86 (Autumn 1988), 323. James Robertson's slave, Robert, was among the first party of settlers in Nashville, Tennessee, in 1779. See Anita S. Goodstein, "Black History on the Tennessee Frontier, 1780–1810," *Tennessee Historical Quarterly* 38 (Winter 1979), 402.

50. For background on the conventions see Patricia Watlington, *The Partisan Spirit: Kentucky Politics, 1779–1792* (New York: Atheneum for the Institute of Early American History and Culture at Williamsburg, Virginia, 1972), 77–198 *passim*.

51. Joan Wells Coward, *Kentucky in the New Republic: The Process of Constitution Making* (Lexington: University Press of Kentucky, 1979), 21.

52. Ibid., 36.

53. *Lexington Kentucke Gazette*, 2 February 1788.

54. Ibid.

55. Ibid.

56. Coward, *Kentucky in the New Republic*, 38.

57. Daniel Drake, *Pioneer Life in Kentucky, 1785–1800*, ed. Emmet Field Horine (New York: Henry Schuman, 1948), 209.

58. Ibid.

59. Coward, *Kentucky in the New Republic*, 38.

60. Ibid.

61. Thomas Speed, *The Political Club, Danville, Kentucky, 1786–1790: Being an Account of an Early Kentucky Society from the Original Papers Recently Found* (Louisville: John P. Morton and Company, 1894), 143–151.

62. Ibid., 151. For additional information on slavery in early Kentucky see Marion B. Lucas, *From Slavery to Segregation, 1760–1891: A History of Blacks in Kentucky*, 2 vols. (Frankfort: Kentucky Historical Society, 1992), Jeffrey Brooke Allen, "Means and Ends in Kentucky Abolitionism, 1792–1823," *The Filson Club History Quarterly*, 50 (October 1983), 365–81, and Jeffrey Brooke Allen, "The Origins of Proslavery Thought in Kentucky, 1792–1799," *The Register of the Kentucky Historical Society*, 78 (Spring 1979), 75–90.

63. The Christmas Conference described slavery as being contrary to the law of God and outlined the method for Methodists "to extirpate slavery." Quoted in Norman W. Spellmann, "The Formation of the Methodist Episcopal Church," in Emory Stevens Bucke, ed., *The History of American Methodism* (New York: Abingdon Press, 1964), 1:227. See also David T. Bailey, *Shadow On the Church: Southwestern Evangelical Religion and the Issue of Slavery, 1783–1860* (Ithaca and London: Cornell University Press, 1985), 30–51, and Coward, *Kentucky in the New Republic*, 38–47; John B. Boles, *The Great Revival, 1787–1805: The Origins of the Southern Evangelical Mind* (Lexington: The University Press of Kentucky, 1972); Christine Leigh Heyrman, *Southern Cross: The Beginning of the Bible Belt* (Chapel Hill and London: The University of North Carolina Press, 1997); Cynthia Lynn Lyerly, *Methodism and the Southern Mind, 1770–1810* (New York and Oxford: Oxford University Press, 1998).

64. Vernon P. Martin, "Father Rice, the Preacher who Followed the Frontier," *The Filson Club History Quarterly* 29 (October 1955), 325–27.

65. Robert V. Remini, "The Early Heroes of Kentucky," *Register of the Kentucky Historical Society* 90:3 (July 1992), 232.

66. George Nicholas to James Madison, 2 January 1789, in *The Papers of James Madison*, eds. Robert A. Rutland et al. (Charlottesville: University Press of Virginia, 1977), 11:408.

67. *Lexington Kentucky Gazette*, 19 November 1791.

68. Ibid.

69. Ibid., 15 October 1791.

70. Ibid., 31 December 1791. Virginians, at the insistence of Robert Carter Nicholas, George Nicholas's father, inserted the clause "when they enter into a state of society" into their Declaration of Rights to emphasis the point that slaves had not entered into a state of society and therefore were removed from the declaration. Kevin B.C. Gutzman, *Virginia's American Revolution: From Dominion to Republic, 1776–1840* (Lanham, MD: Lexington Books, 2007), 27–28.

71. *Lexington Kentucky Gazette*, 24 December 1791.

72. Ibid., 10 March 1792.

73. Ibid., 24 December 1791.

74. Ibid., 10 March 1792.

75. Ibid.

76. Ibid., 10 March 1792 and 24 December 1791.

77. Ibid., 24 December 1791.

78. Ibid., 10 March 1792.

79. Ibid.

80. Ibid.

81. Ibid.

82. Ibid.

83. Hubbard Taylor to James Madison, 16 April 1792, in *The Papers of James Madison*, eds. Robert A. Rutland et al. (Charlottesville: University Press of Virginia, 1983), 14:289.

84. Ibid.

85. "Slaves," in the George Nicholas Papers, The University of Chicago Library, Chicago, IL.

86. Nicholas to Madison, 2 May 1792, Rutland et al., *Madison Papers*, 14:297.

87. David Rice, *Slavery Inconsistent with Justice and Good Policy, Proved by a Speech in the Convention Held at Danville, Kentucky* (Philadelphia: Printed by Parry Hall, 1792), *Early American Imprints, Series 1: Evans, 1639–1800*, no. 24742, p. 36.

88. Nicholas to Madison, 2 May 1792, Rutland et al., *Madison Papers*, 14:297.

89. Rice, "Slavery Inconsistent," 24.

90. Ibid., 25.

91. Ibid.

92. *A Constitution or Form of Governmen [sic] for the State of Kentucky* (Lexington, KY: Printed by John Bradford, 1792), in Clifford K. Shipton, ed., *Early American Imprints, Series 1: Evans, 1639–1800*, no. 24443.

93. Nicholas to Madison, 2 May 1792, in Rutland et al., *Madison Papers*, 14:297.

94. Hubbard Taylor to Madison, 16 April 1792, in Ibid., 14:290.

95. *Annals of Congress*, 1st Cong., 2nd sess., 2267.

96. Ibid., 2269.

97. *The Territorial Papers of the United States*, ed. Clarence Edwin Carter (Washington, DC: Government Printing Office, 1937), 5:10.

98. Ibid., 5:5.

99. *Annals of Congress*, 5th Cong., 2nd sess., 1313. George Thatcher of Massachusetts moved to make it illegal to bring slaves into the territory, but no member of the House seconded his motion.

100. Carter, *Territorial Papers*, 5:27. The territorial bill passed the House on 27 March 1798 without a recorded vote. *Annals of Congress*, 5th Cong., 2nd sess., 1318.

Chapter Nine

Western Anxieties and the
Military Debate

For most western inhabitants in the 1790s, safety from Indian attacks was of paramount importance. In 1790, Judge Harry Innes, writing Secretary of War Henry Knox from Danville, estimated the number of people killed in or while migrating to the Kentucky District since 1783 at 1,500—an increase of more than 1,000 from his estimate in 1787—and "upwards of 20,000 Horses have been taken and carried off—and other property such as money—merchandize—Household Goods—and waring [wearing] apparel hath been carried off and destroyed by these Barbarians to at least 15,000 [pounds]."[1] A memorial to Congress from the "Representatives of the Territory Southwest of the Ohio" in early 1794 asking for "a more effectual system of defense"[2] recounted such misfortunes as "the murder of two hundred people of all descriptions, and the loss of two thousand horses, worth on average, fifty dollars each."[3]

Kentuckians and Virginians living along the Ohio River, as well as those settlers moving into what would become southern Ohio, faced several hostile tribes. Angered at what they viewed as an unreceptive Congress under the Articles of Confederation, which had treated them as conquered nations rather than as possessors of the land, and upset with unscrupulous land speculators, these tribes, including the Shawnee and Miami, sought to make the Ohio River the boundary between their lands and American settlements by attacking settlers on both sides of the waterway.[4] Further to the south, Indian affairs faced similar uncertainties, as Georgia and North Carolina, ignoring the dictates of a weak central government, sought to implement their own Indian policies.[5] By the time George Washington took office in April 1789, the United States confronted a growing problem in the West, and during the congressional debates on how best to serve the defensive needs of the West

that followed the Virginian's and the new government's inauguration, southern congressmen would display a stronger commitment to the West.[6]

Congress began debating frontier defense following Secretary Knox's
submission of a "plan for the arrangement of the militia in the United States"
in January 1790.[7] His proposal, actually an "idea . . . whether an efficient
military branch of Government can be invented, with safety to the great
principle of liberty," elicited considerable debate among members of the
First Congress, who chose to avoid reaching a decision on the controversial
matter by sending it to committee.[8] Despite the efforts of this and other
committees, Congress could never agree on the plan and, partly out of necessity, passed "An Act for regulating the military establishment of the United
States," which President Washington signed on 30 April 1790.[9]

For westerners, the militia debate in Congress was yet another example of
Atlantic seaboard residents' insensitivity to their interests. As events on the
western frontiers escalated, especially after Northwest Territory governor
and superintendent of Indian Affairs Major General Arthur St. Clair's defeat
in an engagement with Indian forces in early November 1791, an anti-war
mood settled over parts of the country.[10] Representative Fisher Ames of
Massachusetts, a supporter of the federal Constitution and an ardent champion of commercial interests, was one person who noticed this "clamor
against the war," attributing it to, among other things, its cost, which he
confessed might "drain the Treasury" if the government were to accept the
westerners' demands to be enlisted as volunteers.[11] North Carolina congressman John Steele likewise heard the "[g]reat complaints" abounding. People,
he reported, disliked "the expensiveness of the i[ndian] war, and not much
appearance of justice."[12]

In Philadelphia, the *Gazette of the United States* and especially the *National Gazette* facilitated a dialogue on the Indian war. Generally, arguments
against the war centered on its justness, cost, and execution. "Have we purchased the territory from them on which we have lately erected several new
forts?" asked one concerned commentator.[13] "Have they not the same right to
their hunting grounds . . . that we have to our houses and farms?" he wondered.[14] A New Jersey contributor, concentrating on the cost of the war,
noted that Congress should have expended the money that it raised through
its "impositions on commerce" with greater frugality and care.[15] Writing
from Albany, a New Yorker laid the entire blame on the federal government's "ill policy, or want of energy" in addressing, in his opinion, the root
cause of the entire problem—the continued British presence in the Northwest
Territory.[16]

With such lingering doubts affecting his section of the country, Pittsburgh
resident Hugh Henry Brackenridge felt it necessary to respond in the *Philadelphia National Gazette*. His "Thoughts on the present Indian War" and
"Farther and Concluding Thoughts on the Indian War" sought to inform the

reader about "the justness of our cause in the war against the Indians" by exploring the "ruthful disposition of a savage" and by reacquainting the reader with the almost righteousness of their desired actions.[17] His remarks did not go unanswered, however, as one contributor noted that "[t]he Indians are denominated [by Brackenridge's] 'beasts of prey' and we are encouraged 'to penetrate the forests where they hunt, and extirpate the race.' Good God! Is this our temper towards these unfortunate people?"[18]

Even President George Washington apparently sensed the unease of the country—and in Congress—over his administration's actions.[19] Commenting that "it appears adviseable" to refresh the public recollection, he instructed Secretary Knox on 16 January 1792 to prepare a statement regarding "the measures which have been taken from time to time for the re-establishment of peace and friendship" with the western tribes.[20] Knox quickly completed his assigned task, releasing it to the press ten days later.[21]

Westerners had for years been arguing that the proper way to contain the Indians was not by establishing more forts and posts, but by using seasoned woodsmen as scouts, who would watch the passes, and small groups of rangers, whose members would protect the settlements. "I am confident," wrote Harry Innes of Kentucky in the summer of 1791, "that if the Government would pursue this mode of attacking the Indians by detachment on Horseback it will have the desired effect and compel them to peace. It fills them with Terror and keeps them watching at home."[22]

Two months after General Arthur St. Clair's humiliating January 1792 defeat, the Second Congress began discussing a bill reported from committee by James Madison for "making further and more effectual provision for the Protection of the Frontiers of the United States."[23] The bill, as the administration had requested, called for "the raising of three additional regiments of infantry and a squadron of light dragoons, amounting in all to three thousand and forty men, exclusive of commissioned officers."[24] At the time of St. Clair's defeat, the United States had only two regiments, each including fewer than 1,000 noncommissioned officers and privates.[25]

Leading off the debate on 26 January, Elias Boudinot of New Jersey insisted that victory over the Indians could only be gained by "justice and moderation," not by the sword.[26] He therefore introduced into the House a motion calling for the removal of the second section of the bill increasing the size of the army to five regiments.[27] Although debate often centered on the morality of the Indian policy of the United States government, Madison would later characterize the debate that ensued as "whether the militia or regular troops were to be preferred in carrying on the Indian war?"[28] Jefferson had hoped that St. Clair's defeat would induce Congress to forget about enlarging the army and instead "confide more in Militia operations," an approach westerners seemed to support.[29] For his part, Madison was realistic enough to know that "much will be left to the Judgment of the President."[30]

In the end, arguments for the use of regular troops prevailed over the use of militia in Congress, as President Washington and Secretary Knox desired.[31] As Pennsylvanian Albert Gallatin noted, however, the outcome may have been due more to fear among southerners that if they did not support Knox's plan, monetary support for the defense of western settlers among northerners, particularly New Englanders, might have evaporated.[32]

Notwithstanding James Madison's characterization, the debate did touch upon East-West relations. "Instead of being ambitious to extend our boundaries," one unnamed member commented, "it would answer a much better national purpose to check the roving disposition of the frontier settlers, and prevent them from too suddenly extending themselves to the Western water."[33] It would be "more useful to the community," he declared, to keep the settlers living nearer the settled parts of the country and thereby lessen the chances that the country would become involved in "unnecessary and expensive wars with the Indians."[34] Later, another unnamed member suggested that an army would serve as an effective barrier between the two hostile groups. "[T]he advocates for a cessation of hostilities would oblige the frontier settlers to abandon their lands," he declared.[35] "But by what new-invented rule of right should the inhabitants of Kentucky, and the other frontier settlers, be laid under a greater obligation than any other citizens of the United States to relinquish a property legally acquired by fair purchase?" he wondered.[36]

Well aware of the West's importance to the country, Thomas Jefferson worked as secretary of state to reduce the causes of western settlers' frustrations with the federal government. In Jefferson's opinion, the encroachment of settlers on Indian land had precipitated many of the Indian raids against western settlers. As such, he supported all efforts, including the government "think[ing] itself bound, not only to declare to the Indians that such settlements are without the authority or protection of the United States, but to remove them also by the public force."[37] He further congratulated territorial officials for their "admonitions against encroachments," which, he predicted, would "have a beneficial effect—the U.S. find an Indian war too serious a thing, to risk incurring one merely to gratify a few intruders with settlements which are to cost the other inhabitants of the U.S. a thousand times their value in taxes for carrying on the war they produce."[38] Nevertheless, Jefferson's approach gained few southern supporters.

The debate over the proper mode of defense for the West reemerged in late December 1792, when North Carolina representative John Steele moved that a committee "be appointed to reduce the military establishment of the United States."[39] The Department of War's "inefficiency" and the burdens that the department had placed on frontier inhabitants were, for Steele, sufficient reasons for the House to take up the matter.[40] A supporter of the militia, the North Carolina congressman condemned the present system of frontier protection, noting that "the whole Continent has been roused up against it."[41] "On this motion . . . ," he declared, "will depend . . . whether we are to continue a fruitless warfare in the present mode for seven or ten years, or shall we adopt a better system . . . which would completely check the Indians; nay, it would entirely exterminate them, if that was thought to be necessary."[42]

Not everyone present in the House was pleased to revisit the issue of militia versus regular army. Representative Thomas Hartley of Pennsylvania, who could not recall one instance "where regulars had engaged the Indians without beating them," objected to the timing of the bill.[43] Negotiations between the government and various tribes, he explained, were ongoing, and any changes now might upset those negotiations. After all, "[i]t is a well known maxim in politics," he reminded his listeners, "that a peace can always be easiest obtained by a nation which is prepared for war."[44]

Speaking several days later, Thomas Hartley's fellow Pennsylvanian William Findley tried to depict the measure as a watershed moment in the history of the young country. "To say that those States who have frontiers, ought to be left to protect themselves, is a very anti-Federal sentiment," he proclaimed.[45] "Do . . . [you] not observe that the fate of the Government is deeply involved in the decision?" he inquired of his fellow representatives.[46] As if anticipating Findley's federalist conclusions, Georgian John Milledge had declared earlier in the debate that residents of his state had ratified the federal Constitution "from a hope that we should be protected."[47] Fellow Georgian Francis Willis, decrying the horrific situation on his state's frontier, subsequently informed fellow members that they had, in fact, not authorized enough regular troops to defend the entire frontier area.[48]

Still, for some participants in the debate, the question was simple: Who was the greater aggressor on the frontier—the settlers or the Indians? Jeremiah Wadsworth of Connecticut found blame difficult to place, but noted that "[t]he murder of the Moravian Indians, [and] the proclamation of Congress against our own people . . . show that the Indians have ground for complaint."[49] Proceeding to cite "representations" from Judge Innis dated between 1783 and 1790, he noted that it was difficult for local officials in Kentucky to restrain settlers "from the commission of crimes against the peace of the country."[50] Virginian Andrew Moore was likewise suspicious of the settlers. The duplicity of settlers, in his opinion, was "a good reason why the protection of those frontiers should not be intrusted to the militia."[51] "Shall we intrust the conduct of that matter to the very persons whom it has been alleged are often the aggressors?" he asked.[52]

As for the merits of regular army versus militia, Wadsworth, joined by middle state representatives Jonathan Dayton of New Jersey and Pennsylvanians William Findley and Thomas Hartley, repeatedly belittled the militia. Wadsworth considered the militia wasteful, noting that "[t]he militia of Kentucky have cost more blood and wealth than all the American war."[53] Dayton, for his part, questioned the veracity of certain militia victories, insinuating that at least one affair, Major John Adair's skirmish with Miami chief Little Turtle on 6 November 1792, was more the result of luck than of skill.[54] Wadsworth likewise questioned North Carolinian Hugh Williamson's version of events surrounding Adair and his mounted Kentucky militia's victory.[55] Williamson had earlier introduced the episode into the debate to highlight militia accomplishments, but it apparently did not impress all present in the House chamber.[56] Certainly not as antagonistic toward the militia as Dayton and Wadsworth had been, Findley and Hartley simply questioned the feasibility, and accompanying "uncertainty," of repeatedly calling out the militia.[57] They viewed it as an "injustice" to the families for "calling out heads of families from one part of the frontier."[58]

Throughout the debate, Madison had remained silent. Finally, on 5 January 1793, he addressed the House. The discussion, he noted, was simply a continuation of the militia versus regular army debate of the previous session. However, what distinguished the current debate, he explained, was the consensus among members that the president possessed the power to reduce the size of the military. "[I]f the force of the country can be continued on as respectable a footing as at present," he therefore thought it economically "inexcusable" for Congress to insist that the president bring the army to full strength.[59] Concluding, he suggested "compleating the effective force by the addition of volunteer militia—organized compleatly the regular troops already raised—and to restrict them to the number that they at present consist of."[60]

For the first time, Madison had taken a public stand against the regular army and had tacitly embraced the westerners' position on the use of the militia. Why he acted this way is unclear. Richard H. Kohn argues that he did so for political reasons, as the fledgling political parties, he explained, were beginning to make their appearances.[61] Participants, including Fisher Ames of Massachusetts, certainly believed that Madison had engaged in political posturing.[62] Still, Madison's close connection with the western frontier cannot be discounted. Prior to the final vote on Steele's motion, Madison had supported a motion calling for a time limit on recruiting enlisted personnel for the regular army, a measure similar to what Madison had earlier advocated. Although the motion failed, 14 southerners and the two Kentuckian members aligned themselves with it.[63]

In his closing remarks, Steele summed up what the House had accomplished by revisiting the issue. "[T]he public," he told his fellow lawmakers,

> will know that we have asserted the sense of the people against standing armies, that we are anxious to defend the frontiers against their enemies; that we have recommended a system of economy and efficiency, instead of profu-

sion and delay; that we have recommended a system calculated to produce victory and peace, instead of disgrace and war, and that we wish to rescue the Government from the intoxication of the times, and all the apery of military establishments.[64]

When the vote on the motion was finally taken on 8 January 1793, its outcome was already known. Three days earlier, the Committee of the Whole had rejected the bill, as only twenty-one members had risen in its favor.[65] When the House voted for the final time, one member, James Madison, abstained, giving the measure only twenty supporters. Thirty-six members voted against it. Although a majority of southerners aligned themselves with the current system, as they had the previous year, more southerners, including Madison, now seemed to have adopted the conclusions of western residents regarding the militia.[66]

This emerging unity among southerners regarding the western bias toward the militia held true in early June 1794 as the first session of the Third Congress came to an end. On 6 June, Virginian William B. Giles reacted with "utmost surprise" to a Senate change in a House bill to protect settlers on the southwestern frontier.[67] In the House version of the bill, "An act for the more effectual protection of the Southwestern frontier settlers," the president was "authorized to call out, from time to time, as occasion may require, any number of militia . . . not exceeding . . . ten thousand . . . to carry on offensive operations against the Creek and Cherokee nations or tribes of Indians."[68] The Senate proposed to eliminate this authorization in favor of 1,140 infantrymen.[69]

Giles, who predicted that "the amendment of the Senate would sit very badly indeed upon" the stomachs of representatives whose constituencies included frontier settlers, was not the only member to react strongly to the Senate proposal.[70] Fellow Virginian John Nicholas, the brother of Kentuckian George Nicholas, declared "that a bill had been wanted to *protect* the frontiers, but, by this amendment, the bill would *scourge* them [emphasis original]."[71] North Carolinian Joseph McDowell, who noted that he had "lived long on the frontier,"[72] voiced exasperation at a proposal that, he proclaimed, would burden the federal government with "an useless expense, or the people with a kind of defence which they dislike" when the militia "were the only proper forces to oppose the Indians with success."[73] Alexander Gillon of South Carolina confirmed that opinion, declaring that "[i]t was a body of militia that was wanted."[74]

The final comments against the Senate proposal came from Thomas P. Carnes of Georgia. "The only use that Continental troops can be," he declared, "is to defend posts; and it has been found, by the experience of several years, that posts do more mischief than service."[75] Settlers, he noted, became complacent around forts, forgetting that "Indian parties slip in between them."[76] "The consequence," he told his colleagues, "is, that they are frequently murdered; while the only service performed by the Continentals is, that when the militia pursue the Indians, they are prevented by the former from crossing what is called the line [the boundary between settled areas and Indian lands]."[77] Exasperated, he asked "that the gentlemen would frankly say, once and for all, that the Georgians did not deserve protection, and then the State would know what was to be done."[78]

Unlike previous instances where the House had sided with the regular army over the militia, representatives this time insisted on keeping their chamber's wording of the bill. Forty-two members refused to "concur with the Senate in the said amendment," whereas twenty-six members supported it.[79] Of the members supporting the amendment, only four were from southern states—Maryland, with three, and South Carolina, with one. Southerners opposing the amendment outnumbered northerners nearly two-to-one, as twenty-seven southerners joined fourteen northerners and one Kentuckian to defeat the amendment.[80]

For the past several months, tensions throughout the country had been high, as Americans worried about how the newly inaugurated British and French war would affect the United States. Embargoes, non-intercourse measures, harbor defense, and, of course, the status of the military suddenly became important topics as rumors of war abounded.[81] Throughout it all, the South remained committed to the use of militia over regular troops. Opinions among New Englanders and middle state residents, however, had started to change. Well aware that merchants in their region had recently lost numerous vessels to the British in the West Indies, New England congressmen began "to take the lead in defensive preparations, and to acquire merit with the people by anticipating their wishes."[82] Only four out of seventeen New Englanders opposed the Senate amendment to the House bill.[83] Among middle state members, who had steadfastly supported the regular army, their near unanimity had come to an end, as only nine of the nineteen members sided with the Senators in their amendment.[84]

Senators' insistence that their amendment prevail resulted in a conference between the two chambers.[85] The following day, when the House conference managers solicited the approval of members for their report, members generally voted as they had on 6 June, the major exception being the addition of three southerners in support of the Senate's version. Two representatives from South Carolina, who had not been present on 6 June, and Abraham Baldwin of Georgia, who switched his vote, joined the previous four southerners in opposing the decision of the House to insist on its version of the bill.[86] The Senate likewise insisted on its version, and the bill eventually died.[87]

When the Third Congress reconvened for its second session in early November 1794, members soon returned to their discussions of military issues and western defense. This time, however, their discussions were buoyed by good news—General Anthony Wayne had in late August defeated an Indian force in northwestern Ohio at the rapids of the Maumee River. The general's victory would eventually lead to the signing of the Treaty of Greenville, which established a definite boundary in the Northwest Territory between the native tribes and settlers. [88]

In addition to General Wayne's victory, House members were also, by February 1795, excited by rumors of a "treaty said to be entered into between this country [United States] and Britain." [89] Jay's Treaty, negotiated by Chief Justice John Jay and signed on 19 November 1794, called for the British to evacuate their posts in the Northwest Territory by 1 June 1796. The British occupation of these posts, which was a violation of the 1783 Treaty of Paris ending the American Revolution, had been an irritant to the United States, since British troops had supported native tribesmen in their hostilities against American settlers. House members, led by James Madison, would eventually spend considerable time debating the treaty, with most of the discussions dealing with procedural issues. [90]

With the hope of more promising news in the future, House members once again entered into a two-day discussion in early February on the future of the United States military. At issue was a select committee's report, of which the House quickly disposed, proposing a reduction in the size of the military to just two regiments. [91] Jonathan Dayton of New Jersey immediately proposed that the "Military Establishment of the United States be continued, and the corps composing the same completed by enlistments for a term not exceeding three years." [92] Although Dayton assured his fellow House members that he acted only to ensure the "effectual protection of the frontiers," he justified his support for the regular army by arguing that his resolution would cause the least inconvenience to the militia and prove to be the most cost-effective method for the United States. [93] "There needed no proof," he explained, "that calls for the services of militia were always attended with great embarrassment to our fellow citizens who composed it, and with a waste of money which the other system would not occasion." [94]

The day after Dayton introduced his resolution William B. Giles of Virginia proposed that Dayton's time frame for the continuation of the military establishment—three years—be changed. [95] Like the select committee's report, the House showed little interest in this type of change. [96] Instead, members chose to support Dayton's resolution after having concluded a discussion in which the role of the militia was debated. [97] Pennsylvanian Thomas Scott reiterated how expensive it was for the United States to rely on the militia. "The mounted volunteers from Kentucky," he told his listeners, "had cost as much to the public in four months [due to the terms of their temporary enlistment] as an equal number of regular troops did in twelve months." [98] Fellow Pennsylvanian Thomas Hartley criticized the militia for its difficulty to be raised, explaining, "It was a hard thing to call out the militia from their work."[99]

Toward the end of the debate, however, Thomas P. Carnes of Georgia lashed out against members who insisted on the adequacy of the regular army. "Georgia and the Southwestern Territory," he stated, "have a frontier of at least eight hundred miles in extent. The number of troops proposed in the resolution is entirely inadequate to the defence of this frontier in general. We have had regulars in Georgia for several years, without the State receiving any benefit whatever from them."[100] For the Georgian the "neglect shown by the Government to the safety of the Southwestern frontier . . . amount[ed] to a disgrace upon Government."[101] As a remedy he proposed that "fire and sword" be turned on Indian towns when any murders occurred.[102] If Indian leaders could expect this type of reaction every time, "they would soon learn to be quiet," he exclaimed.[103]

The tone of the debate became harsher when Marylander William Vans Murray rose in response to Carnes's remarks. He leveled a blistering assessment of the Georgia militia by relating the story of 600 Georgia militia members who went in "pursuit of a party of Indians, and, after coming on their trail, refused to go farther, and went home again."[104] For this reason, Murray explained, regular troops would be a better form of protection than militia.[105]

Carnes could not let Murray's words stand unchallenged. "As to the men who returned from the Indian trail," he told members, "the case was this. The Governor had entered into a correspondence with the Executive at Philadelphia, and it having been understood that the marching of the militia would be disagreeable to him, they were recalled on their way to the Indian country."[106]

After a subsequent exchange between Carnes and Samuel Smith of Maryland, the discussion ended, and the House, without a recorded vote, agreed to Dayton's resolution. Members then ordered Dayton, Smith and Jeremiah Wadsworth of Connecticut to prepare a bill in accordance with the resolution.[107] The select committee reported its bill on 11 February, with the House considering it two days later.[108] Despite several unsuccessful attempts by James Madison and others through the amendment process to offset the dangers of a standing army, such as requiring that the federal government could only deploy troops "for the protection and security of the United States against foreign invasion, and against the Indian tribes," the House passed the bill with little discussion on 14 February.[109] Madison had considered his amendment important, since the bill, unlike previous military acts, lacked this direction "limiting the use of the army to the protection of the Frontiers."[110] Madison attributed the defeat of his amendment to a consensus among members that "the Executive ought to be free to use the regular troops, as well as the Militia in support of the laws against our own Citizens," perhaps a consequence of the Whiskey Rebellion.[111] After the House approved on 2 March "sundry amendments" attached to the bill by the Senate, the president signed it, titled "An Act for continuing and regulating the Military Establishment of the United States, and for repealing sundry acts heretofore passed on that subject," the following day.[112]

The rumored treaty with Great Britain had also entered into the discussion. When James Madison rose in favor of reducing the size of the army, he cited the treaty, arguing that "it might be inferred that the Indian hostilities on the Northwest of the Ohio would slacken."[113] His assumption was quickly challenged by Theodore Sedgwick of Massachusetts, who declared "that it would be improper to diminish the preparation for war on account of any report afloat of a treaty with Britain."[114] William Findley of Pennsylvania, speaking the following day, likewise thought members were acting prematurely. "What is this change?" he asked them.[115] "General Wayne has gained one victory, but is this a conquest? . . . The prospect of a treaty seemed to be considered as an essential change of situation; but supposing the reports of this to be well founded, it certainly was not yet confirmed on our part."[116] Echoing the sentiments of Findley, fellow Pennsylvanian Thomas Scott thought that circumstances had actually "changed for the worse."[117]

Just weeks before the Third Congress ended, members became engaged in a discussion over Indian lands in Georgia. On 17 February, President George Washington informed Congress that the Georgia legislature had passed two acts "of such magnitude . . . [to the] peace and welfare of the United States" that he thought it necessary to inform House and Senate members.[118] According to the president, the legislation concerned the appropriation and sale of Indian lands "within the territorial limits claimed by that State."[119] By means of these two acts, which Georgia senator James Jackson laid before the Senate on 27 February, the Georgia Legislature sold to four companies approximately thirty-five million acres in the Yazoo River country—present-day Alabama and Mississippi—for $500,000.[120] The House subsequently directed five of its members to examine the matter and report their findings.[121]

The select committee reported its findings seven days later.[122] Committee members had prepared four resolutions. The first resolution, which "recommended that the President . . . use all Constitutional and legal means to prevent the infraction of the treaties made with the Indian tribes by the citizens of the United States" passed "without a division."[123] The second resolution, which likewise received the consent of the House, recommended that the president enter into treaties with Indian tribes that benefited the country rather than individuals or states.[124] A third resolution called on the president to "obtain a cession of the State of Georgia of their claim to the whole, or any part, of the land within the present Indian boundaries."[125] Members subsequently established a select committee to prepare a bill concerning this resolution.[126] The fourth resolution, however, did not receive as much support as the other three resolutions.

This final resolution addressed the issue of armed settlers "on any lands belonging to Indians, out of the ordinary jurisdiction of any State, or of the Territory of the United States South of the river Ohio."[127] Central to the discussion was the punishment for these people. The original resolution placed them under the jurisdiction of the "rules and articles of war" for the United States military.[128] One of the members of the committee, Theodore Sedgwick of Massachusetts, immediately proposed an amendment extending to the military the authority to capture violators but granting to civilian courts the right to try offenders.[129] Before deciding on the amendment, the House directed Sedgwick and two other members to prepare a report, which they did.[130] Their resulting resolutions resembled the previous resolution except for a provision outlining specific penalties for violators.[131]

The initial discussion on the select committee's resolutions centered on whether a settler could cross the line separating settled areas and Indian treaty lands without violating the proposed law. Abraham B. Venable of Virginia did not think so and consequently proposed an amendment that would exempt settlers from "the operation of the law who were in pursuit of Indians that had committed actual hostilities on the frontier."[132] Responding to the criticism, Sedgwick stated that, although not granted explicitly, the "inherent rights of nature" granted every man the right "to pursue and punish those who had robbed him."[133] Still, some members, including Thomas Blount of North Carolina, Christopher Greenup of Kentucky, and Andrew Moore of Virginia, thought a more explicit statement necessary.[134]

One member, James Hillhouse of Connecticut, objected to the idea of permitting settlers to cross the line for any reason. "What use was there for expending millions every year in defence of the frontier people, if they were to be at liberty to cross the Indian line as often as they pleased, and to do what was to all intents and purposes carrying on war?" he asked his fellow members.[135] "If they will fight, let us recal our forces and leave them to fight for themselves."[136] Despite his efforts, the House assembled as the Committee of the Whole and voted thirty-six to twenty-eight in favor of Venable's amendment.[137]

The following day, on 28 February, the House once again took up the resolutions, with Venable's amendment receiving most of the attention. The Virginia congressman began the debate by reminding members that the "Indians may come over any part of it [the line], while the citizens of the United States are not to be allowed to cross it one mile in pursuit. Even a man in pursuit of savages who may have carried off his wife and children, may be stopped," he exclaimed.[138]

Few members rose to oppose the amendment. One member who did, Fisher Ames of Massachusetts, denied Venable's interpretation of the resolution, instead agreeing with Sedgwick that it did contain "the right of a man to pursue the Indians in order to recover his wife and children."[139] He specifically objected to the proposed amendment because it would "legalize all those acts of violence and revenge, that, for a century past, have deluged the frontier with blood."[140] Likewise, Jeremiah Wadsworth of Connecticut objected to the amendment as being nothing more than an instrument of "conquest."[141] South Carolinian Robert Goodloe Harper, who stated that he respected the "sentiments of patriotism that gave rise" to the amendment, could not, however, support it.[142] "He had a high respect for the inhabitants, there were many very worthy people among them, but likewise many others of a very different kind," he explained to members.[143] Despite their best intentions, "[t]his amendment," he told members, "will set open a door to all sorts of fraud and mischief."[144]

Several members, however, came to the defense of the frontier settlers. Joseph McDowell of North Carolina spoke of the daily and weekly murders of settlers on the southwestern frontier. "Do the United States avenge these murders?" he asked.[145] "No" was his answer to his own question. "Instead of any satisfaction to the people, their characters are abused on this floor," he declared.[146] Similarly, William B. Giles of Virginia objected to the harsh criticism of frontier settlers offered by some members of the House. "An hundred years hence these people would preponderate over this part of the Continent," he told members.[147] As for himself, he thought it a good idea to "carefully avoid any thing that might offend the Western people."[148]

After the debate had ended, the House voted on Venable's amendment. As Wadsworth had predicted, the amendment failed to pass. Only thirty-nine members voted for it, whereas forty-six members voted against it. Seventy percent of southerners supported the amendment. Only eight southerners voted against it, with four of the eight from South Carolina.[149] James Madison was one of the southerners who voted against the amendment. Although he had earlier suggested making Indian towns off limits, he really believed "that no law of any kind would be able to hinder people from crossing the line in pursuit of Indians, who might have carried off their families."[150]

Following the vote on Venable's amendment, the House moved quickly to approve the resolutions and assign them to a committee for the purpose of molding them into a bill. Before the final adoption, however, members did approve a compromise amendment proposed by Thomas P. Carnes of Georgia. It stated that settlers could cross the line if they were "in continuation of a pursuit to a distance not exceeding [left blank, not specified] miles beyond the line of the particular Indians who shall, have recently committed murder, or may be carrying off captives or plunder."[151] With the session drawing to an end, the House hurriedly completed its work on the bill on 2 March.[152] The Senate, however, expunged much of the bill, leaving only a statement about the amount of money the federal government would expend on Indian supplies for 1795.[153] On 3 March, the last day of the Third Congress, the House approved the Senate's changes, and President Washington signed the bill into law.[154]

Only a few days after the Fourth Congress convened, William Loughton Smith of South Carolina, on 10 December 1795, introduced a set of resolutions that reintroduced the issue of "security of the frontiers, and for protecting the Indians against certain lawless inhabitants of the frontier."[155] Once again the issue of the integrity of frontier inhabitants confronted members of the House.

The debate over frontier security began one week later with Thomas Blount of North Carolina, brother of William Blount, the governor of the Territory South of the River Ohio, declaring that the people living on the frontier had taken "very great offence" to the remarks of some members of Congress.[156] Presumably the offending words had been spoken during the previous Congress, since Blount had learned of the verbal transgressions during a recent visit to the area.[157] He immediately moved that certain offensive language be removed from Smith's resolution. Georgian John Milledge readily agreed, noting "the impropriety and imprudence of offending the frontier people, many of whom, if not the best, were among the best people in the United States."[158] John Heath of Virginia and Uriah Tracy of Connecticut agreed, as would the House moments later, to support the motion provided that members remembered, as Heath explained, "that there are lawless persons on the frontiers, who have committed very great enormities against the Indians."[159] With this issue settled, the House directed the resolution, now containing the less offending words "for the protection of the Indians from any injuries by any of the inhabitants of the Unites States," to a committee for the purpose of crafting a bill.[160]

Debate on the bill began 2 February 1796 but would not be continued until April 9, as the House directed most of its attention toward the treaty that John Jay had negotiated with Great Britain. The initial discussion centered on a demarcation line separating frontier residents from Indian lands. John Nicholas of Virginia quickly offered an amendment that would have made the line less definitive in anticipation of future treaties with Indian tribes. The motion failed, as members, including Christopher Greenup of Kentucky, argued that such action would only create "uncertainty" on the frontier.[161] John Milledge next tried to remove a prohibition against "the citizens of the United States from crossing the line for the purpose of hunting and destroying the game."[162] He predicted that if the House included the provision, it would "be necessary to remove all the citizens on the frontiers at least twenty miles within the line."[163] Connecticut member James Hillhouse reminded Milledge and others that the United States had already stipulated this point in its treaties with the Indians. The House subsequently rejected Milledge's amendment.[164]

The April debate centered on what to do with settlers who encroached on Indian lands. The bill's stipulation that such individuals should forfeit all right to preempt Indian land caused alarm among some members. Virginian John Nicholas warned members that if this penalty remained part of the bill, "[i]t would irritate them [western settlers] very highly, and would unite them against the Government. If they had behaved improperly, they had had [*sic*] strong incentives to it, and so far from its being justifiable to increase their punishment, he thought they ought to be treated with delicacy."[165] A few members, including Madison, James Holland of North Carolina, and Georgian John Milledge, objected to the concept of forfeiture, arguing that it "certainly" went "against the spirit of the constitution."[166] Those members who spoke in support of forfeiture did so mainly for pragmatic reasons. Explaining why he supported the provision, Jeremiah Crabb of Maryland noted that "[i]t would prevent that kind of abuse which was apt to kindle a war on the frontier."[167] A few minutes later, Connecticut representative James Hillhouse noted that such a war would not fall "upon the offenders, for they will no more be found than the wolves, but upon the innocent frontier inhabitants, their wives and children."[168] On April 11, Thomas Blount unsuccessfully moved that the penalty be struck from the bill.[169] Twenty-five southerners, joined by one Kentuckian and ten others, voted in favor of the motion. Twenty-five New Englanders, joined by eleven southerners, a majority from Maryland, and eleven middle states residents, led the charge against the measure.[170] Without further discussion, the House passed the bill two days later.[171] The Senate passed the bill without amendment on 14 May, and President Washington signed "An Act to regulate Trade and Intercourse with the Indian Tribes, and to preserve Peace on the Frontiers" into law five days later.[172]

With the conclusion of this episode, southerners had once again demonstrated their commitment to the West and to westerners. Although not all southerners supported the western settlers' position on the militia, many southerners during these early congressional debates on the use of regular army troops versus frontier militia units had shown an increasing willingness to embrace western opinion on the use of militia, a necessary development if the two sides were to work together in the future. Similarly, the reaction of many southerners to perceived northern attacks on westerners' character signaled the commencement of a warmer relationship between the regions. Even though political leaders would continue to debate these issues for many years, the initial discussion benefited the western and southern interest.

NOTES

1. G. Glenn Clift, ed., "The District of Kentucky 1783–1787 as Pictured by Harry Innes in a Letter to John Brown," *Register of the Kentucky Historical Society* 54 (October 1956), 369;

Harry Innes to Henry Knox, 7 July 1790, in *Documentary History of the First Federal Congress, March 4, 1789–March 3, 1791*, eds. Charlene Bangs Bickford and Helen E. Veit (Baltimore: The Johns Hopkins University, 1986), 5:1322–23.

2. *Annals of Congress*, 3rd Cong., 1st sess., 697.

3. Ibid., 696.

4. Gerard Clarfield, "Protecting the Frontiers: Defense Policy and the Tariff Question in the First Washington Administration," *The William and Mary Quarterly*, Third Series, 32:3 (July 1975), 444–45; *Journals of the Continental Congress, 1774–1789*, ed. Worthington C. Ford et al. (Washington, DC: Government Printing Office, 1922), 25:685–86.

5. Article IX under the Articles of the Confederation extended to the states control over the Indians living within their boundaries, which further hindered the central government's attempts to formulate a unified Indian policy, especially in the South. See David Andrew Nichols, *Red Gentlemen & White Savages: Indians, Federalists, and the Search for Order on the American Frontier* (Charlottesville and London: University of Virginia Press, 2008), 44.

6. For a general overview of Indian relations in the West see R. Douglas Hurt, *The Indian Frontier, 1763–1846* (Albuquerque: University of New Mexico Press, 2002), 103–8; Reginald Horseman, *Expansion and American Indian Policy, 1783–1812* (East Lansing: Michigan State University Press, 1967), 3–52; and Francis Paul Prucha, *American Indian Policy in the Formative Years: The Indian Trade and Intercourse Acts, 1790–1834* (Cambridge: Harvard University Press, 1962) 28–40.

7. *Annals of Congress*, 1st Cong., 2nd sess., 1113.

8. Ibid., 1114; Don Higginbotham, "The Federalized Militia Debate: A Neglected Aspect of Second Amendment Scholarship," *William and Mary Quarterly*, 3rd series, 55 (January 1998), 51–53.

9. "An Act for Regulating the Military Establishment of the United States, 30 April 1790," in *The Public Statutes at Large of the United States, From the Organization of the Government in 1789 to March 3, 1845*, ed. Richard Peters (Boston: Charles C. Little and James Brown, 1845), 1:119–21.

10. On the morning of 4 November 1791, Indians surprised St. Clair's force encamped along the Wabash River. St. Clair and a few score of men escaped unharmed, but most of his command was not so lucky. The confrontation has the distinction of being the worst defeat of the United States Army at the hands of a Native American military force. Washington, subsequently, demanded and received St. Clair's resignation from the army. Jeffrey P. Brown, "Arthur St. Clair and the Establishment of U.S. Authority in the Old Northwest," in *Builders of Ohio: A Biographical History*, eds. Warren Van Tine and Michael Pierce (Columbus: Ohio State University Press, 2003), 30–31. Clarfield locates the strongest support for the war in Georgia, Kentucky, South Carolina, and Virginia. Still, one could hear criticism in these places. For an example, see "A Citizen of Georgia to George Washington, 1 March 1792," in *The Papers of George Washington. Presidential Series*, eds. Robert F. Haggard and Mark A. Mastromarino (Charlottesville and London: University Press of Virginia, 2002), 10:1–2. Clarfield, "Protecting the Frontier," 447.

11. Fisher Ames to Thomas Dwight, 13 January 1792, in *Works of Fisher Ames, As Published by Seth Ames*, ed. W.B. Allen (Indianapolis: Liberty Fund, 1983), 2:891. Thomas Jefferson and James Madison also noticed the disquiet. See Jefferson to Thomas Mann Randolph Jr., 11 December 1791, in *The Papers of Thomas Jefferson*, ed. Charles T. Cullen (Princeton: Princeton University Press, 1986), 22:389, and Madison to Henry Lee, December 18, 1791, in *The Papers of James Madison*, eds. Robert A. Rutland et al. (Charlottesville: University Press of Virginia, 1983), 14:155.

12. John Steele to Joseph Winnston [Winston], 15 January 1792, in *Circular Letters of Congressmen to Their Constituents, 1789–1829*, ed. Noble E. Cunningham Jr. (Chapel Hill: Published for the Institute of Early American History and Culture, Williamsburg, VA, by the University of North Carolina Press, 1978), 1:9.

13. *Philadelphia National Gazette*, 9 January 1792. Also see *Philadelphia National Gazette*, 12 January, 26 January, and 6 February 1792 and *Philadelphia Gazette of the United States*, 14 January 1792.

14. *Philadelphia National Gazette*, 9 January 1792.

15. Ibid., 19 January 1792.

16. Ibid., 9 January 1792.

17. Ibid., 2 February and 6 February 1792.

18. Ibid., 6 February 1792.

19. "Editorial Note", in *The Papers of George Washington. Presidential Series*, ed. Mark A. Mastromarino (Charlottesville and London: University Press of Virginia, 2000), 9:504. On 26 December 1791, Knox had submitted to Washington two statements dealing with the St. Clair debacle. The first discussed the preparations that the administration had undertaken for the campaign; the second outlined a new plan for confronting the warring tribes. See *American State Papers: Indian Affairs*, 4:197–99. Washington placed Knox's statements before Congress on 11 January 1792. See *Journal of the Senate of the United States*, 2nd Cong., 1st sess., 11 January 1792, 370. [Hereafter cited as *Senate Journal*.]

20. George Washington to Henry Knox, 16 January 1792, in *The Writings of George Washington from the Original Manuscript Sources, 1745–1799*, ed. John C. Fitzpatrick (Washington, DC: [United States Government Printing Office, 1939], 31:459.

21. *Philadelphia National Gazette*, 30 January 1792, and *Philadelphia Gazette of the United States*, 1 February 1792. These Philadelphia newspapers were just two of several papers to publish Knox's statement. Newspaper editors in Boston, New York, and Alexandria, Virginia, also carried the secretary's remarks. See "Editorial Note," Mastromarino, *Washington Papers*, 9:504–5.

22. Harry Innes to Thomas Jefferson, 27 August 1791, in Cullen, *Jefferson Papers*, 22:86.

23. *Journal of the House of Representatives of the United States*, 2nd Cong. 1st sess., 25 January 1792, 498. [Hereafter cited as *House Journal*.]

24. *Annals of Congress*, 2nd Cong., 1st sess., 337. Knox called for the establishment of five regiments by raising the number of noncommissioned officers, privates, and musicians in the army to 5,160. "The Plan," *American State Papers: Indian Affairs*, 4:199.

25. *American State Papers: Indian Affairs*, 4:196.

26. *Annals of Congress*, 2nd Cong., 1st sess., 337.

27. Ibid.; George Adams Boyd, *Elias Boudinot: Patriot and Statesman, 1740 to 1821* (Princeton: Princeton University Press, 1952; reprint, New York: Greenwood Press, 1969), 198.

28. Madison, "Military Establishment," in Rutland et al. eds., *Madison Papers*, 14:437.

29. Jefferson to Thomas Mann Randolph, Jr., 11 December 1791, in Cullen, *Jefferson Papers*, 22:389; George Nicholas to John Brown, 31 December 1790, in Huntley Dupre, ed., "Three Letters of George Nicholas to John Brown," *The Register of the Kentucky State Historical Society*, 41:134 (January 1943), 6. In May 1791, Kentucky militia under the command of General Charles Scott crossed the Ohio River in a punitive raid against the local tribes. Kentuckians viewed this raid as evidence of the martial ability of the militia, since the raiders killed scores of Indians, destroyed numerous villages, and burned many crops. See Nicholas to Madison, 20 June 1791, in Rutland et al., *Madison Papers*, 14:32–33; Andro Linklater, *An Artist in Treason: The Extraordinary Double Life of General James Wilkinson* (New York: Walker & Company, 2009), 107.

30. Madison to Edmund Pendleton, 21 January 1792, in Rutland et al., *Madison Papers*, 14:195.

31. *Annals of Congress*, 354–55. On 30 January 1792, sixteen southerners joined eighteen northerners in refusing to strike "three additional regiments of infantry" from the measure. Only eight southerners, including five representatives from North Carolina, voted for it. The final bill, which passed the House on February 1, received the support of 14 southerners; seven southerners voted against it. John Brown, representing the Kentucky district of Virginia, voted for the bill. Representatives from the middle states overwhelming supported the measure, voting eleven to three in its favor. The bill encountered intense opposition from the chamber's New England members, who voted nine to three against the bill. The ten-man southern delegation in the Senate divided equally on the question. As in the House, the strongest overall support for the bill came from the middle states, where all seven senators present voted for the measure. Again, New Englanders opposed the measure, with seven voting against it and only three voting for it. *Senate Journal*, 2nd Cong., 1st sess., 17 February 1792, 393.

32. Albert Gallatin to Jean Badollet, 21 January 1792, quoted in Richard H. Kohn, *Eagle and Sword: The Federalists and the Creation of the Military Establishment in America, 1783–1802* (New York: The Free Press, 1975), 122. In the Senate, seven out of ten New Englanders opposed the bill. In the House, ten of the twelve northerners who opposed the bill likewise came from a New England state. See *Senate Journal*, 2nd Cong., 1st sess., 17 February 1792, 293; *Annals of Congress*, 355.

33. *Annals of Congress*, 338.

34. Ibid.

35. Ibid., 344.

36. Ibid.

37. Thomas Jefferson to Henry Knox, 10 August 1791, in Cullen, *Jefferson Papers*, 22:27.

38. Jefferson to David Campbell, 27 March 1792, in *The Papers of Thomas Jefferson*, ed. Charles T. Cullen (Princeton: Princeton University Press, 1990), 23:346. Everyone did not support Jefferson's position. See Virginian Robert Rutherford's comments to Washington, 13 March 1792, in Haggard et al., *Washington Papers*, 10:97.

39. *Annals of Congress*, 2nd Cong., 2nd sess., 750.

40. Ibid., 762.

41. Ibid., 763. It probably was not the whole country, but it certainly could have been the West, where letters continued to extol the abilities of the militia over the regular army. See John Sevier to James Madison, 30 October 1792, in Rutland et al., *Madison Papers*, 14:393; Arthur Campbell to George Washington, 1 January 1793, in *The Papers of George Washington. Presidential Series*, ed. Philander D. Chase, vol. 12, "January–May 1793," eds. Christine Sternberg Patrick et al. (Charlottesville and London: University Press of Virginia, 2005), 12:62; Robert Anderson to Charles Pinckney, 20 September 1792, in *American State Papers: Indian Affairs*, 4:317–18.

42. Annals of Congress, 2nd Cong., 2nd sess., 764.

43. Ibid., 765.

44. Ibid.

45. Ibid., 789.

46. Ibid.

47. Ibid., 785.

48. Ibid., 783.

49. Ibid., 774. The massacre of nearly 60 Christian Delaware Indians at the Moravian mission at Gnadenhutten, Ohio, by Pennsylvania militia occurred in early March 1782. For a brief account of the tragedy see Beverly W. Bond Jr., *The Foundations of Ohio*, vol. 1 of *The History of the State of Ohio*, ed. Carl Wittke, 6 vols. (Columbus: Ohio State Archaeological and Historical Society, 1941), 1:231–32.

50. *Annals of Congress*, 2nd Cong., 2nd sess., 774.

51. Ibid., 791.

52. Ibid.

53. Ibid., 776.

54. Ibid., 767.

55. Ibid., 775.

56. Ibid., 766. On 19 December 1792, Secretary Knox placed before the Senate several letters on Indian affairs, including Adair's letter of 6 November 1792 to General James Wilkinson describing the skirmish. *Senate Journal*, 2nd Cong., 2nd sess., 19 December 1792, 464. For a copy of the letter, see *American State Papers: Indian Affairs*, 4:335.

57. *Annals of Congress*, 2nd Cong., 2nd sess., 779.

58. Ibid., 797.

59. "Military Establishment," in Rutland et al., *Madison Papers*, 14:437.

60. Ibid.

61. Kohn, *Eagle and Sword*, 148.

62. Ames to Thomas Dwight, January 1793, in Allen, *Works of Fisher Ames*, 2:960.

63. *Annals of Congress*, 2nd Cong., 2nd sess., 801–2. The vote among New England members was close, with eight members voting in favor of the motion and nine against it. Once again, the middle states overwhelmingly opposed any changes to the regular army, voting

fourteen to two against the motion. Nine southerners opposed it as well. As to Kohn's point about politics entering the debate, an analysis of the pro-administration versus anti-administration voting does not show a clear pattern. Not all members' allegiances to the administration are known, but among southerners who supported the motion, four were pro-administration and five were anti-administration. Four pro-administration and two anti-administration southerners opposed the measure. Among New Englanders, four pro-administration members supported the motion and six opposed it, whereas only two anti-administration members supported it. In the middle states, where opposition to the measure was the strongest, seven pro-administration and four anti-administration members voted against it. Only one pro-administration member voted for it. In this case, regional biases appear stronger than pro-administration and anti-administration alignments. Political affiliations based on those provided in the *Biographical Directory of the United States Congress, 1774–Present*, http://bioguide.congress.gov/biosearch/biosearch.asp.

64. *Annals of Congress,* 2nd Cong., 2nd sess., 793.

65. Ibid., 801.

66. Ibid., 801–2. Nine southerners, along with the two Kentuckian members, voted for the motion. Thirteen southerners opposed it. Again, the middle state representatives overwhelmingly supported the current military arrangement, voting thirteen to two against the motion. The vote narrowed among New England members, who voted ten to seven against it. Prior to the final vote, Madison had supported a motion calling for a time limit on recruiting enlisted personnel for the regular army, which failed. When the House voted for the final time on Steele's motion, he chose to abstain.

67. *Annals of Congress*, 3rd Cong, 1st sess., 775.

68. Ibid., 774. The House passed the bill on 29 May 1794. *House Journal*, 3rd Cong., 1st sess., 29 May 1794, 185.

69. *Annals of Congress*, 3rd Cong., 1st sess., 124.

70. Ibid., 775.

71. Ibid. [emphasis original].

72. Ibid.

73. Ibid., 776.

74. Ibid., 777.

75. Ibid.

76. Ibid.

77. Ibid.

78. Ibid.

79. Ibid., 778–79.

80. Ibid., 779.

81. Stanley Elkins and Eric McKitrick, *The Age of Federalism* (New York and Oxford: Oxford University Press, 1993), 405. Even Madison wondered whether Great Britain desired war with the United States. See Madison to Jefferson, 12 March 1794, in *The Papers of James Madison*, eds. Thomas A. Mason et al. (Charlottesville: University Press of Virginia, 1985), 15:278.

82. Madison to Jefferson, 12 March 1794, in Mason et al., *Madison Papers*, 15:278.

83. *Annals of Congress*, 3rd Cong., 1st sess., 779.

84. Ibid. A similar voting pattern occurred on 30 May, when thirty-one southerners and one Kentuckian nearly single-handedly defeated a Senate bill to increase the army by "ten thousand men." Five New Englanders and thirteen middle state members supported their southern colleagues, whereas sixteen New Englanders and twelve middle state representatives supported the Senate measure. See *Annals of Congress*, 735–39.

85. *House Journal*, 3rd Cong., 1st sess. 6 June 1794, 208–9.

86. *Annals of Congress*, 3rd Cong., 1st sess., 781–82. The vote on 7 June was thirty to twenty-eight. Ten northerners joined twenty southerners in voting for the House version, thus maintaining the two-to-one ratio present on 6 June.

87. *Senate Journal*, 3rd Cong., 1st sess., 7 June 1794, 114.

88. For background on the Battle of Fallen Timbers and the Treaty of Greenville see Paul David Nelson, *Anthony Wayne: Soldier of the Early Republic* (Bloomington: Indiana University Press, 1985), 261–83 passim.

89. *Annals of Congress*, 3rd Cong., 2nd sess., 1164.

90. For the debate in the House on the execution of the British treaty see *Annals of Congress*, 4th Cong., 1st sess., 969–1298 passim.

91. *Annals of Congress*, 3rd Cong., 2nd sess., 1163–64.

92. Ibid., 1163.

93. Ibid., 1164.

94. Ibid.

95. Ibid., 1165.

96. Ibid., 1166.

97. Ibid., 1172.

98. Ibid., 1169.

99. Ibid., 1166.

100. Ibid., 1170.

101. Ibid.

102. Ibid., 1171.

103. Ibid.

104. Ibid.

105. Ibid.

106. Ibid.

107. Ibid., 1172.

108. *House Journal*, 3rd Cong., 2nd sess., 11 February and 13 February 1795, 323, 325.

109. Footnote one, in Mason et al., *Madison Papers*, 15:465; *Annals of Congress*, 3rd Cong., 2nd sess., 1221–23.

110. Madison to Jefferson, 15 February 1795, in Mason et al., *Madison Papers*, 15:474. The South was the only region of the country that supported Madison's amendment (twenty-four to ten). The New England and middle states (six to twenty and five to thirteen, respectively) overwhelmingly opposed the measure. Surprisingly, the two Kentuckian members divided on the issue. See *Annals of Congress*, 3rd Cong., 2nd sess., 1222–23.

111. Madison to Jefferson, 15 February 1795, in Mason et al., *Madison Papers*, 15:474.

112. *Annals of Congress*, 3rd Cong., 2nd sess., 1275; *House Journal*, 3rd Cong., 2nd sess., 3 March 1795, 359. *Senate Journal*, 3rd Cong., 2nd sess., 2 March 1795, 179. For a copy of the law, see *Annals of Congress*, 3rd Cong., 2nd sess., 1515–19. In 1796, Congress resolved the issue of a peacetime army by establishing a military structure that would essentially remain intact "for the next century." See Kohn, *Eagle and Sword*, 186.

113. *Annals of Congress*, 3rd Cong., 2nd sess., 1164.

114. Ibid.

115. Ibid., 1167.

116. Ibid., 1167–68.

117. Ibid., 1169.

118. *House Journal*, 3rd Cong., 2nd sess., 17 February 1795, 331.

119. Ibid.

120. *Senate Journal*, 3rd Cong., 2nd sess., 17 February 1795, 172–73. For an examination of the Yazoo land fraud see C. Peter Magrath, *Yazoo: Law and Politics in the New Republic; The Case of Fletcher v. Peck* (Providence, RI: Brown University Press, 1966).

121. *House Journal*, 3rd Cong., 2nd sess., 17 February 1795, 331.

122. Ibid.

123. Ibid.

124. *Annals of Congress*, 3rd Cong., 2nd sess., 1252, 1255.

125. Ibid., 1256.

126. Ibid.

127. Ibid., 1254.

128. Ibid.

129. Ibid.

130. Ibid.
131. Ibid., 1259. The third resolution presented by Sedgwick's select committee stated that "every person apprehended . . . shall be tried in manner and form as is expressed in . . . 'An act to regulate trade and intercourse with the Indian tribes.'" Section ten of the act assigned jurisdiction to the "Superior Courts of each of the said Territorial districts, and the Circuit Courts and other Courts of the United States." President George Washington signed this bill into law on 1 March 1793. See *The Public Statutes At Large*, 1:329–32.
132. *Annals of Congress*, 3rd Cong., 2nd sess., 1259.
133. Ibid.
134. Ibid., 1260.
135. Ibid., 1259–60.
136. Ibid., 1260.
137. Ibid., 1261.
138. Ibid., 1264.
139. Ibid.
140. Ibid.
141. Ibid., 1265.
142. Ibid., 1268.
143. Ibid.
144. Ibid.
145. Ibid., 1265.
146. Ibid.
147. Ibid.
148. Ibid.
149. Ibid., 1269. Both the *Annals of Congress* and the *Journal of the House of Representatives* for 28 February 1795 state that thirty-nine members voted for the Venable amendment; however, the recorded vote in both sources list forty members. The recorded votes in both sources agree on the number of members voting against the amendment.
150. Ibid., 1268.
151. Ibid., 1269–70. The House filled in the blank on 2 March at the clerk's table and then passed the bill. The specific number is not known. *House Journal*, 3rd Cong., 2nd sess., 28 February 1795, 352.
152. *House Journal*, 3rd Cong., 2nd sess., 2 March 1795, 353.
153. *Senate Journal*, 3rd Cong., 2nd sess., 2 March 1795, 182.
154. *House Journal*, 3rd Cong., 2nd sess., 3 March 1795, 358. For a copy of the act see *The Public Statutes At Large*, 1:443. The haste of both chambers to pass the bill caused some confusion among members of the Fourth Congress. It seems a few members mistakenly thought that some of what the House had debated had been included in the act. See *Annals of Congress*, 4th Cong., 1st sess., 152.
155. *Annals of Congress*, 4th Cong., 1st sess., 131.
156. Ibid., 151.
157. Ibid.
158. Ibid.
159. Ibid., 151–52.
160. Ibid., 153.
161. Ibid., 287.
162. Ibid.
163. Ibid.
164. Ibid., 287–88.
165. Ibid., 896.
166. Ibid., 900.
167. Ibid., 897.
168. Ibid., 898.
169. Ibid., 905.
170. Ibid.
171. *House Journal*, 4th Cong., 1st sess., 13 May 1796, 510.

172. *Senate Journal*, 4th Cong., 1st sess., 14 May 1796, 257. For a copy of the law see *The Public Statutes At Large*, 1:469–74.

Chapter Ten

A Change in Emphasis

For more than a decade, James Madison and similarly minded southerners had focused their attention westward toward the area below the Ohio River and had worked hard to foster a strong relationship with the people who decided to make their homes in this wilderness. They hoped that this relationship would strengthen the South's standing in the national government. However, beginning with Jay's and Pinckney's treaties, western concerns seemed to lose their urgency for Madison and other southern leaders, whose reactions seemed less intense, less emotional. Whether success had brewed disinterest or promoted a feeling that westerners could now be taken for granted is unclear, but what is certain is that it started when southern leaders began to engage in party politics with their political enemies.

Despite being decidedly "not favorable to it," George Washington submitted John Jay's Treaty of Amity, Commerce, and Navigation with Great Britain to the Senate, meeting in special session, on 8 June 1795.[1] The president had sent the chief justice to London to ease the extremely tense relationship that had developed between the two countries concerning a variety of issues, including the continued presence of British troops in the Northwest Territory. He now concluded that the issue could no longer remain "unsettled" and that the United States had no choice but to ratify the treaty.[2] In the Senate, pro-administration forces concurred, ratifying the document on 24 June after agreeing only to one reservation.[3]

Public reaction to Jay's Treaty did not commence until Philadelphian Benjamin Franklin Bache published it in his *Aurora General Advertiser* in late June.[4] The Senate had sworn its members to secrecy when it began deliberations on the treaty and then to a pledge "not to authorize or allow any copy of the said communication, or of any article thereof" once it had ratified the treaty.[5] Not all members agreed with such restrictions, however, as South

Carolinian Pierce Butler informed Madison of the details of the treaty throughout the proceedings and Virginian Stevens T. Mason supplied Bache with the text of the treaty for publication.[6] A handful of southerners, along with one Kentuckian and two New Englanders, even tried during the session to remove the restriction but failed.[7]

At first, public reaction across the country was overwhelmingly unfavorable toward the treaty. By the end of July, Washington had received resolutions against the treaty from residents of Boston, Charleston, Philadelphia, Portsmouth (New Hampshire), and Richmond.[8] The following month, residents of Fredericksburg and Norfolk (Virginia), Lexington (Kentucky), St. John's Parish (South Carolina), Savannah (Georgia), and Warrenton (North Carolina), among others, wrote remonstrances to the president expressing their opposition to the treaty.[9] In addition, concerned citizens passed letters among themselves, even on occasion writing the president personally.[10]

Initial reaction seemed more like shock. "The spirit of the treaty, commercial and political," wrote Philadelphian Tench Coxe, "is as rigidly selfish as the navigation act of Great Britain—for tho some things are granted they are mere Indian presents, for which a greater value was to be placed within their reach at the Moment of Donation."[11] The Right Reverend James Madison, president of the College of William and Mary and an Episcopal bishop, unloaded on his cousin of the same name. "[T]he Treaty," he wrote, "must be considered by every disinterested American, not only as insidious, but as scarcely wearing even the Blush of that Equality & Reciprocity, without which, it were infinitely better to have no Treaty at all."[12] Over the next few months, people would continue to express their opinions on the treaty across the country, but their tone would moderate.[13]

As some of the resolutions against the treaty indicated, opponents decided to oppose it on constitutional grounds, although some critics, including Jefferson, viewed it as "really nothing more than a treaty of alliance between England and the Anglomen of this country against the legislature and people of the United States."[14] Still, the constitutional issues that the treaty raised stirred treaty opponents in their determination to defeat it. "[I]f the treaty can once be brought before the house of Representatives upon its intrinsic contents," noted one of Virginia's nineteen congressmen, William Branch Giles, "a great majority will probably appear against it. The only difficulty will be, to convince the house of its constitutional right to exercise its discression respecting the instrument itself."[15] Echoing Giles's sentiments, Jefferson, perhaps too confident, predicted that "the popular branch of our legislature will disapprove of it, and thus rid us of this infamous act."[16] Explaining the strategy to Giles, Jefferson noted that "the true theory of our constitution, that when a treaty is made, involving matters confided by the constitution to the three branches of the legislature conjointly, the representatives are as free as the President & Senate were to consider whether the national interest requires or forbids their giving the forms & force of law to the articles over which they have a power," an argument that Madison made during the Virginia ratifying convention.[17] During debates in the House over the treaty, Madison presented the issue more succinctly: "whether the general power of making Treaties supersedes the power of the House of Representatives, particularly specified in the Constitution, so as to take to the Executive all deliberative will, and leave the House only an instrumental and ministerial instrumental agency?"[18] Parts of the treaty, such as article eight, which required that the two countries jointly fund the "[e]xpences attending the . . . Commissions" established by the treaty, decidedly trespassed, as far as treaty opponents were concerned, on the constitutional duties of the House, thus making the House's consent to the treaty necessary.[19] In the end, however, the constitutional position failed to persuade enough members of the House, as that body voted fifty-one to forty-eight in favor of authorizing the appropriations required by the British treaty.[20]

The extended debate over the treaty in the House touched on a variety of issues, particularly its commercial terms and position on the rights of neutral carriers, but it did not mirror previous debates in which southerners had worried about how the issue before them might affect the West.[21] On the rare occasion when the West entered the discussion, congressmen concentrated their remarks on article three, which extended to the British the right to traverse the Mississippi River.[22] For Madison, the article was "singularly reprehensible," especially in light of the fact that under the Treaty of Paris of 1783, Great Britain would have been "deprived, by her real boundary, of all pretensions to a share in the banks and waters of the Mississippi."[23] The few defenders of the provision, such as Joshua Coit of Connecticut, did so on the grounds that "it only recognizes the principle established in the Treaty of 1783, that its navigation shall be common to both parties."[24]

Outside of Congress, Kentuckian George Nicholas bemoaned British good fortune, exclaiming that Jay's Treaty, along with "the peace between France and Spain, have I make no doubt, destroyed all just expectation of obtaining the navigation of the M—i [Mississippi] by negociation."[25] Madison expressed similar sentiment in an October 1795 petition that he anonymously wrote to the Virginia General Assembly, which was published in the *Petersburg [Virginia] Intelligencer* and other newspapers throughout Virginia, New York and Pennsylvania.[26] Madison viewed the treaty as a deliberate attempt on the part of Great Britain to derail any agreement with Spain concerning the Mississippi River, declaring that it was "not likely to conciliate those from whom an amicable adjustment of the navigation of the Mississippi is expected."[27] Residents of Lexington, Kentucky, likewise believed the treaty doomed any effort to settle amicably "our differences with Spain on [the navigation of the Mississippi]."[28]

Notwithstanding Madison's melancholy position, Spain and the United States did conclude a treaty that opened the Mississippi River to American commerce.[29] A miscalculation on the part of Spanish officials led them to believe that the United States and Great Britain had settled all their outstanding differences through their recently concluded treaty and that the two countries now posed a direct threat to Louisiana and Florida, and with the negotiations for the British treaty occurring closely after the Citizen Genet affair in 1793, they seemingly had plenty of reasons to worry.[30] Although Edmond-Charles Éduoard "Citizen" Genet's scheme to seize Louisiana and Florida for his native France, which was undergoing its own revolution, had fallen apart by 1794, the French minister's activities did revive concerns over the peaceful intentions of western residents.[31] Spanish officials could not help but worry about "the very disquieting movements of the Americans" in the West, despite assurances from the federal government that western residents would be stopped if they engaged in any activity threatening Spanish possessions.[32] Spanish officials still felt it necessary to have their "Agent 13," General James Wilkinson of the United States Army, advise them about "whatever may be concocted, either in Kentucky or in Cumberland, contrary to the interests of Spain."[33]

The Spanish government was not the only government to worry about the restless nature of western residents. In late August 1794, Secretary of State Edmund Randolph, having met with Spanish commissioner Josef de Jaudenes about the state of negotiations between their two governments, pleaded with Jefferson to serve as a special envoy to Spain. Kentuckians, he declared, "demand a conclusion of the negotiations [concerning the Mississippi River] or a categorical answer from Spain."[34] Continuing, the secretary painted a dire picture. "What if the government of Kentucky should force us either to support them in their hostilities against Spain, or to disavow and renounce them? War at this moment with Spain would not be war with Spain alone: the lopping off of Kentucky from the union is dreadful to contemplate, even if it should not attach itself to some other power. The people there ripen daily, I fear, for one or the other of these alternatives."[35] Although Jefferson declined the appointment, stressing his determination to refrain from "anything public," the Washington administration remained determined to seize the initiative and restart negotiations with Spain.[36] Eventually, Washington turned to his country's minister to Great Britain, Thomas Pinckney, who concluded a treaty with Spain in October 1795.

Washington presented the Treaty of San Lorenzo (often referred to as Pinckney's Treaty), which opened the Mississippi River to American commerce, to the Senate on 26 February 1796, and the Senate ratified it during the first week of March.[37] Slightly more than a month later, on 13 April, the House met to decide how to proceed with the funding for the various treaties before it. Besides the treaties with Great Britain and Spain, the House also had recently concluded treaties between General Anthony Wayne and certain Indian tribes in the Northwest Territory and between the United States and the dey of Algiers.[38] Representative Theodore Sedgwick of Massachusetts immediately proposed that the House bundle all four treaties together for the purpose of having just one vote.[39] Mistrust underscored Sedgwick's motion. As fellow Bay State resident William Lyman noted, "attempts had been made . . . to mislead and deceive the people into an opinion and belief that unless the British Treaty should be carried into effect, the Spanish and other Treaties would also be negative[d]."[40] Albert Gallatin of Pennsylvania was more direct. "It had been declared, that if the British Treaty was not carried into effect, gentlemen would be justified in voting against the other Treaties."[41] Virginia congressman William Branch Giles agreed that an overpowering sense of mistrust had enveloped Congress, noting that "the people are told that the execution of the one, is essentially dependent on the execution of the other."[42]

With mistrust strong among members, Sedgwick's motion necessitated two days of debate, as supporters of the Spanish treaty sought to sooth the concerns of the supporters of the British treaty. Their main argument, as articulated by Madison, was that "[t]he treaty had excited no opposition, and would probably pass through the House without debate, and a select committee could prepare and bring in a bill for carrying it into effect, whilst the British Treaty should be under discussion."[43] British treaty supporters countered by noting that the United States faced a 1 June deadline to fund the treaty and, taking a slap at those members who had argued in favor of beginning debate with the Spanish treaty because of its importance to their constituents, they argued that "they came there to legislate for the whole and not a part of the Union."[44] In the end, however, the House decided to unbundle the treaties and commence debate on the Spanish treaty.[45]

Madison's assessment of the overall support for the Spanish treaty was correct, as once the House stopped acting "like angry children . . . [declaring] that because they could not get all they wanted they would not have a part," the House with minimal discussion voted to carry the treaty into effect.[46] Within a matter of minutes, the House also approved the Algerian treaty and Wayne's Treaty of Greenville. Somewhat surprising, however, was House members' apparent lack of concern over how the Spanish and British treaties conflicted in their treatments of the Mississippi River. In its treaty, Spain had granted the right to navigate the Mississippi River in its entirety only to the "subjects and citizens of the United States," whereas the United States, in the British treaty, had opened the river to British citizens.[47] Spain had reserved the right to extend navigation rights to other parties but had not done so at the time the treaty came before the House, nor would it do so in the future. Even before the terms of the Spanish treaty were known, Madison and others had wondered just how the two treaties might conflict. "Its [the Spanish treaty's] aspect on the Mississippi article in the British treaty will be particularly interesting," Madison noted in anticipation of receiving the document for the first time.[48] Once people learned of the terms of the Spanish treaty, it became necessary that they "ascertain whether it clashes with the British treaty as to the Missisipi."[49] Apparently, the two treaties were "so far . . . from harmoniseing," that they decided to simply ignore the incongruities and pretend that they did not exist, as evidenced by action in the Senate.[50] When the treaty came before that chamber, senators at first felt that they needed to attach a "declaratory proviso to the ratification," but after second thought, they decided "to presume a construction that would avoid the inconsistency."[51] Had not "[Thomas] Pinckney considered the article as admitting a construction reconcileable with the British article," they rationalized.[52]

With Pinckney's Treaty, westerners had finally gained what they had been so intent on acquiring—complete access to the entire Mississippi River and right of deposit (store goods for export) at New Orleans. The provisions dealing with the Mississippi River in Jay's Treaty had worried westerners and southerners, but Pinckney had allayed their apprehensions. In the end, however, it was the political drama surrounding Jay's Treaty that directed the attention of southerners away from Pinckney's Treaty and from celebrating what the Spanish treaty meant for them and the West. Politics had left them with little time to enjoy their success.

Just days before the House first began debate on the four treaties, Washington had laid before Congress documents attesting to the desire of the residents of the Territory South of the River Ohio to be admitted into the Union as a state.[53] For many residents of the territory, this part of the process probably seemed like a formality, for they had already conducted a census, written a constitution, elected state officials, and chosen their United States senators.[54] Knowledge of what the "settlements on the Holston, French Broad, Cumberland and their waters" had done had already reached the members of Congress by early March, so Washington's message was not unexpected.[55] The House subsequently referred the communication from the president to a five-member committee, which reported on 12 April a resolution "that the State of Tennessee is hereby declared to be one of the sixteen United States of America."[56]

The House did not take up the report of the committee until 5 May, having devoted most of its energy in April to a discussion of the British treaty. When the House finally addressed the issue of Tennessee statehood, it did so amid speculation that Washington would not seek a third term as president.[57] Suddenly, Tennessee statehood became entangled in the first competitive presidential election in the history of the United States. "It is now pretty certain" Madison noted to Monroe in late February, "that the president will not serve beyond his present term. . . . The republicans knowing that Jefferson alone can be started with hope of success mean to push him."[58] Tennessee, with at least three but possibly four electoral votes, became in some ways the subject of the opening salvo of the 1796 presidential contest. "Of this, their proceedings on the organizing and admitting the territory of the United States [Tennessee] into the Union as a state, is a singular instance. . . . No doubt this is one twig of the electioneering cabal for Mr. Jefferson," noted Connecticut Federalist Chauncy Goodrich.[59] Federalists worried about the Republican leanings of Tennessee and worked to prevent the territory's erection into a state before the presidential election.[60] Upon failing to prevent Tennessee statehood, Federalist congressman Jonathan Dayton of Massachusetts remarked that "the admission of Tennessee into the Union must render Mr. Adams's success less certain than before the event."[61]

Federalists adopted several arguments to deny statehood to Tennessee. First, they contended that only Congress could initiate statehood. Tennessee's actions in 1795 and 1796, conducting a census and drafting a constitution without the express consent of Congress, established a dangerous precedent for all the "other States [that] would be rising up in the Western wilderness," averred South Carolinia Federalist Robert Goodloe Harper.[62] Federalists also wondered whether it would be better to erect two or more states from the Southwest Territory and not just one, as "the inhabitants of the Western or Mero district almost universally answered in the negative" to statehood.[63] Finally, they argued "that the census was not to be relied on" for the requisite 60,000 inhabitants for statehood or for determining the number of representatives in the House.[64] Although most members agreed that Tennessee should have only one representative, not the two representatives that residents had requested, the validity of the census became the crux of the Federalist argument against Tennessee statehood. Over in the Senate, Federalist members succeeded where their House colleagues had failed and included in their chamber's statehood bill a provision that required a new enumeration of the inhabitants of the territory "before they could be admitted."[65] However, the House, which had passed its version of the bill by a vote of forty-three to thirty, refused to agree to the Senate's version.[66] Finally, with only days left in the session, the Senate backed down, and on the last day of the session, 1 June, Washington signed into law "An Act for the Admission of the State of Tennessee into the Union."[67]

With the legitimacy of the census emerging as the central issue in Tennessee's bid for statehood, House members directed most of their comments to it. When they did take time to address other issues, they spoke to the character of the people living in the territory. Two New England members chose to address the loyalty of territorial residents. Henry Dearborn, a Republican from Massachusetts, broached the subject apparently in the belief that it might sway some members to vote for statehood. "He could not see," it was reported, "the propriety of adopting any measure which might irritate them.

They formed an extensive frontier—were very far detached from the Atlantic States. We should rather, he said, think of conciliating them than irritating them."[68] A short time later, Jonathan Dayton, the Federalist speaker of the House from New Jersey, expanded on what Dearborn had said in an apparent effort to sway opinion away from statehood. Although acknowledging that the people of the Southwest Territory harbored no "hostile or menacing measure," he could not help but wonder about a region in "a part of which resided many whose attachment to another government was well known," an obvious reference to various Spanish intrigues.[69] Could Congress trust a people, he wondered, who considered themselves an independent state? What was to stop them, he asked, from refusing "to become a party to this Confederacy, or they might, in offering to enter into the Union, annex to the offer such terms and conditions as should give them advantages over the other States, and they might even treat and ally themselves with any foreign Power."[70] Coming to the defense of territorial residents later that same day, Nathaniel Macon of North Carolina expressed shock that anyone could have suggested such a thing. "There was no more likelihood," he declared, "of their going over to any other Government, than there was of any other State doing the same thing."[71]

For his part, Madison offered a lackadaisical defense, painting a picture of a people "in a degraded situation."[72] The people of the territory, he noted, lacked a basic American right—"the right of being represented in Congress."[73] "An exterior power," he told his fellow members, "had authority over their laws."[74] Skeptical, Federalist Theodore Sedgwick of Massachusetts responded that Madison was simply trying to misrepresent the situation. "What had been said by the gentleman from Virginia . . . ," he reminded listeners, "would not only apply to 60,000 but to six persons. The question was whether they were in a situation in which they could claim to be a State," he declared.[75] Even with regard to Tennessee, an important addition to the southern power structure, the intensity of previous debates now seemed a thing of the past.

Other events that year seemed to further the distrust enveloping the two political parties. That summer, French general Georges-Henri-Victor Collot appeared in the West on a mission for the French minister to the United States, Pierre Auguste Adet, "to furnish him with a minute detail of the political, commercial, and military state of the western part of that continent."[76] The general's activities, which included discussions with some of the region's important political figures, caused considerable consternation within the Washington administration, as they provoked the administration to send "a confidential person" to spy on the general as he travelled.[77] Although nothing came of the general's fact-finding mission, it alarmed Federalists, who believed that it was simply one more example of the dangerous relationship developing between France and Republicans.[78]

The war between revolutionary France and Great Britain had strained political relationships, as each political party viewed the other as the puppet of one or the other European power. When the French minister published a letter that he had written in November to Secretary of State Timothy Pickering, touching on the close relationship that the United States and France had once enjoyed and ending with the words, "Let your Government return to itself, and you will still find in Frenchmen faithful friends and generous allies," he provoked allegations from Federalists that France was colluding with the Republicans to ensure a victory for Jefferson in the presidential election.[79] Even Washington believed that the French were "disposed to play a high game."[80] John Adams's victory in the presidential election did not end the Federalists' assault on the Republicans, as they filled newspapers throughout the summer of 1797 with tales of French and Republican machinations against the United States.[81]

News of William Blount's conspiracy seemed only to intensify the newspaper offerings. Blount, one of Tennessee's initial two senators, had become involved in a plan to interest Great Britain in seizing Spanish possessions in Florida and Louisiana and opening their rivers to American commerce.[82] Westerners had heard rumors that France intended to force Spain to return to it the lands that it once possessed west of the Mississippi River and the port of New Orleans.[83] With France in control of New Orleans, the Spanish treaty that Pinckney had negotiated in 1795 would be worthless, and westerners would again have no outlet for their products.[84] The conspirators also sought to alarm residents of Kentucky and Tennessee by alleging that "all property in these countries will be of no value, as it will be in the neighborhood of a hostile and warlike people who will favor the liberation of all the slaves," a reference to France's abolition of slavery in 1794.[85] Against these concerns, Knoxville tavern keeper John Chisholm, a British subject, hatched his plan and enticed Blount to join his plot, which Blount soon came to direct.[86] Chisholm, at least, had hoped that "the Frontier People would generally join in" on the British-led assault on Spanish possessions.[87] Eventually, letters among the conspirators found their way into the hands of government officials.[88] Confronted with evidence of treason by one of its members, the Senate expelled Blount "with only one dissenting voice" on 8 July 1797.[89]

The "Blount Conspiracy" shocked Americans, as newspapers across the country followed the proceedings of the Senate and House of Representatives, where members hurriedly voted to impeach the Tennessee senator "without a division" on 7 July.[90] Blount's political affiliation with the Republicans allowed many northern and some southern newspapers to attack Jefferson and lay blame at the foot of the French.[91] "It can be little doubted, from his [Blount's] long connection with the French party," declared an unknown editorial writer in the *Washington [D.C.] Gazette*, "that he has been made acquainted with the secret views of the directory, and his pecuniary embarrassments render him a fit man to be employed in the most desperate projects."[92] "There are some reasons," an unknown person in New York wrote, "for believing the French, in collusion with the Spanish Minister, contrived the scheme, to furnish pretexts for keeping the garrisons on the Mississippi, in defiance of the [Pinckney's] treaty, and to increase jealousies and enmities between the United States and Great Britain, with a view to defeat the object of the late [Jay's] treaty or any further and closer connection."[93] Adams's treasury secretary believed that he saw in Blount's activities the beginnings of a French and Spanish "western or ultra-montane republic."[94] One Virginian even went so far as to theorize that Blount devised his plot as retribution for Jefferson's loss in the presidential election.[95] When a House committee determined that "it was not a French plot with Mr. Jefferson at the bottom," "some long faces" appeared among those who had believed otherwise.[96]

Besides Jefferson and the Republicans, the Blount affair cast a pall of suspicion over westerners in general and Tennesseans in particular. For treasury secretary Wolcott, the episode showed how "precarious[ly] . . . the western country is attached to the existing government."[97] A New Yorker viewed many people in the region as simply willing pawns of "adventurers in land jobbing."[98] The appearance of a newspaper article from Knoxville dated 18 September and published in newspapers from Georgia to Connecticut caused quite a stir among some readers. The article described the hero's welcome that Blount received when he returned to Tennessee after being expelled from the Senate. "We are happy to say," the article concluded, "that Mr. Blount has received on his journey through this state, the most flattering and hearty welcome from every description of citizens; a welcome justly due from a grateful people to the father, friend and protector of their state."[99] One disgusted New Yorker wrote in reply that Blount's reception "is proof that his projects have either met with the approbation of his neighbors, or at least have not been considered as criminal. Indeed many of them are doubtless his accomplices."[100] Of course, not everyone believed in the culpability of westerners. William Polk of North Carolina, for example, reasoned that no one associated with Blount possessed any "hostile views toward the Spanish settlements or . . . knew any thing of Blount[']s plan."[101]

Surprisingly, Jefferson and Madison, who had retired from the House in March, remained fairly aloof during the Blount episode. Jefferson's position as president of the Senate allowed him to be aware of the evidence that the House managers had collected against Blount, but this information did not elicit any strong opinions on his part, only an interest in the propriety of impeaching a person who had already been expelled from office and the satisfaction of knowing that the trial would justify the Senate's convening in December 1797.[102] He was, however, definitely aware of the Federalists' attacks against him, as was Madison, who believed that a majority of Federalists in Congress were simply using the issue for political gain until their constituents tired of the whole affair.[103] Like most Americans, Jefferson and Madison were interested in the allegations against Blount; however, Blount's misfortunes did not appear to worry them too much, nor did the aspersions cast against westerners because of Blount necessitate in their minds a need to defend the integrity of westerners. They and other southerners had done so in the past, but not this time.

Blount's actions were not the only western activities that worried Americans in 1797. The Treaty of San Lorenzo, which the Senate had ratified in March 1796, stipulated that Spain must evacuate its forts above the thirty-first parallel "within the term of six months" after the ratification of the treaty.[104] By early 1797, the forts, primarily at Natchez and Walnut Hills (present-day Vicksburg), still remained in Spanish hands for a variety of stated reasons, including the fear of British attacks on Upper and Lower Louisiana and a purported surprise attack on the part of the United States against unnamed Spanish possessions.[105] This delay in the transfer worried local residents and the American sent to survey the new boundary line, Andrew Ellicott.[106] Ellicott's reports, which included repeated examples of Spanish duplicity and mistreatment of Americans, only added to the apprehensions that many Americans felt.[107]

In June, a drunken Baptist preacher, Barton Hannon, instigated a "revolt" against Spanish authority at Natchez.[108] According to Ellicott, Hannon's sermon on 4 June stirred a desire for the liberty of conscience "in its fullest extent" among the Americans present.[109] A few days later, Hannon, while drunk, entered into a theological debate with some Irish Roman Catholics, who proceeded to thrash him. Confronting Manuel Gayoso de Lemos, the Spanish governor, Hannon demanded justice while maintaining the right to seek satisfaction himself.[110] Gayoso promptly had him arrested, which enraged the Americans in the area, who viewed the governor's actions as an effort "to enforce the laws of Spain, both civil and religious with rigour" in an area whose location placed it above the thirty-first parallel.[111] As a result of the increased hostility toward him, Gayoso took refuge in a nearby fort.[112] A committee of local residents subsequently formed and restored order.[113] In July, local residents further enhanced their control by forming a second committee, often referred to as the Committee of Safety, that, according to Ellicott, "put the finishing stroke to the Spanish authority, and jurisdiction in the area."[114] Events in the district, however, remained tense throughout the remainder of the year.[115]

Several newspapers across the United States followed the events at Natchez. One account, originating from Baltimore on 18 October and reportedly based on firsthand accounts, was reprinted in several newspapers, including the *Times and Alexandria [Virginia] Advertiser*.[116] Although failing to discuss Hannon's role, it did showcase the efforts of the Americans and their neighbors to "assume all the power."[117] Hannon's role in precipitating events did not go unnoticed in the press, however, as some newspapers did mention the presence of a "Baptist preacher."[118] Generally, newspaper accounts painted a picture of uneasiness among the residents of Natchez while highlighting their desire to become a part of the United States. Surprisingly, few newspapers carried reports, which seem to have originated in Charleston, of a harmless skirmish between Natchez area residents and Spanish troops on 14 June.[119]

In Philadelphia, President John Adams sought a congressional solution to the problems at Natchez. In June, he asked Congress to erect a government at Natchez, whose residents he declared to be "generally well affected and much attached to the United States."[120] Military matters concerned Congress more, and it failed to act on Adams's request before its session ended on 10 July. In late January 1798, the president once again addressed the Natchez situation with Congress.[121] Perhaps prodded by the timely arrival in early February of a petition from the residents of Natchez, Congress finally acted, but before it addressed any bill, word arrived that Spain had relinquished its forts on the Mississippi River to the United States.[122]

Until that moment, Jefferson and Madison had believed that the administration was manipulating events through its agents at Natchez to embroil the United States in a war with Spain. The day after Adams made his second request to Congress, Jefferson wrote Madison that "very acrimonious altercations are going on between the Spanish minister & Executive, and at the Natchez something worse than mere altercations. If hostilities have not begun there, it has not been for want of endeavors to bring them on by our agents."[123] Madison agreed, declaring that "a war with Spain will be provoked by the present administration."[124] Both men believed that regional interests dictated the administration's efforts as a war with Spain, as part of a larger confrontation with France, would provide New England privateers with a better "prospect of plunder."[125] Although the reports that Spain had relinquished its forts were welcome news, Jefferson gave all the credit for this accomplishment not to Adams's administration, but to the "moderation of the Spanish government."[126] Throughout it all, the two Virginians expressed no concern for western interests, except for a quip by Jefferson that if the administration were to accomplish its goal of starting a war with Spain, "our Southern states might have something to conquer and amuse themselves by land."[127] Westerners, on the other hand, remained worried about the possibility of war with France and its effects on their commercial highway, the Mississippi River.[128]

In late February, the Senate finally began work on a territorial bill for the Natchez region, but members soon encountered a complication—the failure of Georgian officials and their state's western land claimants to resolve legal questions stemming from the Yazoo land fraud scandal. Although the Georgian legislature had rescinded the Yazoo Act of 1795 during its legislative session the following year, speculators who had acquired land from the four Yazoo companies established by the 1795 act believed that Georgia had unjustly wronged them.[129] Senators, unsure as to the legal right of the United States to the land around Natchez, decided to appoint "Commissioners to negotiate with Georgia for the sale of her western Territory—and with the individual purchasers under Georgia for their rights."[130] During debate on the bill to establish a government at Natchez, Georgian Josiah Tattnall, who had worked with his predecessor James Jackson in the state legislature to rescind the Yazoo Act, had sought to delay the creation of a territorial government until "the consent of the State of Georgia shall be obtained, by cession or otherwise, [regarding] all that tract of country bounded on the west by the Mississippi."[131] He managed to gain, however, only eight supporters, five from southern states and two from western states.[132] The final version of the bill passed the Senate on 5 March by a vote of twenty to eight. Six of the original eight senators who had supported Tattnall still remained opposed to the bill and were joined in their opposition by two senators from New England, which increased the total number of senators from that region who opposed the bill to three.[133]

When debate on the bill began in the House in late March, John Milledge of Georgia immediately attacked the Senate's efforts at treating the territorial claims of Georgia and of individual purchasers equally. Including such language in the bill as Henry Tazewell had outlined, the Georgian noted that it would "sanction claims which had been declared not to exist."[134] He further declared that if the House were to retain the language, it would become an "obstacle in the way of cession of either the territory or jurisdiction."[135]

Federalist Robert Goodloe Harper of South Carolina believed that Milledge had mischaracterized Georgia's position on the Yazoo affair. He argued that the government of the United States should recognize all claimants, whether state or private, to the territory. How "could [Georgia] take offense at this"? he wondered, but his query fell on deaf ears. The other members who spoke on this issue, primarily southerners, tended to view it with some suspicion, as northerners, particularly those from Massachusetts, had been principal investors in the early companies or their offshoots.[136] Virginia's Abraham Venable believed that the "words were introduced with a view of indemnifying the purchasers of these lands," an assertion validated by Harper's admission that "[t]hese men . . . have no hope while Georgia possesses this territory."[137] Venable sardonically noted that since the original purchasers had declined the return of their $500,000, "choosing rather to risk the whole than give up their claim, it may be expected they will be high in their demands."[138] Another Virginian, John Nicholas, questioned the wisdom of allowing commissioners to negotiate for the territory, since they might pledge the United States "to provide money to any amount which it may please . . . [them] to stipulate for."[139] He further argued that if members believed that the inclusion of others besides Georgia in the negotiations was so important, they should take time to address the issue in a separate bill.[140] Despite Harper's pleas, members in the end agreed with Milledge and removed the controversial wording.[141]

Having succeeded in his first attempt at modifying the bill in favor of Georgia, Milledge next attempted to accomplish what his counterpart in the Senate had not—the erection of a temporary government "as soon as the consent of the Legislature of Georgia shall be obtained."[142] Milledge believed that the United States only had a "pretended claim . . . to this country" and that to erect a government "would be stepping beyond the Constitution."[143]

Harper, the first to respond, rejected Milledge's claim that the United States did not possess title to the territory, as would several northern congressmen who followed in the debate.[144] Still, he chose to oppose the amendment on the ground that the bill contained a clause that protected Georgia's "right of the jurisdiction or the soil of this territory."[145] Expediency, he declared, called for the establishment of a government at Natchez. "[I]f this country were invaded by Indians, or involved in a civil war," he told members, "we could not have the benefit of the navigation of [the Mississippi River]."[146] Besides, "if it was found in the end that the United States had no title to it, the Government which had been established could be withdrawn."[147]

Northerners tended to agree with Harper, reiterating the South Carolinian's point that a government for the inhabitants of the area "required [the] immediate attention" of Congress. The three southerners who spoke on the issue, on the other hand, viewed things differently. Nicholas, like Milledge, questioned the validity of the United States' claim to the territory, arguing that without the amendment, the bill sanctioned the "forcible possession of [the territory]" on the part of the United States.[148] Such an action, Nicholas declared, would be tantamount to the federal government taking over "a certain district in Virginia . . . [because it was] not so well governed as it might be, and, as the people would be happier under the Government of the United States."[149] Nathaniel Macon of North Carolina definitely agreed with Nicholas that the bill was not friendly toward Georgia.[150] Another Georgian, Abraham Baldwin, declared it a "dereliction of principle" "[i]f the proposed Government was proceeded with without the consent of Georgia."[151] The southerners' arguments, which centered on constitutional and states' rights principles, did not prevail, however, as the House voted forty-six to thirty-four against Milledge's amendment.[152]

As soon as the House had resolved this issue, George Thatcher of Massachusetts ignited another controversy by proposing that Congress prohibit slavery in the new territory on the grounds that it violated the "rights of man."[153] Again, Robert Goodloe Harper responded first. Speaking more as a southerner than as a Federalist, he declared that "it would be very improper to make such a regulation, as that species of property already exists, and persons emigrating there from the Southern States would carry with them property of this kind."[154] To agree to such a motion, he declared, would "be a decree of banishment to all the people settled there, and of exclusion to all those intending to go there."[155]

Three other southerners joined Harper in opposing the motion. Whereas John Rutledge, Jr., a Federalist from South Carolina, complained about northern congressmen "on every occasion, . . . [bringing] forward the Southern States in an odious light," Nicholas and William Branch Giles, both Virginians, argued that such a prohibition would harm not only the slave-holding states, but also the slaves themselves. "[I]f the slaves of the Southern States were permitted to go into this Western country," Giles noted, "by lessening the number in those States, and spreading them over a larger surface of the country, there would be a greater probability of ameliorating their condition, which could never be done whilst they were crowded together as they now are in the Southern States."[156] Nicholas, admitting that the southern states were unfortunate "to be overwhelmed with this kind of property," proceeded to ask whether "it would not be doing service not only to them but to the whole Union, to open this country, and by that means spread the blacks over a large space, so that in time it might be safe to carry into effect the plan which certain philanthropists have so much at heart, and to which he had no objection."[157]

By far the most vocal supporter of the motion was its author. Thatcher rejected the Virginians' arguments, declaring "that colonizing these people tended to increase the race far beyond what it would be when penned closely together."[158] "They wished to get rid of them," he remarked, "and to plague others with them. But they had them, and if they determined to keep them, he wished only they should be plagued with them."[159] Besides, he informed members, if this amendment so alarmed southerners because it would deter "emigrants from the Southern States, who cannot work for themselves. . . . [Then i]f this be true, it makes the people of the Southern States only fit to superintend slaves. The language of this is, that these people cannot subsist, except they have slaves work for them."[160] Several northerners, however, spoke against the motion, worrying that it might produce some "bad effects," including "[a]n immediate insurrection."[161] Despite Thatcher's effort at rallying support, only 12 members voted for his motion.[162] Slavery remained a topic of debate, however.

After a weekend off, the House reconvened on Monday, 26 March, and approved two changes to the bill. The first amendment ensured to the people of the Mississippi Territory, the agreed on name for this new area, the rights and privileges enjoyed by the people living in the Northwest Territory. The

second change, authored by Harper of South Carolina, prohibited the importation of slaves from "without the limits of the United States."[163] Thatcher
moved that the words "without the limits of the United States" be deleted, but
his motion failed for lack of a second.[164] The next day, the House passed the
reshaped Senate bill, and the Senate concurred in the changes two days
later.[165]

The Mississippi territorial bill was the last major western issue before the
Louisiana Purchase. By the mid-1790s, western issues that had once aroused
the passion of southerners seemed less important. European events, particularly the difficulties that developed between the United States and France as
a result of Jay's Treaty, and domestic political considerations, especially
Jefferson's disillusionment with the national government, began to redirect
the attention of men like Madison away from the West. With Kentucky and
Tennessee, they now had two states upon which they could depend. With the
Mississippi Territory, they could even anticipate more states in the future. At
last, they could feel comfortable redirecting their attention eastward once
again.

NOTES

1. George Washington to Edmund Randolph, 22 July 1795, in *The Writings of George
Washington from the Original Sources, 1745–1799*, ed. John C. Fitzpatrick (Washington, DC:
Government Printing Office, 1940), 34:244; *Annals of Congress*, Senate, 4th Cong., special
sess., 855.

2. Washington to Randolph, 22 July 1795, in Fitzpatrick, *Writings of Washington*, 34:244.

3. *Annals of Congress*, 862. The vote in favor of consent included four southerners and
one Kentuckian. Two New Englanders and one middle state resident joined six southerners and
one Kentuckian in voting against consent. All but one member who voted for consent, James
Gunn of Georgia, were pro-Washington administration in their political leanings. All of the
members who voted against consent were anti-Washington administration in their political
leanings. Political affiliations based on those provided in the *Biographical Directory of the
United States Congress, 1774–Present,* http://bioguide.congress.gov/biosearch/biosearch.asp.
The Senate rejected article twelve, which dealt with the commercial rights of the United States
in the West Indies. See Todd Estes, *The Jay Treaty Debate, Public Opinion, and the Evolution
of Early American Political Culture* (Amherst: University of Massachusetts Press, 2006), 29.

4. "Editorial Note," in *The Papers of James Madison*, eds. J.C.A. Stagg et al. (Charlottesville: University Press of Virginia, 1989), 16:141; Estes, *Jay Treaty Debate*, 34.

5. *Journal of the Executive Proceedings* of the *Senate of the United States*, 4th Cong.,
special sess., 8 June and 25 June 1795. [Hereafter cited as *Senate Executive Journal*.]

6. "Editorial Note," in Stagg et al., *Madison Papers*, 16:141; Todd Estes, "Shaping the
Politics of Public Opinion: Federalists and the Jay Treaty Debate," *Journal of the Early Republic* 20:3 (Autumn 2000), 399.

7. *Senate Executive Journal*, 4th Cong., special sess., 13 June 1795; Pierce Butler to
Madison, 26 June 1795, in Stagg et al., *Madison Papers*, 16: 25–26.

8. Boston Citizens to George Washington, 15 July 1795, Charleston, South Carolina,
Citizens to Washington, 22 July 179, Philadelphia Citizens to Washington, 25 July 1795,
Portsmouth, New Hampshire, Citizens to Washington, 17 July 1795, Richmond, Virginia,
Citizens to Washington, 31 July 1795, all in *George Washington Papers, 1741–1799* (Wash-
ington, DC: Library of Congress, Manuscript Division, 1964), Film J1, Reel 107.

9. *The American Remembrancer; or, An Impartial Collection of Essays, Resolves, Speeches, etc. Relative, or Having Affinity, to the Treaty with Great Britain, Part 5* (Philadelphia: Printed by Henry Tuckniss for Mathew Carey, 10 October 1795), in *Early American Imprints, Series 1: Evans, 1639–1800*, no. 28389, 2:269–70; Fredericksburg, Virginia, Citizens Committee, 18 August 1795; Norfolk, Virginia, Citizens to George Washington, 6 August 1795; St John's Parish, South Carolina, Citizen's Meeting, 8 August 1795; Savannah, Georgia, Citizens Meeting to Washington, 1 August 1795, all in *George Washington Papers*, Film J1, Reel 107; Warren County, North Carolina, Citizens to Washington, 22 August 1795, in *George Washington Papers at the Library of Congress, 1741–1799: Series 2 Letterbooks*, http://memory.loc.gov/cgi-bin/query/P?mgw:1:./temp/~ammem_i0en::.

10. Madison to Jefferson, 6 August 1795, in Stagg et al., *Madison Papers*, 16:45.

11. Tench Coxe to Jefferson, 30 July 1795, in *The Papers of Thomas Jefferson*, ed. John Catanzariti (Princeton and Oxford: Princeton University Press, 2000), 28:422.

12. Right Reverend James Madison to Madison, 25 July 1795, in Stagg et al., *Madison Papers*, 16:40.

13. For instance, in Richmond, which had been one of the first cities to dispatch a resolution to Washington criticizing the treaty, reappraisal of the treaty would cause one resident to report "that all along between this and the Potomack a degree of anxiety prevails, and that the general opinion is general in favor of the President and the execution of the treaty." See *Newbern North Carolina Gazette*, 14 May 1796. In addition, Oliver Wolcott, Jr., noted that by the end of July, tempers had started to moderate in Philadelphia. See Oliver Wolcott, Jr., to Alexander Hamilton, 30 July 1795, in *The Papers of Alexander Hamilton*, ed. Harold C. Syrett (New York and London: Columbia University Press, 1973), 18:526.

14. Petersburg, Virginia, Citizens Meeting to Washington, 1 August 1795, in *George Washington Papers*, Film J1, Reel 107; Richmond County, Georgia, Citizens Meeting, 1 September 1795, in *George Washington Papers at the Library of Congress, 1741–1799: Series 2 Letterbooks*, http://memory.loc.gov/cgi-bin/query/P?mgw:1:./temp/~ammem_xNRi:::; Warren County, North Carolina, Citizens to Washington, 22 August 1795, in *George Washington Papers at the Library of Congress*; Jefferson to Edward Rutledge, 30 November 1795, in Catanzariti, *Jefferson Papers*, 28:542. Even Washington understood the strategy of the treaty's opponents, writing that "no candid man in the least degree acquainted with the progress of this business, will believe for a moment that the *ostensible* dispute, was about papers, or that the British Treaty was a *good* one, or a *bad* one; but whether there *should be a Treaty at all* without the concurrence of the house of Representatives. Which was striking at once, and boldly too, at the fundamental principles of the Constitution [italics original]." See Washington to Edward Carrington, 1 May 1796, in *The Writings of Washington from the Original Sources, 1745–1799*, ed. John C. Fitzpatrick (Washington, DC: Government Printing Office, 1940), 35:32.

15. William Branch Giles to Jefferson, 15 December 1795, in Catanzariti, *Jefferson Papers*, 28:555. Thomas J. Farnham, in "The Virginia Amendments of 1795: An Episode in the Opposition to Jay's Treaty," *The Virginia Magazine of History and Biography* 75:1 (January 1967), 75–88, traces the efforts of some Virginians to interject the constitutional issue into the House of Representatives through the introduction of four proposed constitutional amendments approved by the Virginia legislature in late 1795.

16. Jefferson to Edward Rutledge, 30 November 1795, in Catanzariti, *Jefferson Papers*, 28:542.

17. Jefferson to William Branch Giles, 31 December 1795, in Ibid., 28:565; *The Documentary History of the Ratification of the Constitution*, eds. John P. Kaminski and Gaspare J. Saladino (Madison: State Historical Society of Wisconsin, 1993), 10:1241.

18. *Annals of Congress*, 4th Cong., 1st sess., 437–38.

19. *American State Papers, Foreign Affairs*, 1:522.

20. *Annals of Congress*, 4th Cong., 1st sess., 1291.

21. Debate on Jay's Treaty began in the House on 14 April and lasted until 30 April. See *Annals of Congress*, 4th Cong., 1st sess., 969–1298 passim.

22. The article stated: "The River Mississippi shall however, according to the Treaty of Peace be entirely open to both Parties; And it is further agreed, That all the ports and places on

its Eastern side, to whichsoever of the parties belonging, may freely be resorted to, and used by both parties, in as ample a manner as any of the Atlantic Ports or Places of the United States, or any of the Ports or Places of His Majesty in Great Britain." See *American State Papers, Foreign Affairs*, 1:520.

23. *Annals of Congress*, 4th Cong., 1st sess., 979, 980.

24. Ibid., 1145.

25. Nicholas to Madison, 6 November 1795, in Stagg et al., *Madison Papers*, 16:119.

26. "Draft of Petition to the General Assembly of the Commonwealth of Virginia," in Ibid., 62–68.

27. *The American Remembrancer; or, An Impartial Collection of Essays, Resolves, Speeches, etc. Relative, or Having Affinity, to the Treaty with Great Britain, Part 9* (Philadelphia: Printed by Henry Tuckniss for Mathew Carey, 28 November 1795), in *Early American Imprints, Series 1: Evans, 1639–1800*, no. 28389, 3:3–6. Madison also believed that the British government sought through Jay's Treaty to prevent or at least hinder any future agreements between the United States and France or any other European country. See Madison to an Unidentified Correspondent, 23 August 1795, and Madison to Monroe, 20 December 1795, in Stagg et al., *Madison Papers*, 16:58, 170.

28. *The American Remembrancer, Part 5*, 2:269.

29. For the text of the Treaty of San Lorenzo, see *American State Papers, Foreign Affairs*, 1:546–49.

30. Donald E. Chipman and Harriett Denise Joseph, *Spanish Texas, 1519–1821*, rev. ed. (1992; repr., Austin: University of Texas Press, 2010), 226.

31. Genet sought two things from the United States. First, he wanted a new treaty reflecting France's interpretation of the existing treaties between the two countries, which more than likely would have meant war between the United States and Great Britain. Secondly, he sought to seize Spanish possessions with the help, he imagined, of disgruntled westerners. To this point, he tried organizing two armies that would launch attacks against Spanish Louisiana and Florida, but the two armies never materialized. Stanley Elkins and Eric McKitrick, *The Age of Federalism* (New York and Oxford: Oxford University Press, 1993), 330–36; George C. Herring, *From Colony to Superpower: U.S. Foreign Relations Since 1776* (Oxford: Oxford University Press, 2008), 71.

32. Baron de la Carondelet to the Duke de la Alcudia, 31 July 1793, in "Selections from the Draper Collection in the Possession of the State Historical Society of Wisconsin, to Elucidate the Proposed French Expedition under George Rogers Clark against Louisiana, in the Years 1793–94." *Annual Report of the American Historical Association for the Year 1896, in Two Volumes* (Washington, DC: Government Printing Office, 1897), 1:998 (hereafter cited as *Annual Report*). The Washington administration took the activities of Genet seriously, instructing state and federal officials throughout the West, especially in Kentucky and the Tennessee settlements, that the "enterprise is not to be tolerated in the least degree." See *American State Papers, Foreign Affairs*, 1:254, 255, 458 (quotation). In early 1794, the threatening actions of Georgians against Spanish possessions in Florida would likewise attract the attention of federal officials. See *American State Papers, Foreign Affairs*, 1:459–60. Finally, in June 1794, Congress passed a neutrality act that codified much of what Washington had stated in his 1793 proclamation on neutrality and thereby made much of what Genet had attempted to accomplish illegal. See *Statutes At Large*, 3rd Cong., 1st. sess., 1:381–84.

33. Baron de la Carondelet to Manuel Gayoso de Lemos, 29 October 1793, in *Annual Report*, 1:1020; Andro Linklater, *An Artist in Treason: The Extraordinary Double Life of General James Wilkinson* (New York: Walker Publishing Company, 2009), 128. Genet's scheme did arouse interest in the West. In December 1793, residents of Lexington, Kentucky, drafted two resolutions, one addressed to the people living "west of the Allegany and Apalachian mountains" and the other to the president and Congress. In the remonstrance to the president and Congress, the Kentuckians expressed their dissatisfaction regarding the lack of "effectual measures" to secure access to the Mississippi River and implored that negotiations with Spain be rapidly concluded. In their appeal to the people of the West, they hinted that the time had come to end negotiations. "The present crisis," they declared, "is favorable. Spain is engaged in a war which requires all her forces. If the present golden opportunity be suffered to

pass without advantage, and she shall have concluded a peace with France, we must then contend against her undivided strength." See *American State Papers, Miscellaneous*, 1:929, 930. Several days later, with emotions still apparently intense, the publisher of the *Lexington Kentucky Gazette*, John Bradford, decided that it would be prudent to refuse to publish a letter from local merchant Charles De Pauw, titled "That the Republicans of the Western Country are ready [to go down] the Ohio and Mississippi," because "it would excite opposition in the Executive of this State." See John Bradford to M. De Pauw, 19 December 1793, in *Annual Report*, 1:1023–24.

34.   Edmund Randolph to Jefferson, 28 August 1794, in Catanzariti, *Jefferson Papers*, 28:117.

35.   Ibid, 118.

36.   Jefferson to Randolph, 7 September 1794, in Ibid., 28:148. Washington acted on the belief that Spain's commissioners had intimated to Randolph that if the United States were to act quickly, an opportunity to restart negotiations existed. See *Senate Executive Journal*, 3rd Cong., 2nd sess., 163.

37.   *Senate Executive Journal*, 4th Cong., 1st sess., 200, 203.

38.   For the text of The Treaty of Greenville, see *American State Papers, Indian Affairs*, 1:562–64; for the text of A Treaty of Peace and Amity with the dey of Algiers, see *American State Papers, Foreign Affairs*, 1:530–32.

39.   *Annals of Congress*, 4th Cong., 1st sess., 940.

40.   Ibid., 953.

41.   Ibid., 965.

42.   William Branch Giles to Jefferson, 26 March 1796, in *The Papers of Thomas Jefferson*, eds. Barbara B. Oberg et al. (Princeton and Oxford: Princeton University Press, 2002), 27:48.

43.   *Annals of Congress*, 4th Cong., 1st sess., 955.

44.   Ibid., 946. According to the treaty, the British pledged to evacuate their forts in the Northwest Territory by 1 June 1796, and several members, including William Vans Murray of Maryland, worried that "frivolous and entangling preliminary questions" would jeopardize that timeframe. For quotation see Ibid. For the deadline, see *American State Papers, Foreign Affairs*, 1:520.

45.   *Annals of Congress*, 4th Cong., 1st sess., 966.

46.   Ibid., 969.

47.   *American State Papers, Foreign Affairs*, 1:547, 520.

48.   See Madison to Monroe, 26 January 1796, in Stagg et al., *Madison Papers*, 16:203.

49.   Madison to Monroe, 26 February 1796, in Ibid., 16:232.

50.   Giles to Jefferson, 26 March 1796, in Oberg, *Jefferson Papers*, 29:48.

51.   Madison to Jefferson, 6 March 1796, in Stagg et al., *Madison Papers*, 16:247.

52.   Ibid.

53.   *Annals of Congress*, 4th Cong., 1st. sess., 892. Actually, not everyone favored statehood, as two counties, Davidson and Tennessee, voted against it. See *American State Papers, Miscellaneous*, 1:146.

54.   *American State Papers, Miscellaneous*, 1:146, 147; Paul H. Bergeron, Stephen V. Ash, Jeanette Keith, *Tennesseans and Their History* (Knoxville: The University of Tennessee Press, 1999), 63–66.

55.   Robert G. Harper to His Constituents, 9 March 1796, in "Papers of James A. Bayard, 1796–1815," ed. Elizabeth Donnan, *Annual Report of the American Historical Association for the Year 1913, in Two Volumes* (Washington, DC: Government Printing Office, 1913), 2:14.

56.   Ibid., *Annals of Congress*, 4th Cong., 1st sess., 916.

57.   Washington issued his "Farewell Address" on 17 September 1796. See Fitzpatrick, *Writings of Washington*, 35:214–38.

58.   Madison to Monroe, 26 February 1796, in Stagg et al., *Madison Papers*, 16:232.

59.   Chauncey Goodrich to Oliver Wolcott, Sr., 13 May 1796, in *Memoirs of the Administration of Washington and John Adams, Edited from the Papers of Oliver Wolcott, Secretary of the Treasury*, ed. George Gibbs (New York: William Van Norden, Printer, 1846), 1:338–39.

60.   Federalists had never established a stronghold in the territory prior to statehood. See William J. Cooper, Jr., *Liberty and Slavery: Southern Politics to 1860* (Columbia: University of

South Carolina Press, 1983), 86; Stanley J. Folmsbee, Robert E. Corlew, and Enoch L. Mitchell, *Tennessee: A Short History* (Knoxville: The University of Tennessee Press, 1969), 110.

61. Jonathan Dayton to Wolcott Jr., 15 September 1796, in Gibbs, *Memoirs of the Administrations*, 1:383.

62. *Annals of Congress*, 4th Cong., 1st. sess., 1304.

63. Ibid., 1324. Of the three counties that comprised the Mero District, the statehood desires of only two counties are known. Residents of both counties overwhelmingly voted against the proposition. See *American State Papers, Miscellaneous*, 1:147; Bergeron, *Tennesseans and Their History*, 63.

64. *Annals of Congress*, 4th Cong., 1st. sess., 1323.

65. Ibid., 1473, 109. Federalist Rufus King of New York reported the bill with the enumeration provision from committee on 18 May 1796. See Ibid., 97. Observing the proceedings, James White, the non-voting delegate from the Territory South of the River Ohio, believed that it was a foregone conclusion that the Senate would "think very differently" from the House and amend the House bill to include a new census requirement. See James White to John Overton, 13 May [1796], in Murdock Collection, Overton Papers, Tennessee Historical Society, Nashville, TN.

66. *Annals of Congress*, 4th Cong., 1st sess., 1328–29, 1487. Five Republicans joined ten Federalists in voting for the Senate's bill. Among southerners, two Federalists and four Republicans voted for the bill, and one Federalist and two Republicans voted against it. Kentucky's two senators split their votes, as the Republican voted for the bill and the Federalist voted against it. See Ibid., 109.

67. Ibid., 1489; *Statutes At Large*, 1:491–92.

68. *Annals of Congress*, 4th Cong., 1st sess., 1315.

69. Ibid., 1317. Neither Dearborn nor Dayton voted when the House passed its statehood bill on 6 May.

70. Ibid.

71. Ibid., 1327.

72. Ibid., 1309.

73. Ibid.

74. Ibid.

75. Ibid., 1317.

76. [Georges-Henri-] Victor Collot, *A Journey in North America*, Containing a Survey of the Countries Watered by the Mississippi, Ohio, Missouri, and Other Affluing Rivers; With Exact Observations on Course and Soundings of These Rivers; and on the Towns, Villages, Hamlets and Farms of that part of the New-World; Followed by Philosophical, Political, Military and Commercial Remarks and by a Projected Line of Frontiers and General Limits, Illustrated by 36 Maps, Plans, Views and Divers Cuts (Paris: Printed for Arthus Bertrand, Bookseller, 1826), 1:i. Online facsimile edition at www.americanjourneys.org.

77. Gibbs, *Memoirs of the Administrations*, 1:352; J. Wendell Knox, *Conspiracy in American Politics, 1787–1815* (1966; New York: Arno Press, 1972), 92–93.

78. Albert Gallatin and William Findley, both Pennsylvanian Republicans, were alleged to have supplied Collot with letters for his trip. See Gibbs, *Memoirs of the Administrations*, 1:351.

79. Pierre Auguste Adet to Timothy Pickering, 15 November 1796, in *American State Papers, Foreign Affairs*, 1:583. For details on the reaction in the press, see Knox, *Conspiracy in American Politics*, 93–95.

80. Washington to Hamilton, 21 November 1796, in Fitzpatrick, *Writings of Washington*, 35:288.

81. Knox, *Conspiracy in American Politics*, 97.

82. Blount outlined the plans in a letter to James Carey. See William Blount to James Carey, 21 April 1797, in *George Washington Papers, 1741–1799* (Washington, DC: Library of Congress, Manuscript Division, 1964), Film J1, Reel 110. By mid-1797, newspapers were beginning to deny the rumors. See *Columbian Museum and Savannah Advertiser*, 23 May 1797.

83. Folmsbee, *Tennessee: A Short History*, 128.

84. Nicholas Romayne to Blount, 15 March 1797, in *Annals of Congress*, 5th Cong., 2nd sess., 2345.

85. Ibid; Lawrence C. Jennings, *French Anti-Slavery: The Movement for the Abolition of Slavery in France* (Cambridge: Cambridge University Press, 2000), vii.

86. Folmsbee, *A Short History of Tennessee*, 127–29.

87. Frederick J. Turner, ed., "Documents on the Blount Conspiracy, 1795–1797," *The American Historical Review* 10:3 (April 1905), 604.

88. Harper to His Constituents, 24 July 1797, in "Papers of James Bayard," 40.

89. Timothy Pickering to Rufus King, 8 July 1797, in *The Life and Correspondence of Rufus King: Comprising His Letters, Private and Official, His Public Documents and His Speeches*, ed. Charles R. King (New York: G. P. Putnam's Sons, 1895), 2:196; *Annals of Congress*, 1st sess., 44.

90. *Annals of Congress*, 5th Cong., 1st sess., 460. The House adjourned on 10 July, having established a committee to draft the articles of impeachment. The Senate did not receive the five articles of impeachment until 7 February 1798. See Ibid., 466; *Journal of the Senate of the United States*, 5th Cong., 2nd sess., 435–37. [Hereafter cited as *Senate Journal*.]

91. Knox, *Conspiracy in American Politics,* 100–102.

92. *Newbern North Carolina Gazette*, 5 August 1797.

93. *Charleston City Gazette and Daily Advertiser*, 12 August 1797.

94. Wolcott Jr. to Wolcott Sr., 4 July 1797, in Gibbs, *Memoirs of the Administrations*, 1:548.

95. *Wilmington [North Carolina] Gazette*, 26 October 1797.

96. John Dawson to James Madison, 10 December 1797, in *The Papers of James Madison*, eds. David B. Mattern et al. (Charlottesville and London: University Press of Virginia, 1991), 17:58.

97. Wolcott Jr. to Wolcott Sr., 4 July 1797, in Gibbs, *Memoirs of the Administrations*, 1:548.

98. Charleston *City Gazette and Daily Advertiser*, 12 August 1797.

99. *Alexandria [Virginia] Advertiser*, 9 October 1797.

100. *Federal Gazette and Baltimore Daily Advertiser,* 19 October 1797.

101. William Polk to William Richardson Davie, 9 August 1797, in the William Richardson Davie Papers, 1782–1799, Manuscript Department, William R. Perkins Library, Duke University.

102. Jefferson to Monroe, 8 February 1798, in *The Papers of Thomas Jefferson*, ed. Barbara B. Oberg (Princeton and Oxford: Princeton University Press, 2003), 30:90; and Jefferson to John Taylor, 23 December 1797, in *The Papers of Thomas Jefferson*, ed., Barbara B. Oberg (Princeton and Oxford: Princeton University Press, 2001), 29:588. All of the members of the House managing the trial of Blount in the Senate were Federalists. See *Annals of Congress*, 5th Cong., 2nd sess., 953, 957.

103. Jefferson to Monroe, 5 April 1798, in Oberg, *Jefferson Papers*, 30:247; Madison to Jefferson [ca. 18 February 1798], in Mattern et al., *Madison Papers*, 17:82.

104. *American State Papers, Foreign Relations*, 1:547.

105. Andrew Ellicott, *The Journal of Andrew Ellicott, late Commissioner on behalf of the United States during part of the year 1796, the years 1797, 1798, 1799, and part of the year 1800: For Determining the Boundary between the United States and the Possessions of His Catholic Majesty in America, containing Occasional Remarks on the Situation, Soil, Rivers, Natural Productions, and Diseases of the Different Countries on the Ohio, Mississippi, and Gulf of Mexico, with Six Maps* (Philadelphia: Budd & Bartram, 1803; reprint, New York: Arno Press, Inc., 1980), 102; *American State Papers, Foreign Relations*, 2:78–79. Robert V. Haynes argues that Spain was having second thoughts about the treaty, which it had hoped would draw the United States away from Great Britain and more into its political and economic orbit. Secondly, Spain's inability to sell Louisiana to the French meant that the Americans would remain neighbors, a situation that alarmed Spanish officials. See Haynes, *The Mississippi Territory and the Southwest Frontier, 1795–1817* (Lexington: University Press of Kentucky, 2010), 14.

106. *American State Papers, Foreign Relations*, 2:79.

107. Ibid., 2:78.

108. Ellicott referred to the Baptist preacher as "Hannah." See Ellicott, *Journal*, 96.

109. Ellicott, *Journal*, 97; Jim Fraiser, *Mississippi River Country Tales: A Celebration of 500 Years of Deep South History* (Gretna, LA: Pelican Publishing Company, Inc., 2001), 32.

110. Ellicott, *Journal*, 100.

111. Ibid., 101.

112. On 12 June, approximately three hundred armed men met to plan an attack on the Spanish fort, but they changed their minds when they learned that the Spaniards had refortified it. See Haynes, *The Mississippi Territory*, 16.

113. Ellicott, *Journal*, 101, 114–17. Gayoso agreed to certain conditions drafted by the Americans, and the Americans, in return, agreed to obey Spanish law. See Haynes, *Mississippi Territory*, 17. As constituted in July, the committee consisted of four British and two United States citizens. In September, elections were held for an enlarged committee, consisting of five British citizens and four Americans. This committee became the de facto government of Natchez until the arrival of the first territorial governor, Winthrop Sargent, in August 1798. See Ethan A. Grant, "Anthony Hutchins: A Pioneer of the Old Southwest," *The Florida Historical Quarterly*, 74:4 (Spring 1996), 417–19.

114. Ellicott, *Journal*, 117. On 29 July 1797, Gayoso left Natchez for New Orleans, where he assumed the position of governor of Louisiana. See Haynes, *Mississippi Territory*, 17.

115. D. Clayton James, *Antebellum Natchez* (Baton Rouge: Louisiana State University Press, 1968), 72–74; Haynes, *The Mississippi Territory*, 18–23.

116. *Times and Alexandria [Virginia] Advertiser*, 21 October 1797.

117. Ibid.

118. *Columbian Mirror and Alexandria [Virginia] Gazette*, 31 August 1797.

119. *New York Weekly Museum*, 16 September 1797. For an account of the skirmish, see James, *Antebellum Natchez*, 70.

120. *American State Papers, Foreign Relations*, 2:20.

121. Ibid., 78.

122. *Annals of Congress*, 5th Cong., 2nd sess., 960; *Philadelphia Gazette and Universal Daily Advertiser*, 16 February 1798.

123. Jefferson to Madison, 24 January 1798, in Oberg, *Jefferson Papers*, 30:53.

124. Madison to Jefferson, 12 February 1798, in Mattern et al., *Madison Papers*, 17:78.

125. Ibid.; Madison to Monroe, 5 February 1798, in Ibid., 17:74; Jefferson to Thomas Mann Randolph, 22 February 1798, in Oberg, *Jefferson Papers*, 30:127.

126. Jefferson to John Wayles Eppes, 18 February 1798, in Oberg, *Jefferson Papers*, 30:115.

127. Jefferson to Randolph, 22 February 1798, in Ibid., 30:127.

128. *Stewart's [Lexington] Kentucky Herald*, 3 July 1798.

129. For an overview of the Yazoo land fraud, see Thomas Perkins Abernethy, *The South in the New Nation, 1789–1819* (Baton Rouge: Louisiana State University Press, and the Littlefield Fund for Southern History of the University of Texas, 1961), 136–68.

130. Henry Tazewell to Madison, 18 March 1798, in Mattern et al., *Madison Papers*, 17:96.

131. *Annals of Congress*, 5th Cong., 2nd sess., 514. James Jackson had resigned his Senate seat in order to fight the Yazoo land companies, and with the aid of Tattnall, he succeeded. See James H. Broussard, *The Southern Federalists, 1800–1816* (Baton Rouge: Louisiana State University, 1978), 248; The Georgia legislature subsequently elected Tattnall to Jackson's vacant seat. See *The New Georgia Encyclopedia*, q.v. "Josiah Tattnall," http://www.georgiaencyclopedia.org.

132. *Annals of Congress*, 5th Cong., 2nd sess., 515. Both members of the Georgia, Tennessee, and Virginia delegations voted for the amendment. They were joined by one North Carolinian and one New Hampshirite.

133. Ibid., 515. The territorial limits of the proposed territory consisted of the western boundary at the Mississippi River, the eastern boundary at the Chattahooche River, the southern boundary at the thirty-first parallel, and the northern boundary at the point where the Yazoo River emptied into the Mississippi River. See *Statutes At Large*, 5th Cong., 2nd sess., 1:549–50.

134. *Annals of Congress*, 5th Cong., 2nd sess., 1277.

135. Ibid., 1279.

136. John Thomas Noonan, Jr., *Bribes: The Intellectual History of a Moral Idea* (Berkley: University of California Press, 1984), 437.

137. *Annals of Congress*, 5th Cong., 2nd sess., 1278. Senator Tazewell of Virginia believed that business interests had "converted Congress into a Company of Land Speculators." See Tazewell to Madison, 18 March 1798, in Mattern et al., *Madison Papers*, 17: 96.

138. *Annals of Congress*, 5th Cong., 2nd sess., 1278. Actually, the state refunded about $300,000 to receptive investors. Some investors, however, chose to retain their titles, preferring to transfer them to other investors. See Noonan, *Bribes*, 437.

139. *Annals of Congress*, 5th Cong., 2nd sess., 1299.

140. Ibid.

141. Ibid., 1280.

142. Ibid., 1283.

143. Ibid., 1298, 1299.

144. Ibid., 1299–1300.

145. Ibid., 1300.

146. Ibid., 1301.

147. Ibid.

148. Ibid., 1302.

149. Ibid.

150. Ibid., 1303.

151. Ibid., 1305.

152. Ibid., 1306. The breakdown of the vote is not recorded.

153. Ibid. In late January and early February, Thatcher had led an attempt in the House to have debated the petition of Jacob Nicholson, Jupiter Nicholson, Joe Albertson, and Thomas Pritchet of North Carolina. Seeking relief from Congress, the four men claimed that their owner had manumitted them and that they had been unjustly re-enslaved. The House rejected the motion by a vote of thirty-three to fifty.

154. Ibid.

155. Ibid. Residents of the Natchez district desired the continuation of slavery in their district. See "Memorial to Congress by Permanent Committee of the Natchez District," [23 October 1797], in *The Territory of Mississippi*, ed. and comp., Clarence Edwin Carter, vol. 5 of *The Territorial Papers of the United States* (Washington, DC: Government Printing Office, 1937), 10.

156. *Annals of Congress*, 5th Cong., 2nd sess., 1307, 1309.

157. Ibid., 1310.

158. Ibid., 1311.

159. Ibid.

160. Ibid.

161. Ibid., 1309, 1308.

162. Ibid., 1312. The *Annals of Congress* did not indicate the number of congressmen who voted against the motion.

163. Ibid., 1313. Why Harper introduced the amendment is unclear. Harper's biographer, Joseph W. Cox, provides no answer. W. E. B. Du Bois speculated that Harper did so in order to further the slave trading interests in Charleston, a common conclusion among historians, but as Lacy K. Ford notes, South Carolina only reopened its external and internal slave trades in late 1803, six years after the Mississippi territorial bill. Ford also points out that the reopening of the trade was due in large part to the Louisiana Purchase. See Joseph W. Cox, *Champion of Southern Federalism: Robert Goodloe Harper of South Carolina* (Port Washington, NY: National University Publications, 1972), 55–56; W. E. Burghardt Du Bois, *The Suppression of the African Slave-Trade to the United States of America, 1638–1870* (New York: Longmans, Green and Co., 1896), 88–89; Lacy K. Ford, *Deliver Us from Evil: The Slavery Question in the Old South* (Oxford: Oxford University Press, 2009), 97–103.

164. *Annals of Congress*, 5th sess., 2nd sess., 1313.

165. Ibid. 1318, 533. The final votes were unrecorded in both chambers.

Chapter Eleven

Looking East

From his home in Kentucky, a despondent George Nicholas outlined in a letter to his good friend in Virginia, James Madison, the effects of John Jay's recently announced treaty with Great Britain. "As far as I can understand the question," he declared, "unless some stand is made against the treaty, the powers of the general government will be unlimited, and the P. [president] and S. [Senate] may assume to themselves, such parts of them as they please."[1] The "only constitutional power" standing in their way, the Kentuckian explained to Madison, was the Virginian's own congressional chamber, the United States House of Representatives.[2] "If they give way, the constitution is a dead letter; and like the house of commons in England, their only business will be, to pass laws to carry into execution, the wicked schemes of others. . . . As our dependence is on the house of representatives, so our great hope that they will do what is right arises from an expectation that you will zealously urge them to do so."[3]

Despite Madison's best efforts, he could not convince fellow House members to block the British treaty. Nicholas's insight, however, into the role that the House of Representatives had been performing, mainly as a restraint on northern—increasingly Federalist—perceived excesses, would find expression in Thomas Jefferson and James Madison's later alarm over the actions of Congress during the Adams administration. Ironically, Madison's retirement from Congress in March 1797, due in part to his frustration with "the unsteadiness, the follies, the perverseness, & the defections" among his friends in the House, occurred just as, in the opinion of the two Virginians, Federalists in Congress were launching their attack on the Constitution.[4] In response, Madison, Jefferson, and other concerned southerners, now confident of a strong relationship with the West, redirected their attention eastward to confront the dangers brewing closer to home.

Jefferson's uneasiness surfaced in late May 1797 with a federal circuit court grand jury pronouncement against Representative Samuel J. Cabell, Jefferson's congressman. On 22 May, Supreme Court associate justice James Iredell, fulfilling his duties as a circuit court judge, charged the grand jury in the federal district of Virginia, sitting in Richmond, to remain vigilant against anything that might disunite Americans, including "differences of opinion," which he believed corroded the country so much that it was like "inviting some foreign nation to foment and take advantage of our internal discords."[5] In Justice Iredell's opinion, internal discord posed a danger to the continued existence of the United States, and Americans, therefore, needed to avoid it at all cost. It was better, he reasoned, for an individual who disagreed with government policy to "submit to it with diffidence and respect" than to voice opposition to it.[6] Although Iredell had refrained from naming any specific individual in his charge, the grand jury, apparently energized by Justice Iredell's sentiments, proceeded to label Cabell's circular letter to his constituents "ruinous to the peace, happiness and independence of the United States" and consequently charged him with the common-law crime of seditious libel.[7]

The grand jury's presentment angered Cabell, who placed all the blame on Iredell, and upset Jefferson and other Virginians.[8] Henry Tazewell, one of Virginia's two senators, viewed the grand jury's action as political censorship, arguing that jury members had "made their own opinions the standard of Truth."[9] He further proclaimed the pronouncements of federal judges nothing more than "an Engine of the Executive . . . [that are used] for oppressive purposes."[10] Jefferson concurred with Tazewell, writing that "[t]he charges of the federal judges have for a considerable time been inviting the Grand juries to become inquisitors on the freedom of speech, of writing and of principle of their fellow citizens."[11]

By August, Jefferson was busy writing the draft of a petition defending Cabell that he intended to submit anonymously to the Virginia House of Delegates. He informed Madison and James Monroe of his intentions and solicited their advice, which they freely offered.[12] In December, someone, probably Wilson Cary Nicholas, the brother of Kentuckian George Nicholas, presented the completed petition to the delegates, who after three failed attempts to scuttle the resolution passed it in January 1798 by a vote of ninety-two to fifty-three and agreed to have one thousand copies produced for distribution.[13] The Virginia Senate failed to act on it, however, despite its popularity in the local newspapers.[14] For Jefferson, the outcome of this dispute was extremely important, for he was beginning to distrust the national government. "The system of the General government is to seize all doubtful ground," he declared to Monroe, and it was, therefore, up to the states to "retain as complete authority as possible over their own citizens."[15]

A few months later, in early March, President John Adams received the dispatches sent to him by his commissioners in Paris. They spoke of a recalcitrant French government unwilling to receive them, let alone negotiate with them without the payment of a bribe. In addition, Adams learned that France had issued a new decree that made it nearly impossible for Americans to ship their products safely. Unsure what his response should be, Adams welcomed advice from his advisors, who generally advocated war with France. Unwilling to take that ultimate step, he called on Congress to augment the country's defenses. Congress responded by establishing a Department of the Navy, authorizing the purchase of more naval vessels, augmenting the size of the army, appropriating money to update harbor defenses, erecting foundries for the manufacture of cannon, abrogating existing treaties with France, and approving the arming of merchant vessels. Congress also went beyond Adams's initial request by passing the Alien, the Sedition, and the Naturalization acts, which targeted aliens and restricted Americans' expression concerning Congress and the president.[16]

Of course, not all southerners viewed the actions of the federal government as dangerous, as some legitimately worried about a French invasion of the United States while others fretted over a rumored invasion of the South by black French troops under the command of the Saint-Domingue leader Toussaint L'Ouverture, but southern Republicans did look at these laws with "astonishment."[17] Since January, the letters of the two leaders of the Republicans, Jefferson and Madison, had reflected their anxieties over a possible war with France and its repercussions for the United States. Adams's release of the commissioners' dispatches and his war-like requests of Congress intensified their concerns. With the Senate proceeding rapidly on the president's agenda, they placed hope in the House of Representatives, but with too few supporters, they could not forestall the efforts of the "war-party."[18] When Jefferson learned of Federalist intentions to introduce alien, sedition, and naturalization bills into Congress, he knew that the Federalists had under the guise of public safety targeted their legislation at Republicans or their friends.[19] Madison, just as alarmed, declared the Alien bill a "monster" and wondered how such legislation "could have been engendered in either House [of Congress]."[20] With the country seemingly marching toward war with France, Madison could only hope that the Federalists' legislative victories would eventually alarm Americans.[21]

In the meantime, with correspondents predicting the ruin of the country "if the people do not come forward & exercise their rights," Jefferson finally convinced Madison that the two of them should take up their pens in protest.[22] The Virginia and Kentucky Resolutions, the results of their individual efforts, proclaimed the states as final arbiters of the Constitution. However, with no official support materializing in the South and only harsh criticism emanating from northern legislatures, Jefferson and Madison managed to find limited comfort in the petitions and remonstrances against the Alien and Sedition acts appearing in the states of New Jersey, New York, and Pennsylvania.[23] Still, by early February 1799, Jefferson had convinced himself that the public was on the verge of casting off its Federalist moorings and was about to "fall into the republican scale."[24] The nearly year-long congressional campaigns in 1798 and 1799 revealed that Jefferson was perhaps too optimistic in his pronouncement.[25]

The Republicans' anxiety continued into 1799. In early March, Madison received a passionate letter from John Taylor of Caroline beseeching him to run for the Virginia General Assembly. "The public sentiment in Virginia," Taylor declared, "is at a crisis—at the next assembly it will take permanent form, which will fix the fate of America. There will be no member capable of counterpoising Mr: [Patrick] Henry, unless you will come; and if you do, his defeat at this crisis will certainly happen, and will suddenly invigorate the efforts of republicanism throughout the union."[26] Worried about the continuance of the Union, the popular Virginian had aligned himself with the Federalist party. Madison agreed to stand for election, and his victory on 24 April elicited cries of relief.[27] "I congratulate my Countrey on your return to our state Counsels in this important crisis," wrote Edmund Pendleton.[28] One happy correspondent, John G. Jackson, Madison's brother-in-law, explained his excitement by proclaiming that "[r]epublicanism is gaining ground very fast in this District [Harrison County]. . . [and that] the time is not far distant when the Freemen of America will see through the flimsy veil of modern Federalism & spurn the Enemies of their Liberties."[29]

In August, Wilson Cary Nicholas, who had just learned of the death of his brother George in Kentucky and would soon be travelling to that state, inquired of Jefferson whether a coordinated response to the negative reaction that the Virginia and Kentucky Resolutions had engendered throughout the country might be in order.[30] Jefferson liked the idea "of pursuing the same tract at the ensuing session of their [Kentucky and Virginia] legislatures" and immediately contacted Madison, who would join Nicholas in the Virginia legislature in December, and James Monroe.[31] In early September, Jefferson, Madison and Monroe, without Nicholas, sat down to discuss the points that Jefferson had suggested in his August letter to Madison. Apparently Jefferson's reference to secession as a possible remedy worried Madison, for Jefferson, in a letter to Nicholas recounting the events of the meeting, noted that he "recede[d] readily, not only in deference to his [Madison's] judgment, but because, as we should never think of separation but for repeated and enormous violations so these, when they occur, will be cause enough of themselves."[32] With the plan in place, it fell to Madison to prepare the draft for presentation to the Virginia legislature and for Nicholas, if he so desired, the draft for Kentucky, because, as Jefferson noted, "how could you better while away the road from hence to Kentucky than in meditating this very subject and preparing something yourself, than whom nobody will do it better."[33]

Madison did not begin work on the Virginia response, the Report of 1800, until December 1799, when the legislature was set to convene. He easily ushered the lengthy document through the House of Delegates on 17 January. The Senate followed the lead of the House a few days later.[34] Earlier in November, the Kentucky legislature had approved its latest response, which included the remedy of nullification.[35] In addition, while he had been busy with the Report of 1800, Madison had also managed the election of James Monroe as governor.[36]

Before the legislature convened in December, Madison had received suggestions from people inside and outside the state that Virginia Republicans begin planning for the upcoming presidential election in 1800. From his home in Charleston, Charles Pinckney informed Madison that "[i]t was now a proper time to push every measure favourable to the republican interest & to strengthen it's [*sic*] friends."[37] In particular, he urged Madison to induce the legislature to change the way that the state selected presidential electors. It was "of the absolute necessity . . . that the Electors of a President & Vice President shall be elected by joint Ballot by your state legislature," he wrote.[38] Local congressman John Dawson concurred. "An election by the legislatures [Virginia and North Carolina] would," he wrote, ". . . secure every vote."[39] Just enough members of both chambers agreed with the sentiment in these letters and, in January 1800, switched the state to an at-large system to select its electors.[40] Madison, who had served on the committee that drafted the electors bill, would subsequently become one of the Republicans' twenty-one electors in Virginia.[41]

In early December, Jefferson, while presiding over the Senate in Philadelphia, received urgent messages from two of his contacts in Kentucky. Harry Innes, the only federal judge in Kentucky at the time, had written the vice president about a subject that he deemed "of importance to the Western Country & to the Union too."[42] John Breckinridge, who had introduced Jefferson's 1798 resolution into the Kentucky legislature, was just as dramatic, viewing the topic as so "disagreeable . . . [that it might] endanger or destroy that Harmony of sentiment which now prevails here."[43] What these two Kentuckians decried was the possibility that Congress might attach Kentucky and Tennessee to North Carolina when it created a new circuit court. In the past, Jefferson, and Madison for that matter, would have responded reasonably quickly to such urgent cries for help. This time, Jefferson's response in late January to both men took the form of a polite dismissal. After acknowledging the "wilder" aspects of the proposal, Jefferson assured Innes that his fears were baseless and that Congress would never pass such a scheme.[44] To Breckinridge, Jefferson expressed hope that someday the western country would have its own judicial district but for now "partiality to a general & uniform system . . . [must] yield to geographical & physical impraticabilities."[45] The rather nonchalant way in which Jefferson responded to this western "crisis" demonstrated how much the urgency of past western issues had eased by 1800 for the two leading Republicans, Jefferson and Madison.

What really concerned Madison and Jefferson in 1800 was the presidential election. Having secured Virginia's electoral votes, they now had to worry about Jefferson's electoral position in the other states.[46] Aaron Burr's orchestration of Republican support in New York excited the two Virginians, but Burr's suspicious nature, especially his concern that the southern states would fail to cast all their electoral votes for him as previously agreed, required Madison to expend time placating Burr and his fellow New Yorkers.[47] Among the southern states, North Carolina was the only state that seemed to worry them. As Jefferson viewed the situation, Federalists would win election as electors and control the state's electoral vote, because, in his opinion, North Carolinians voted for Federalists out of "necessity because of few other candidates."[48] Just to the south, despite the strong Federalist tradition in South Carolina, Jefferson and Madison were confident that Republican support in the countryside would offset Federalist successes in Charleston in that fall's legislative elections and that the new legislature would subsequently cast the state's electoral votes for Jefferson and Burr.[49] The western states of Kentucky and Tennessee rarely entered into the discussion, except when they were awaiting the official results. Even then, no one seemed to doubt the political leanings of the two states.[50] This expectation had shown itself that summer, as newspapers were already confidently predicting that Kentucky and Tennessee would cast all their electoral votes for Jefferson.[51] With the results finally known and Kentucky unanimously in the Jefferson column, one happy Kentuckian wrote, "This proves the prediction made long since to be true, that Kentucky would be a DEAD shot."[52]

The unwelcome tie in the Electoral College frustrated the two Republican leaders, but Jefferson's ultimate victory in the House of Representatives ended their long wait. During his initial years as president, Jefferson moved aggressively, attempting the removal of Federalist judges, reducing the national debt, waging war against the Barbary pirates, and, in 1803, orchestrating a treaty with France for the purchase of Louisiana. Having only recently won the loyalty of the trans-Appalachian West, southerners would now, with the Louisiana Purchase, begin the task of securing the loyalty of the trans-Mississippi West and creating the Old South.

NOTES

1. George Nicholas to James Madison, 6 November 1795, in *The Papers of James Madison*, eds. J. C. A. Stagg et al. (Charlottesville: University Press of Virginia, 1989), 16:119.

2. Ibid.

3. Ibid.

4. Madison to Thomas Jefferson, 1 May 1796, in Ibid., 16:343. On the Constitution, see Jefferson to Madison, 21 March 1798, in *The Papers of James Madison*, eds. David B. Mattern et al. (Charlottesville and London: University Press of Virginia, 1991), 17:99, and Madison to Jefferson, 2 April 1798, in Mattern et al., *Madison Papers*, 17:104.

5. *The Documentary History of the Supreme Court of the United States, 1789–1800*, ed. Maeva Marcus (New York and Oxford: Columbia University Press, 1990), 3:177.

6. Ibid., 3:176.

7. *Federal Gazette and Baltimore Daily Advertiser*, 31 May 1797. Cabell was never prosecuted. Leonard W. Levy, *Seasoned Judgment: The American Constitution, Rights and History* (New Brunswick, NJ: Transaction Press, 1995), 403.

8. Phillip I. Blumberg, *Repressive Jurisprudence in the Early American Republic: The First Amendment and the Legacy of English Law* (Cambridge: Cambridge University Press, 2010), 74. Iredell subsequently denied all responsibility. See *Federal Gazette and Baltimore Daily Advertiser*, 11 July 1797.

9. Henry Tazewell to Madison, 4 June 1797, in Mattern et al., *Madison Papers*, 17:18.

10. Ibid.

11. Jefferson to Peregrine Fitzhugh, 4 June 1797, in *The Papers of Thomas Jefferson*, ed. Barbara B. Oberg (Princeton and Oxford: Princeton University Press, 2002), 29:417.

12. Jefferson to Madison, 3 August 1797, in Mattern et al., *Madison Papers*, 17:35–36; Madison to Jefferson, 5 August 1797, in Oberg, *Jefferson Papers*, 29:505–6; James Monroe to Jefferson, 5 September 1797, in Oberg, *Jefferson Papers*, 29:524.

13. "Editorial Footnote," in Oberg, *Jefferson Papers*, 29:492; *Journal of the House of Delegates of the Commonwealth of Virginia, begun and held at the capitol, in the city of Richmond, on Monday, the fourth day of December, one thousand seven hundred and ninety-seven* (Richmond: Printed by Augustine Davis, Printer to the Commonwealth, 1798), in *Early American Imprints, Series 1: Evans, 1639–1800*, no. 34936, 40–63 passim. The various resolutions argued that Congress, not the Virginia legislature, was the proper forum by which to address the affront to Cabell.

14. For a sampling of newspaper responses, see *Fredericksburg Virginia Herald*, 17 January 1798; *Richmond Virginia Argus*, 28 December 1797; *Alexandria Virginia Advertiser*, 2 January 1798; and *Columbian Mirror and Alexandria [Virginia] Gazette*, 4 January 1798.

15. Jefferson to Madison, 7 September 1797, in Oberg, *Jefferson Papers*, 29:526–27.

16. Stanley Elkins and Eric McKitrick, *The Age of Federalism* (New York and Oxford: Oxford University Press, 1993), 582–90.

17. Ibid., 598; Tazewell to Jefferson, 5 July 1798, in *The Papers of Thomas Jefferson*, ed. Barbara B. Oberg (Princeton and Oxford: Princeton University Press, 2003), 30:441; Jefferson to Madison, 21 March 1798, in Mattern et al., *Madison Papers*, 17:99. South Carolinian Federalists Robert Goodloe Harper and Thomas Pinckney are an example of two southerners who sided wholeheartedly with the Adams administration. See Jefferson to Madison, 29 March 1798, in Mattern et al., *Madison Papers*, 17:102.

18. Jefferson to Madison, 29 March 1798, Madison to Jefferson, 2 April 1798, Jefferson to Madison, 19 April 1798, and Jefferson to Madison, 26 April 1798, all in Mattern et al., *Madison Papers*, 17:101–2, 104, 116, 120.

19. Jefferson contended that the Federalists targeted Albert Gallatin of Pennsylvania with their Naturalization Act, French visitors General Georges-Henri-Victor Collot and Constantin François Chasseboeuf Boisgirais, comte de Volney, with their Alien acts, and Philadelphia newspaper publisher Benjamin Franklin Bache with their Sedition Act. See Jefferson to Madison, 26 April 1798, in Ibid., 17:120.

20. Madison to Jefferson, 20 May 1798, in Oberg, *Jefferson Papers*, 30:359.

21. Ibid.

22. John Dawson to Madison, 5 July 1798, in Mattern et al., *Madison Papers*, 17:162. The exact timeline of their decision to write the Virginia and Kentucky Resolutions is unknown, but Jefferson had been urging Madison to voice in writing his opposition to what had been happening for some time. See "Editorial Note," in Ibid., 17:186.

23. Elkins and McKitrick, *Age of Federalism*, 720; Jefferson to Madison, 30 January 1799, in Mattern et al., *Madison Papers*, 17:223.

24. Jefferson to Madison, 7 February 1799, in Mattern et al., *Madison Papers*, 17:227.

25. Peter S. Onuf and Leonard J. Sadosky, *Jeffersonian America* (Malden, Massachusetts: Blackwell Publishers, Inc., 2002), 21; John G. Jackson to Madison, 14 May 1799, in Mattern et al., *Madison Papers*, 17:249. As a result of the 1798–1799 congressional elections, the Federalists held sixty seats to the Republicans' forty-six in the House of Representatives.

26. John Taylor to Madison, 4 March 1799, in Mattern et al., *Madison Papers*, 17:246.

27. "Note," in Ibid., 17:247.

28. Edmund Pendleton to Madison, 12 May 1799, in Ibid., 17:249.

29. Jackson to Madison, 14 May 1799, in Ibid.

30. Wilson Cary Nicholas to Jefferson, 20 August 1799, in *The Papers of Thomas Jefferson*, ed. Barbara B. Oberg (Princeton and Oxford: Princeton University Press, 2004), 31:172.

31. Jefferson to Nicholas, 26 August 1799, in Ibid., 31:177.

32. Jefferson to Nicholas, 5 September 1799, in Ibid., 31:179.

33. Ibid. It remains a mystery who actually wrote the 1799 Kentucky Resolution, which does incorporate the main ideas of Jefferson. John Breckinridge introduced the resolution, but historians do not credit him with authorship. See James C. Klotter, *The Breckinridges of Kentucky* (Lexington: The University Press of Kentucky, 1986), 22.

34. *Journal of the House of Delegates of the Commonwealth of Virginia. Begun and Held at the Capitol in the City of Richmond, on Monday the Second Day of December, One Thousand Seven Hundred and Ninety Nine* (Richmond: Printed by Meriwether Jones, Printer to the Commonwealth, 1800), in *Early American Imprints, Series 1: Evans, 1639–1800*, no. 38954, 92, 94.

35. Klotter, *The Breckinridges of Kentucky*, 22.

36. *Richmond Virginia Argus*, 10 December 1799.

37. Charles Pinckney to Madison, 30 September 1799, in Mattern et al., *Madison Papers*, 17:272.

38. Ibid.

39. John Dawson to Madison, 28 November 1799, in Ibid. North Carolina would be one of three states in the election, Kentucky and Maryland being the other two, that would retain its district-based system for choosing presidential electors. See Edward J. Larson, *A Magnificent Catastrophe: The Tumultuous Election of 1800, America's First Presidential Campaign* (New York: Free Press, 2007), 65.

40. Madison to Jefferson, 18 January 1800, in Mattern et al., *Madison Papers*, 17:357; *Journal of the House of Delegates*, 91, 95.

41. "Circular Letter from the Chairman of the General Committee of Correspondence," 30 January 1800, in Mattern et al., *Madison Papers*, 17:359; *Journal of the House of Delegates*, 83.

42. Harry Innes to Jefferson, 6 December 1799, in Oberg, *Jefferson Papers*, 31:261.

43. John Breckinridge to Jefferson, 13 December 1799, in Ibid., 31:266–67.

44. Jefferson to Innes, 23 January 1799, in Ibid., 31:336, 344–45. In 1801, Congress did reorganize the court system in the United States and combined Kentucky, Tennessee, and the Ohio country into one circuit court, a solution that Innes had suggested to Jefferson in 1799. See *Statutes At Large*, 6th Cong., 2nd sess., 2:89–91; Innes to Jefferson, 6 December 1799, in Oberg, *Jefferson Papers*, 31:262.

45. Jefferson to Breckinridge, 29 January 1800, in Oberg, *Jefferson Papers*, 31:344.

46. For a sense of the planning and preparation, see Jefferson to Madison, 4 March 1800, Jefferson to Madison, 25 March 1800, Wilson Cary Nicholas to Madison, 22 May 1800, Gabriel Duvall to Madison, 6 June 1800, Jefferson to Madison, 17 September 1800, Charles Peale Polk to Madison, 10 October 1800, Madison to Jefferson, 21 October 1800, and Madison to Jefferson, 11 November 1800, all in Mattern et al., *Madison Papers*, 17:369, 374, 389, 392, 410, 423, 425, 427.

47. David Gelston to Madison, 8 October 1800, Madison to Jefferson, 21 October 1800, Madison to Monroe, [21 October] 1800, Madison to Gelston, 24 October 1800, all in Mattern et al., *Madison Papers*, 17:418–19, 425, 426. Jefferson also wrote Burr apologizing for the pos-

sibility that Republicans had not remained united in the election. See Jefferson to Aaron Burr, 15 December 1800, in *The Papers of Thomas Jefferson*, ed. Barbara B. Oberg (Princeton and Oxford: Princeton University Press, 2005), 32:307.

48. Jefferson to Philip Norborne Nicholas, 7 April 1800, in Oberg, *Jefferson Papers*, 31:485.

49. Jefferson to Madison, 9 November 1800 and 11 November 1800, both in Mattern et al., *Madison Papers*, 17: 433, 437.

50. Jefferson to Madison, 19 December 1800, in Ibid., 17:444.

51. *Charleston South-Carolina State Gazette and Timothy's Daily Advertiser*, 25 June 1800, *Elizabethtown Maryland Herald*, 1 July 1800, *Charleston Carolina Gazette*, 28 August 1800.

52. *Nashville Tennessee Gazette*, 24 December 1800.

Bibliography

PRIMARY SOURCES

Government Documents

Journal of the House of Delegates of the Commonwealth of Virginia, begun and held at the capitol, in the city of Richmond, on Monday, the fourth day of December, one thousand seven hundred and ninety-seven. Richmond: Printed by Augustine Davis, Printer to the Commonwealth, 1798. In *Early American Imprints, Series 1: Evans, 1639–1800*, no. 34936.

Journal of the House of Delegates of the Commonwealth of Virginia. Begun and Held at the Capitol in the City of Richmond, on Monday the Second Day of December, One Thousand Seven Hundred and Ninety Nine. Richmond: Printed by Meriwether Jones, Printer to the Commonwealth, 1799. In *Early American Imprints, Series 1: Evans, 1639–1800*, no. 38954.

United States Congress. *American State Papers: Foreign Affairs.*

———. *American State Papers: Indian Affairs.*

———. *American State Papers: Miscellaneous.*

———. *Annals of the Congress of the United States.* 42 vols. Washington, DC: Gales and Seaton, 1834–1856.

———. *Biographical Directory of the United States Congress, 1774–Present*, http://bioguide.congress.gov/biosearch/biosearch.asp

———. *Journal of the Executive Proceedings of the Senate of the United States.*

———. *Journal of the House of Representatives of the United States.*

———. *Journal of the Senate of the United States.*

United States Department of Commerce. Bureau of the Census. *Historical Statistics of the United States, Colonial Times to 1970.* 2 vols. Washington, DC: United States Government Printing Office, 1975.

———. *Return of the Whole Number of Persons Within the Several Districts of the United States, According to "An Act Providing for the Enumeration of the Inhabitants of the United States," Passed March the First, One Thousand Seven Hundred and Ninety-One.* 1791. Reprint, New York: Norman Ross Publishing Company, 1990.

———. *Return of the Whole Number of Persons Within the Several Districts of the United States, According to "An Act Providing for the Second Census or Enumeration of the Inhabitants of the United States," Passed February the Twenty Eighth, One Thousand Eight Hundred.* 1801. Reprint, New York: Norman Ross Publishing Company, 1990.

United States Department of State. *The Diplomatic Correspondence of the United States of America, from the Signing of the Definitive Treaty of Peace, September 10, 1783, to the*

Adoption of the Constitution, March 4, 1789. Being the Letters of the Presidents of Congress, the Secretary of Foreign Affairs—American Ministers at Foreign Courts, Foreign Ministers near Congress—Reports of Committees of Congress, and Reports of the Secretary of Foreign Affairs on Various Letters and Communications; Together with Letters from Individuals on Public Affairs. 7 vols. Washington, DC: Printed by Francis Preston Blair, 1833–1834.

Manuscript Collections

Arthur Campbell Letters. The Filson Historical Society. Lexington, KY.
Breckinridge Family Papers. Manuscript Division. Library of Congress. Washington, DC.
Breckinridge-Marshall Papers. The Filson Historical Society. Louisville, KY.
Breckinridge Papers. University of Virginia. Charlottesville, VA.
Campbell Family Papers. Manuscript Department. William R. Perkins Library. Duke University. Durham, NC.
David Rowland Letter. Miscellaneous Collection. The Filson Historical Society. Louisville, KY.
David Wood Meriwether Miscellaneous Papers. The Filson Historical Society. Louisville, KY.
Draper Mss. 11CC121 of the Kentucky Papers of the Lyman C. Draper Collection. Wisconsin Historical Society. Madison, WI.
Draper Mss. 19CC38 of the Kentucky Papers of the Lyman C. Draper Collection. Wisconsin Historical Society. Madison, WI.
Draper Mss. 11DD53 of the King's Mountain Papers of the Lyman C. Draper Collection. Wisconsin Historical Society. Madison, WI
Draper Mss. 4XX17 of the Tennessee Papers of the Lyman C. Draper Collection. Wisconsin Historical Society. Madison, WI.
Edward Vernon Howell Papers. Southern Historical Collection. University of North Carolina Library. Chapel Hill, NC.
Fleming-Christian Correspondence. Grisby Papers. Virginia Historical Society. Richmond, VA.
George Nicholas Letters, 1789–1796. Kentucky Historical Society. Frankfort, KY.
George Nicholas Papers. The University of Chicago Library. Chicago, IL.
George Washington Papers, 1741–1799. Washington, DC: Library of Congress, Manuscript Division, 1964, Film J1, Reel 107.
George Washington Papers at the Library of Congress, 1741–1799: Series 2 Letterbooks. http://memory.loc.gov/cgi-bin/query/P?mgw:1:./temp/~ammem_i0en::.
John Brown Miscellaneous Papers. The Filson Historical Society. Louisville, KY.
Murdock Collection. Overton Papers. Tennessee Historical Society. Nashville, TN.
Record Group 11: General Records of the United States Government: Papers of the Continental Congress. Washington, DC: National Archives and Records Administration, M247, r102, i78, v21.
Purviance Family Papers, 1757 (1776–1920) 1932. Manuscript Department. William R. Perkins Library. Duke University. Durham, NC.
William Richardson Davie Papers, 1782–1799. Manuscript Department. William R. Perkins Library. Duke University. Durham, NC.

Newspapers

Alexandria Virginia Advertiser. 1798.
Annapolis Maryland Gazette. 1785, 1787, 1788.
Charleston Carolina Gazette. 1800.
Charleston City Gazette and Daily Advertiser. 1797.
Charleston South-Carolina State Gazette and Timothy's Daily Advertiser. 1800.
Columbian Mirror and Alexandria [Virginia] Gazette. 1797, 1798.
Edenton State Gazette of North Carolina. 1788, 1789.

Elizabethtown Maryland Herald. 1800.
Federal Gazette and Baltimore Daily Advertiser. 1797.
Jamestown [New York] Journal. 1842.
Knoxville [Tennessee] Gazette. 1795.
Lexington Kentucky Gazette. 1788, 1791, 1792, 1794, 1795.
Nashville Tennessee Gazette. 1800.
Newbern North Carolina Gazette. 1796, 1797.
New York Daily Advertiser. 1788.
New York Weekly Museum. 1797.
Philadelphia Gazette and Universal Daily Advertiser. 1798.
Philadelphia Gazette of the United States. 1792.
Philadelphia National Gazette. 1792.
Philadelphia Pennsylvania Journal and Weekly Advertiser. 1781.
Richmond Virginia Argus. 1797, 1799.
Richmond Virginia Gazette and General Advertiser Extraordinary. 1791, 1794.
Savannah Gazette of the State of Georgia. 1785, 1787.
Stewart's [Lexington] Kentucky Herald. 1798.
Times and Alexandria [Virginia] Advertiser. 1797.
Virginia Journal and Alexandria Advertiser. 1785.
Wilmington [North Carolina] Gazette. 1797.

Edited Works

Allen, W. B., ed. *Works of Fisher Ames, As Published by Seth Ames.* 2 vols. Indianapolis: Liberty Fund, 1983.
The American Remembrancer: or An Impartial Collection of Essays, Resolves, Speeches, etc. Relative, or Having Affinity, to the Treaty with Great Britain. Part 5. Philadelphia: Printed by Henry Tuckniss for Mathew Carey, 10 October 1795. In *Early American Imprints, Series 1: Evans, 1639–1800*, no. 28389.
The American Remembrancer: or An Impartial Collection of Essays, Resolves, Speeches, etc. Relative, or Having Affinity, to the Treaty with Great Britain. Part 9. Philadelphia: Printed by Henry Tuckniss for Mathew Carey, 28 November 1795. In *Early American Imprints, Series 1: Evans, 1639–1800*, no. 28389.
Ballagh, James Curtis, ed. *The Letters of Richard Henry Lee.* 2 vols. New York: The Macmillan Company, 1911–1914.
Bickford, Charlene Bangs, et al., eds. *Documentary History of the First Federal Congress of the United States of America, March 4, 1789–March 3, 1791.* 20 vols. Baltimore and London: The Johns Hopkins University Press, 1972– .
Boyd, Julian P., et al., eds. *The Papers of Thomas Jefferson.* 36 vols. Princeton: Princeton University Press, 1950– .
Burnett, Edmund C., ed. *Letters of Members of the Continental Congress.* 8 vols. Washington, DC: Carnegie Institution of Washington, 1921–1936.
Carter, Clarence Edwin, ed. *The Territorial Papers of the United States.* 26 vols. Washington, DC: Government Printing Office, 1934–1962.
Clark, Walter, et al., eds. *State Records of North Carolina.* 30 vols. Various publishers, 1886–1907.
Cobb, Thomas R. B. *Statute Laws of the State of Georgia, in Force prior to the Session of the General Assembly of 1851, with Explanatory Notes and References; Together with an Appendix, Containing the Constitution of the United States; the Constitution of the State of Georgia; the Statute of Frauds and Perjuries; the Habeas Corpus Act; The Judiciary Act of 1799, and the Local Laws of Applicable to Each County, Compiled and Published under the Authority of the General Assembly.* Athens: Published by Christy, Kelsea & Burke, 1851.
Collot, [Georges-Henri-] Victor. *A Journey in North America, Containing a Survey of the Countries Watered by the Mississippi, Ohio, Missouri, and Other Affluing Rivers; With Exact Observations on Course and Soundings of These Rivers; and on the Towns, Villages, Hamlets and Farms of that part of the New-World; Followed by Philosophical, Political,*

Military and Commercial Remarks and by a Projected Line of Frontiers and General Limits, Illustrated by 36 Maps, Plans, Views and Divers Cuts. 2 vols. Paris: Printed for Arthus Bertrand, Bookseller, 1826. Online facsimile edition at www.americanjourneys.org.

A Constitution or Form of Governmen [sic] for the State of Kentucky. Lexington, KY: Printed by John Bradford, 1792. *Early American Imprints, Series 1: Evans, 1639–1800,* no. 24443.

Cunningham, Noble E., Jr., ed. *Circular Letters of Congressmen to Their Constituents, 1789–1829.* 3 vols. Chapel Hill: Published for the Institute of Early American History and Culture, Williamsburg, Virginia, by the University of North Carolina Press, 1978.

Dickoré, Marie, comp. *General James Taylor's Narrative.* N.p,: N.d. Ohio Historical Society Archives/Library Stacks 929.2 T214d.

Donnan, Elizabeth, ed. "Papers of James A. Bayard, 1796–1815." *Annual Report of the American Historical Association for the Year 1913, in Two Volumes.* Washington, DC: Government Printing Office, 1913.

Dupre, Huntley, ed. "Three Letters of George Nicholas to John Brown." *The Register of the Kentucky State Historical Society,* 41:134 (January 1943), 1–10.

Ellicott, Andrew. *The Journal of Andrew Ellicott, late Commissioner on behalf of the United States during part of the year 1796, the years 1797, 1798, 1799, and part of the year 1800: For Determining the Boundary between the United States and the Possessions of His Catholic Majesty in America, containing Occasional Remarks on the Situation, Soil, Rivers, Natural Productions, and Diseases of the Different Countries on the Ohio, Mississippi, and Gulf of Mexico, with Six Maps.* Philadelphia: Budd & Bartram, 1803. Reprint, New York: Arno Press, Inc., 1980.

Farrand, Max, ed. *The Records of the Federal Convention.* 3 vols. New Haven: Yale University Press, 1911.

Fitzpatrick, John C., ed. *The Writings of Washington from the Original Manuscript Sources, 1745–1799.* 39 vols. Washington, DC: United States Government Printing Office, 1931–1944.

Ford, Worthington C., et al., eds. *Journals of the Continental Congress, 1774–1789.* 34 vols. Washington, DC: Government Printing Office, 1904–1937.

Gibbs, George, ed. *Memoirs of the Administration of Washington and John Adams, Edited from the Papers of Oliver Wolcott, Secretary of the Treasury.* 2 vols. New York: William Van Norden, Printer, 1846.

Haggard, Robert F., Mark A. Mastromarino et al., eds. *The Papers of George Washington. Presidential Series. 14 vols.* Charlottesville and London: University Press of Virginia, 1987– .

Hening, William Waller. *The Statutes at Large; Being a Collection of all the Laws of Virginia from the First Session of the Legislature, in the Year 1619.* 13 vols. Various Places: Printed for the editor, 1819–1823. Reprint, Charlottesville: Published for the Jamestown Foundation of the Commonwealth of Virginia by the University Press of Virginia, 1969.

Hutchinson, William T., William M. E. Rachal et al., eds. *The Papers of James Madison.* 17 vols. Chicago: The University of Chicago Press/Charlottesville: University of Virginia Press, 1962–1991.

Johnson, Herbert A., et al., eds. *The Papers of John Marshall.* 12 vols. Chapel Hill: University of North Carolina Press in association with the Institute of Early American History and Culture, Williamsburg, Virginia, 1974–2006.

Johnston, Henry P., ed. *The Correspondence and Public Papers of John Jay.* 4 vols. New York: G. P. Putnam's Sons, 1890–1894.

Kaminski, John P., et al., eds. *The Documentary History of the Ratification of the Constitution.* 26 vols. Madison: State Historical Society of Wisconsin, 1976– .

Keith, Alice Barnwell, ed. *John Gray Blount Papers.* 3 vols. Raleigh: State Department of Archives and History, 1952–1959.

King, Charles R., ed. *The Life and Correspondence of Rufus King: Comprising His Letters, Private and Official, His Public Documents and His Speeches.* 6 vols. New York: G. P. Putnam's Sons, 1894–1900.

Maclay, William. *Journal of William Maclay, United States Senator from Pennsylvania, 1789–1791.* Edited by Edgar S. Maclay. New York: D. Appleton and Company, 1890.

Marcus, Maeva, ed. *The Documentary History of the Supreme Court of the United States, 1789–1800.* 7 vols. New York and Oxford: Columbia University Press, 1985– .

Mays, David John, ed. *The Letters and Papers of Edmund Pendleton, 1734–1803.* 2 vols. Charlottesville: Published for the Virginia Historical Society by the University Press of Virginia, 1967.

"Nourse-Chapline Letters." *Register of the Kentucky State Historical Society,* 31 (April 1933), 152–67.

Palmer, William P., et al., eds. *Calendar of Virginia State Papers and Other Manuscripts.* 11 vols. Richmond: R.U. Derr, Superintendent of Public Printing, 1875–1893. Reprint, New York: Kraus Reprint Corp., 1968.

Peters, Richard, ed. *The Public Statutes at Large of the United States of America, From the Organization of the Government in 1789 to March 3, 1845.* 8 vols. Boston: Charles C. Little and James Brown, 1845–1867.

Preston, Daniel, ed. *The Papers of James Monroe.* 4 vols. Westport, CT: Greenwood Press, 2003– .

Prince, Oliver H. *Digest of the Laws of the State of Georgia, Obtaining All Statutes and the Substance of all Resolutions of a General and Public Nature, and Now in Force, which have been Passed in this State, Previous to the Session of the General Assembly of Dec. 1837, with Occasional Explanatory Notes, and Connecting References, to which is added an Appendix, containing the Constitution of the United States, the Constitution of the State of Georgia as Amended; the Statute of Frauds and Perjuries, the Habeas Corpus Act, [e]tc. Also a Synopsis of the Local Acts, Arranged to Each County, and Classed under Appropriate Heads, with a Copious Index.* 2nd ed. Athens: Published by the author, 1837.

Rice, David. *Slavery Inconsistent with Justice and Good Policy, Proved by a Speech in the Convention Held at Danville, Kentucky.* Philadelphia: Printed by Parry Hall, 1792. *Early American Imprints, Series 1: Evans, 1639–1800,* no. 24742.

Rutland, Robert A., ed. *The Papers of George Mason, 1725–1792.* 3 vols. Chapel Hill: The University of North Carolina Press, 1970.

"Selections from the Draper Collection in the Possession of the State Historical Society of Wisconsin, to Elucidate the Proposed French Expedition under George Rogers Clark against Louisiana, in the Years 1793–94." Vol. 1 of *Annual Report of the American Historical Association for the Year 1896, in Two Volumes.* Washington, DC: Government Printing Office, 1897, 930–1107.

Smith, Paul H., et al., eds. *Letters of Delegates to Congress.* 26 vols. Washington, DC: Library of Congress, 1976–2000.

Smith, Sam B., et al., eds. *The Papers of Andrew Jackson.* 8 vols. Knoxville: University of Tennessee Press, 1980–2010.

Syrett, Harold C., ed. *The Papers of Alexander Hamilton.* 27 vols. New York and London: Columbia University Press, 1961–1987.

Tansill, Charles C., ed. *Documents Illustrative of the Formation of the Union of the American States.* Washington, DC: Government Printing Office, 1927.

Turner, Frederick J., ed., "Documents on the Blount Conspiracy, 1795–1797." *The American Historical Review* 10:3 (April 1905), 574–606.

Wharton, Francis., ed. *The Revolutionary Diplomatic Correspondence of the United States.* 6 vols. Washington, DC: Government Printing Office, 1889.

[Wilkinson, James]. "Letters of James Wilkinson Addressed to Dr. James Hutchinson, of Philadelphia." *Pennsylvania Magazine of History and Biography* 12 (1888), 55–64.

SECONDARY SOURCES

Books and Articles

Abernethy, Thomas Perkins. *The South in the New Nation, 1789–1819.* Baton Rouge: Louisiana State University Press and the Littlefield Fund for Southern History of the University of Texas, 1961.

Alden, John R. *The First South.* Baton Rouge: Louisiana State University Press, 1961.

———. *The South in the American Revolution, 1763–1789.* Baton Rouge: Louisiana *State University Press and the Littlefield Fund for Southern History of the University* of Texas, 1957.

Allen, Jeffrey Brooke. "Means and Ends in Kentucky Abolitionism, 1792–1823." *The Filson Club History Quarterly* 50 (October 1983), 365–81.

———. "The Origins of Proslavery Thought in Kentucky, 1792–1799." *The Register of the Kentucky Historical Society* 78 (Spring 1979), 75–90.

Alvord, Clarence Walworth. *The Illinois Country, 1673–1818.* Chicago: A. C. McClurg & Company, 1922.

Ambler, Charles H. *George Washington and the West.* Chapel Hill: The University of North Carolina Press, 1936.

American National Biography, s.v. "Butler, Pierce."

———. s.v. "Carmichael, William."

———. s.v. "Caswell, Richard."

———. s.v. "Claiborne, William Charles Coles."

Bailey, David T. *Shadow On the Church: Southwestern Evangelical Religion and the Issue of Slavery, 1783–1860.* Ithaca and London: Cornell University Press, 1985.

Banning, Lance, ed. *After the Constitution: Party Conflict in the New Republic.* Belmont, California: Wadsworth Publishing Company, 1989.

Barksdale, Kevin T. *The Lost State of Franklin: America's First Secession.* Lexington: University Press of Kentucky, 2008.

Bartlett, Richard A. *The New Country: A Social History of the American Frontier, 1776–1890.* New York: Oxford University Press, 1974.

Beeman, Richard R. *Plain, Honest Men: The Making of the American Constitution.* New York: Random House, 2009.

Bergeron, Paul H., Stephen V. Ash, and Jeanette Keith. *Tennesseans and Their History.* Knoxville: The University of Tennessee Press, 1999.

Blumberg, Phillip I. *Repressive Jurisprudence in the Early American Republic: The First Amendment and the Legacy of English Law.* Cambridge: Cambridge University Press, 2010.

Blumrosen, Alfred W., and Ruth G. Blumrosen. *Slave Nation: How Slavery United the Colonies and Sparked the American Revolution.* Naperville, Illinois: Sourcebooks, Inc., 2005.

Boggess, Arthur Clinton. *The Settlement of Illinois, 1778–1830.* Chicago: Chicago Historical Society, 1908.

Boles, John B. *The Great Revival, 1787–1805: The Origins of the Southern Evangelical Mind.* Lexington: The University Press of Kentucky, 1972.

Bond, Beverly W., Jr. *The Foundations of Ohio.* Vol. 1 of *The History of the State of Ohio,* edited by Carl Wittke. Columbus: Ohio State Archaeological and Historical Society, 1941.

Bowling, Kenneth R. "Dinner at Jefferson's: A Note on Jacob E. Cooke's 'The Compromise of 1790.'" *William and Mary Quarterly,* Third Series, 28 (October 1971), 629–48.

Boyd, George Adams. *Elias Boudinot: Patriot and Statesman, 1740 to 1821.* Princeton: Princeton University Press, 1952. Reprint, New York: Greenwood Press, 1969.

Brant, Irving. *The Fourth President: A Life of James Madison.* Indianapolis and New York: The Bobbs-Merrill Company, 1970.

———. *James Madison.* Vol. 2, *The Nationalist: 1780–1787.* New York: The Bobbs-Merrill Company, 1948.

Broussard, James H. *The Southern Federalists, 1800–1816.* Baton Rouge: Louisiana State University, 1978.

Brown, John Mason. *The Political Beginnings of Kentucky: A Narrative of Public Events bearing on the History of the State up to the time of its Admission into the American Union.* Louisville: John P. Morton and Company, Printers to the Filson Club, 1889.

Brown, William Dodd, ed. "A Visit to Boonesborough in 1779: The Recollections of Pioneer George M. Bedinger." *The Register of the Kentucky Historical Society* 86 (Autumn 1988), 315–29.

Cadle, Farris W. *Georgia Land Surveying History and Law.* Athens: University of Georgia in Press, 1991.

Carpenter, Jesse T. *The South as a Conscious Minority, 1789–1861: A Study in Political Thought.* New York: The New York University Press, 1930.

Chinn, George Morgan. *Kentucky: Settlement and Statehood, 1750–1800.* Frankford: Kentucky Historical Society, 1975.

Chipman, Donald E., and Harriett Denise Joseph. *Spanish Texas, 1519–1821.* Rev. ed. Austin: University of Texas Press, 2010.

Clarfield, Gerard. "Protecting the Frontiers: Defense Policy and the Tariff Question in the First Washington Administration." *The William and Mary Quarterly,* Third Series, 32:3 (July 1975), 443–64.

Clark, Thomas D. *Agrarian Kentucky.* Lexington: The University Press of Kentucky, 1977.

Clift, G. Glenn, ed. "The District of Kentucky 1783–1787 as Pictured by Harry Innes in a Letter to John Brown." *Register of the Kentucky Historical Society* 54 (October 1956), 369–70.

Coleman, Kenneth. *The American Revolution in Georgia, 1763–1789.* Athens: University of Georgia Press, 1958.

Cooke, Jacob E. "The Compromise of 1790." *William and Mary Quarterly,* Third Series, 27 (October 1970), 523–45.

Cooper, William J., Jr. *Liberty and Slavery: Southern Politics to 1860.* New York: Alfred A. Knopf, 1983.

Copeland, Pamela C., and Richard K. MacMaster. *The Five George Masons: Patriots and Planters of Virginia and Maryland.* Charlottesville: University Press of Virginia, 1975.

Coulter, E. Merton., ed. "Minutes of the Georgia Convention Ratifying the Federal Convention." *Georgia Historical Quarterly* 10 (September 1926), 223–27.

Coward, Joan Wells. *Kentucky in the New Republic: The Process of Constitution Making.* Lexington: University Press of Kentucky, 1979.

Cox, Joseph W. *Champion of Southern Federalism: Robert Goodloe Harper of South Carolina.* Port Washington, NY: National University Publications, 1972.

Craven, Avery O. *The Growth of Southern Nationalism, 1848–1861.* Baton Rouge: Louisiana State University Press and the Littlefield Fund for Southern History of the University of Texas, 1953.

Din, Gilbert C. "War Clouds on the Mississippi: Spain's 1785 Crisis in West Florida." *The Florida Historical Quarterly* 60 (July 1981), 51–76.

Deyle, Steven. "The Irony of Liberty: Origins of the Domestic Slave Trade." *Journal of the Early Republic* 12:1 (Spring 1992), 37–62.

Drake, Daniel. *Pioneer Life in Kentucky, 1785–1800.* Edited by Emmet Field Horine. New York: Henry Schuman, 1948.

Du Bois, W. E. Burghardt. *The Suppression of the African Slave-Trade to the United States of America, 1638–1870.* New York: Longmans, Green and Co., 1896.

Elkins, Stanley, and Eric McKitrick. *The Age of Federalism.* New York and Oxford: Oxford University Press, 1993.

Ernst, Robert. *Rufus King: American Federalist.* Chapel Hill: The University of North Carolina for the Institute of Early American History and Culture at Williamsburg, Virginia, 1968.

Estes, Todd. *The Jay Treaty Debate, Public Opinion, and the Evolution of Early American Political Culture.* Amherst: University of Massachusetts Press, 2006.

———. "Shaping the Politics of Public Opinion: Federalists and the Jay Treaty Debate." *Journal of the Early Republic* 20:3 (Autumn 2000), 393–422.

Faragher, John Mack. *Daniel Boone: The Life and Legend of an American Pioneer.* New York: Henry Holt and Company, 1992.

Farnham, Thomas J. "The Virginia Amendments of 1795: An Episode in the Opposition to Jay's Treaty." *The Virginia Magazine of History and Biography* 75:1 (January 1967), 75–88.

Feldman, Jay. *When the Mississippi Ran Backwards: Empire, Intrigue, Murder, and the New Madrid Earthquakes.* New York: Free Press, 2005.

Few, William, "Autobiography of Col. William Few of Georgia." *Magazine of American History,* VII (November 1881), 343–58.

Finkelman, Paul. "The Northwest Ordinance: A Constitution for an Empire of Liberty." *Pathways to the Old Northwest: An Observance of the Bicentennial of the Northwest Ordinance:*

Proceedings of a Conference held at Franklin College of Indiana, July 10–11, 1987. Indianapolis: Indiana Historical Society, 1988.

——. "Slavery and Bondage in the 'Empire of Liberty.'" In *The Northwest Ordinance: Essays on Its Formulation, Provisions, and Legacy.* Edited by Fredrick D. Williams. East Lansing: Michigan State University Press, 1989.

Foley, William E. *The Genesis of Missouri: From Wilderness Outpost to Statehood.* Columbia: University of Missouri Press, 1989.

Folmsbee, Stanley J., Robert E. Corlew, and Enoch L. Mitchell. *Tennessee: A Short History.* Knoxville: The University of Tennessee Press, 1969.

Ford, Lacy K. *Deliver Us from Evil: The Slavery Question in the Old South.* Oxford: Oxford University Press, 2009.

Fraiser, Jim. *Mississippi River Country Tales: A Celebration of 500 Years of Deep South History.* Gretna, LA: Pelican Publishing Company, Inc., 2001.

Freehling, William W. *The Road to Disunion.* Vol. 1, *Secessionists at Bay, 1776–1854.* New York and Oxford: Oxford University Press, 1990.

Garber, Frank Harmon. "The Attitude of the Constitutional Convention of 1787 toward the West." The *Pacific Historical Review* 5 (December 1936), 349–58.

Goodstein, Anita S. "Black History on the Tennessee Frontier, 1780–1810." *Tennessee Historical Quarterly* 38 (Winter 1979), 401–20.

Grant, Ethan A. "Anthony Hutchins: A Pioneer of the Old Southwest." *The Florida Historical Quarterly* 74:4 (Spring 1996), 405–22.

Gutzman, Kevin R.C. *Virginia's American Revolution: From Dominion to Republic, 1776–1840.* Lanham, MD: Lexington Books, 2007.

Harrison, Lowell Hayes, and James C. Klotter. *A New History of Kentucky.* Lexington: The University Press of Kentucky, 1997.

Haynes, Robert V. *The Mississippi Territory and the Southwest Frontier, 1795–1817.* Lexington: The University Press of Kentucky, 2010.

Herring, George C. *From Colony to Superpower: U.S. Foreign Relations Since 1776.* Oxford: Oxford University Press, 2008.

Heyrman, Christine Leigh. *Southern Cross: The Beginning of the Bible Belt.* Chapel Hill and London: The University of North Carolina Press, 1997.

Higginbotham, Don. "The Federalized Militia Debate: A Neglected Aspect of Second Amendment Scholarship." *William and Mary Quarterly,* 3rd series, 55 (January 1998), 39–58.

Hofstra, Warren R. *A Separate Place, The Formation of Clarke County, Virginia.* Madison: Madison House Publishers, 1999.

Horseman, Reginald. *Expansion and American Indian Policy, 1783–1812.* East Lansing: Michigan State University Press, 1967.

Hurt, R. Douglas. *The Indian Frontier, 1763–1846.* Albuquerque: University of New Mexico Press, 2002.

Jacobs, Clyde E. "Prelude to Amendment: The States before the Court." *The American Journal of Legal History* 12:1 (January 1968), 19–40.

James, D. Clayton. *Antebellum Natchez.* Baton Rouge: Louisiana State University Press, 1968.

Jennings, Lawrence C. *French Anti-Slavery: The Movement for the Abolition of Slavery in France.* Cambridge: Cambridge University Press, 2000.

Jensen, Merrill. *The Articles of Confederation: An Interpretation of the Social-Constitutional History of the American Revolution, 1774–1781.* Madison: The University of Wisconsin Press, 1940.

Jillson, Calvin, and Rick K. Wilson. *Congressional Dynamics: Structure, Coordination & Choice in the First American Congress, 1774–1789.* Stanford: Stanford University Press, 1994.

Jones, Robert Francis. *George Washington: Ordinary Man, Extraordinary Leader.* New York: Fordham University, 2002.

Kaminski, John P. "Controversy Amid Consensus: The Adoption of the Federal Constitution in Georgia." *Georgia Historical Quarterly* 58 (Summer 1974), 244–61.

Kaplan, Charles J., ed. *Indian Treaties, 1778–1883.* New York: Interland Publishing Inc., 1973.

Kentucky: A Guide to the Bluegrass State Compiled and Written by the Federal Writer's Project of the Works Projects Administration for the State of Kentucky, American Guide Series. New York: Harcourt, Brace and Company, 1939.

Kentucky State Parks. "History of the McNitt Massacre, Levi Jackson Wilderness Road State Park." (Unpublished brochure).

Ketcham, Ralph. *James Madison: A Biography.* New York: The Macmillan Company, 1971.

Kleber, John E., ed. *The Kentucky Encyclopedia.* Lexington: The University Press of Kentucky, 1992.

Klotter, James C. *The Breckinridges of Kentucky, 1760–1981.* Lexington: The University Press of Kentucky, 1986.

Knox, J. Wendell. *Conspiracy in American Politics, 1787–1815.* 1966. Reprint, New York: Arno Press, 1972.

Kohn, Richard H. *Eagle and Sword: The Federalists and the Creation of the Military Establishment in America, 1783–1802.* New York: The Free Press, 1975.

———. "The Inside Story of the Newburgh Conspiracy: America and the Coup d'état." *William and Mary Quarterly,* 3rd series, 27:2 (April 1970), 187–220.

Larson, Edward J. *A Magnificent Catastrophe: The Tumultuous Election of 1800, America's First Presidential Campaign.* New York: Free Press, 2007.

Laurel County Historical Society. "The Story of Laurel County" (unpublished brochure).

Lee, Lloyd G. *A Brief History of Kentucky and Its Counties.* Berea, KY: Kentucke Imprints, 1981.

Levy, Leonard W. *Seasoned Judgment: The American Constitution, Rights and History.* New Brunswick, NJ: Transaction Press, 1995.

Lewis, James E., Jr. *The American Union and the Problem of Neighborhood: The United States and the Collapse of the Spanish Empire, 1783–1829.* Chapel Hill: The University of North Carolina Press, 1998.

Linklater, Andro. *An Artist in Treason: The Extraordinary Double Life of General James Wilkinson.* New York: Walker Publishing Company, Inc., 2009.

Lucas, Marion B. *From Slavery to Segregation, 1760–1891: A History of Blacks in Kentucky.* 2 vols. Frankfort: Kentucky Historical Society, 1992.

Lyerly, Cynthia Lynn. *Methodism and the Southern Mind, 1770–1818.* New York and Oxford: Oxford University Press, 1998.

Magrath, C. Peter. *Yazoo: Law and Politics in the New Republic: The Case of Fletcher v. Peck.* Providence, RI: Brown University Press, 1966.

Maier, Pauline. *Ratification: The People Debate the Constitution, 1787–1788.* New York: Simon & Schuster, 2010.

Martin, Vernon P. "Father Rice, the Preacher who Followed the Frontier." *The Filson Club History Quarterly* 29 (October 1955), 324–30.

Matson, Cathy D., and Peter S. Onuf. *A Union of Interests: Political and Economic Thought in Revolutionary America.* Lawrence: University Press of Kansas, 1990.

Mayer, Henry. *A Son of Thunder: Patrick Henry and the American Republic.* New York: Franklin Watts, 1986.

McAfee, Robert B. "The Life and Times of Robert B. McAfee and Family Connections." *Register of the Kentucky State Historical Society* 25:74 (May 1927), 111–43.

McDonald, Forrest. *We The People: The Economic Origins of the Constitution.* Chicago: The University of Chicago Press, 1958.

M'Elwee, W. E. "'The Old Road,' From Washington and Hamilton Districts to the Cumberland Settlement." *American Historical Magazine and Tennessee Historical Society Quarterly* 8 (October 1903), 347–54.

Merritt, Eli. "Sectional Conflict and Secret Compromise: The Mississippi River Question and the United States Constitution." *The American Journal of Legal History* 35:2 (April 1991), 117–71.

Morris, Richard B. *The Forging of the Union, 1781–1789.* New York: Harper & Row, Publishers, 1987.

Morton, Joseph C. *Shapers of the Great Debate at the Constitutional Convention of 1787.* Westport, CT: Greenwood Press, 2006.

Nash, Gary B. *Race and Revolution.* Madison, WI: Madison House, 1990.

Nelson, Paul David. *Anthony Wayne: Soldier of the Early Republic.* Bloomington: Indiana University Press, 1985.

The New Georgia Encyclopedia, q.v. "Josiah Tattnall." http://www.georgiaencyclopedia.org.

Nichols, David Andrew. *Red Gentlemen & White Savages: Indians, Federalists, and the Search for Order on the American Frontier.* Charlottesville and London: University of Virginia Press, 2008.

Noonan, John Thomas, Jr. *Bribes: The Intellectual History of a Moral Idea.* Berkley: University of California Press, 1984.

Onuf, Peter S. "Liberty, Development and Union: Visions of the West in the 1780s." *William and Mary Quarterly,* Third Series, XLIII (April 1986), 179–213.

———. *Statehood and Union: A History of the Northwest Ordinance.* Bloomington: Indiana University Press, 1987.

Onuf, Peter S., and Leonard J. Sadosky, *Jeffersonian America.* Malden, Massachusetts: Blackwell Publishers, Inc., 2002.

Perrin, W. H., J. H. Battle, and G. C. Kniffin, *Kentucky: A History of the State, Embracing a Concise Account of the Origin and Development of the Virginia Colony; Its Expansion Westward, and the Settlement of the Frontier Beyond the Alleghanies; the Erection of Kentucky as an Independent State, and Its Subsequent Development,* 8th ed. Louisville, KY, and Chicago, IL: F. A. Battey and Company, 1888.

Phillips, Paul Chrisler. *The West in the Diplomacy of the American Revolution.* Urbana: The University of Illinois Press, 1913. Reprint, New York: Johnson Reprint Corporation, 1967.

Prucha, Francis Paul. *American Indian Policy in the Formative Years: The Indian Trade and Intercourse Acts, 1790–1834.* Cambridge: Harvard University Press, 1962.

Remini, Robert V. "The Early Heroes of Kentucky." *Register of the Kentucky Historical Society,* 90:3 (July 1992), 225–35.

———. *Henry Clay: Statesman for the Union.* New York: W. W. Norton & Company, 1991.

Rice, Otis K. *The Allegheny Frontier: West Virginia Beginnings, 1730–1830.* Lexington: The University Press of Kentucky, 1970.

———. *Frontier Kentucky.* Lexington: University Press of Kentucky, 1993.

Robertson, James Rood. ed. *Petitions of the Early Inhabitants of Kentucky to the General Assembly of Virginia, 1769 to 1792.* Louisville: John P. Morton & Company, 1914.

Rutland, Robert Allen. *The Ordeal of the Constitution: The Antifederalists and the Ratification Struggle of 1787–1788.* 1965. Reprint, Norman: University of Oklahoma Press, 1983.

Sikes, Lewright B. *The Public Life of Pierce Butler, South Carolina Statesman.* Washington, DC: Rowman and Littlefield, 1979.

Slaughter, Thomas P. *The Whiskey Rebellion: Frontier Epilogue to the American Revolution.* New York: Oxford University Press, 1986.

Speed, Thomas. *The Political Club, Danville, Kentucky, 1786–1790: Being an Account of an Early Kentucky Society from the Original Papers Recently Found.* Louisville: John P. Morton and Company, 1894.

Spellmann, Norman W. "The Formation of the Methodist Episcopal Church." In *The History of American Methodism.* Edited by Emory Stevens Bucke. 3 vols. New York: Abingdon Press, 1964.

Sydnor, Charles S. *The Development of Southern Sectionalism, 1819–1848.* Baton Rouge: Louisiana State University Press and the Littlefield Fund for Southern History of the University of Texas, 1948.

Talbert, Charles G. "Kentuckians in the Virginia Convention of 1788." *Kentucky Historical Society Register* 58 (July 1960), 187–93.

Taylor, Robert M., Jr., ed. *The Northwest Ordinance, 1787: A Bicentennial Handbook.* Indianapolis: Indiana Historical Society, 1987.

Terry, Gail S. "Sustaining the Bonds of Kinship in a Trans-Appalachian Migration, 1790–1811: The Cabell-Breckinridge Slaves Move West." *Virginia Magazine of History and Biography,* 102:4 (October 1994), 455–76.

Van Tine, Warren, and Michael Pierce, eds. *Builders of Ohio: A Biographical History.* Columbus: Ohio State University Press, 2003.

Waldstreicher, David. *Slavery's Constitution: From Revolution to Ratification.* New York: Hill and Wang, 2009.

Warner, Michael S. "General Josiah Harmar's Campaign Reconsidered: How the Americans Lost the Battle of Kekionga." *Indiana Magazine of History*, 83 (March 1987), 43–64.

Warren, Elizabeth. "Senator John Brown's Role in the Kentucky Spanish Conspiracy." *The Filson Club History Quarterly* 36 (April 1962), 158–76.

Watlington, Patricia. *The Partisan Spirit: Kentucky Politics, 1779–1792.* New York: Atheneum for the Institute of Early American History and Culture at Williamsburg, Virginia, 1972.

Williams, Samuel Cole, ed. *Early Travels in the Tennessee Country, 1540–1800, with Introductions, Annotations and Index.* Johnson City, TN: The Watagua Press, 1928.

Wright, Louis B. *Life on the American Frontier.* New York: G. P. Putnam's Sons, 1968.

Index

About the Author

Jeffrey Allen Zemler earned his doctorate in American history from the University of North Texas in 2011. Previously, he had served as research director for Political Research, Inc., where he had the opportunity to write scores of articles on a variety of U.S. and international topics. The author of several articles and book reviews appearing in various peer-reviewed journals, Zemler has concentrated his research on the early westward expansion of the United States. He resides in Texas with his wife, five children, and four dogs.

CPSIA information can be obtained at www.ICGtesting.com
Printed in the USA
BVOW04*0131301113

337533BV00003B/5/P